Angels
and the
Miraculous

Chicken Soup for the Soul: Angels and the Miraculous
101 Inspirational Stories of Faith, Miracles and Answered Prayers
Amy Newmark

Published by Chicken Soup for the Soul, LLC www.chickensoup.com

Front cover photo of man courtesy of iStockphoto.com (©feedough), cloud background courtesy of Getty Images/Richard Newstead (©Richard Newstead)
Back cover and interior illustration of bird courtesy of iStockphoto.com (©vip2807)
Photo of Amy Newmark courtesy of Susan Morrow at SwickPix

Cover and Interior by Daniel Zaccari

Publisher's Cataloging-in-Publication data

Names: Newmark, Amy, editor.
Title: Chicken soup for the soul : angels and the miraculous : 101 inspirational stories of
    faith , miracles and answered prayers / edited by Amy Newmark.
Description: Cos Cob, CT: Chicken Soup for the Soul, LLC, 2023.
Identifiers: LCCN: 2023939366 | ISBN: 978-1-61159-104-0 (paperback) | 978-1-61159-
    341-9 (ebook)
Subjects: LCSH Angels--Literary collections. | Angels--Anecdotes. | Miracles--Literary
    collections. | Miracles--Anecdotes. | BISAC SELF HELP / Motivational and Inspirational
    | SELF HELP / Spiritual | SELF HELP / Personal Growth/Happiness | BODY, MIND &
    SPIRIT / Angels & Spirit Guides | RELIGION / Inspirational |
Classification: LCC BL477 . C457 2023 | DDC 202/.15--dc23

Library of Congress Control Number: 2023939366

PRINTED IN THE UNITED STATES OF AMERICA
on acid∞free paper

30 29 28 27 26 25 24 23   01 02 03 04 05 06 07 08 09

Angels

and the
Miraculous

101 Inspirational Stories of Faith, Miracles and Answered Prayers

Amy Newmark

CSS

Chicken Soup for the Soul, LLC
Cos Cob, CT

Chicken Soup for the Soul

Changing your life one story at a time®
www.chickensoup.com

Table of Contents

❶

~Divine Coincidences~

❷

~Touched by an Angel~

❸

~Divine Intervention~

❹

~Angels in Disguise~

❺

~Messages from Heaven~

6

~Miracles Happen~

7

~Guardian Angels~

8

~Divine Messengers~

9

~Comfort from Beyond~

10

~How Did That Happen?~

Chapter 1

Divine Coincidences

The Little Library

Angels love to create synchronicities because each synchronicity
produces an illumination point for a soul to connect
the dots on life experiences.
~Molly Friedenfeld

It was one of those little libraries that people erect in front of their homes encouraging people to "take a book, leave a book." Ayla, my eight-year-old daughter, stared, fascinated by this bit of pop-up architecture in our neighborhood.

"How does it work?" she asked.

"Well, it's pretty simple. First, you take one of your books, bring it here, open the little door, and put it in. Then, you look through the books and pick one to take home."

Ayla considered this. "So, I bring one of my old books, put it in, and get a new one, right?"

"It's not exactly a new one. It's just new to you. The book you pick will have belonged to some other little girl or boy. That's how it works."

Ayla scowled, clearly not buying into the whole "leave it, take it" idea.

"What if I can't find a book that I want?"

"That's the chance you take."

"Can I take back my book?"

I was beginning to feel like I was being cross-examined by a very shrewd lawyer-in-waiting. "I suppose you could, but it's really all about passing on something that's special to you to someone else so they can experience it, too."

Ayla didn't answer, but I could see that she was not impressed with my "dad logic."

We finished our walk and went our separate ways once we got home. Much later, I realized I hadn't heard or seen Ayla in a while. I found her in her bedroom, seated on the floor, surrounded by her books. All of them.

"Wow. Opening a bookstore?"

Ayla looked at me and rolled her eyes, a habit she had recently picked up from kindergarten. Or maybe my wife.

"I'm trying to find the right book for the tiny library," she slowly enunciated as if explaining it to a child.

"How about that one?" I suggested, pointing.

"Daaaaad, that's my favorite book!"

"Okay, sorry. How about that one?"

Ayla picked up the book, crinkled her nose, and held it at arm's length. "This one's stinky. Even you didn't like it."

"Oh, yeah. Well, let me know if you decide on one."

Not much later, I was mowing the lawn and looked up to see Ayla standing on the front porch, holding a book in one hand and a mermaid footstool in the other. She used the footstool in the bathroom when she brushed her teeth.

"What's with the footstool?"

"I need it to see into the library."

"I could pick you up."

Yet another eye roll. "Dad, I want to do it myself."

I was anxious to see what book Ayla had picked. When we reached the library, she carefully set down the footstool with the smiling mermaid facing out and clambered up.

She opened the glass-pane door slowly, with exquisite care. Then she paused, gazed down at the book in her hand, and slid it inside.

It was her favorite book.

The "take it" part took a long time. Ayla extracted the children's books one by one and carefully examined them, like a jeweler searching for the perfect stone. At last, she found what she was looking for.

But she needed a second opinion.

"What do you think?" she quietly asked.

The title was *Little Stories for Little Girls*. While it was old, the illustrations were colorful and enchanting.

"I think you will enjoy listening to it as much as I will enjoy reading it to you."

"Dad, I know how to read," she reminded me as she closed the little door on the library and backed down the footstool.

Once home, Ayla retired to her bedroom. When I checked on her a little later, she was sitting on the floor, paging through her newest acquisition.

"I saw the book you put in the little library. Why did you decide on that one?"

"I figured that if every kid left their favorite book, there would be plenty of favorite books to take."

I nodded my approval. "I'm glad you did that. You found a pretty special book. How's it shaping up?"

"Great. I have a new friend named Clara."

"That was my grandmother's name."

"I don't remember her."

"You never met. Grandma Clara passed away before you were born. Is Clara a character in one of the stories?"

"No, Dad," Ayla answered matter-of-factly. "She's my new friend. It was her book. See?"

Ayla handed me her book, opening it to the first page, and I began to read the inscription written in flowery cursive.

Dear Little Girl,

This was my book when I was a little girl. Now, it's yours. Even though we'll never meet, we will know each other through these stories. Think of me when you read them.

Your friend,
Clara
Newton, Kansas

"Ummmm, I'd like to show your new book to Mom, okay?"

"Alright, Dad. But hurry."

My wife's reaction to the inscription in Ayla's new book was similar to mine.

"Oh, my! You don't think…"

"I don't know what to think. When Grandma Clara moved in with my sister in Wichita, she donated all her belongings to a rummage sale that her church in Newton was sponsoring. Furniture, appliances, even her books."

"But Newton, Kansas is over a thousand miles away!"

"Sounds crazy, doesn't it? If only there was some way to check if it was Grandma Clara's."

"Handwriting!" my wife exclaimed.

I scoffed at my wife's suggestion. "Grandma Clara's been gone a long time, honey. I doubt if she's going to be sending us a greeting card anytime soon."

Hands on hips, with a look of defiance (and an eye roll — that's where my daughter got it!), my wife shot back, "How about your mom's recipe book, smarty-pants? As I recall, she got it from Grandma Clara, and it's all handwritten. In cursive, no less."

The two of us scrambled to the pantry and retrieved the worn, stained recipe book, its broken binders held together with ancient strips of masking tape.

My wife flipped through the pages, clearly familiar with the ancient tome of recipes.

"Here!" she cried in celebration, reading a recipe title aloud. "Clara's Caramel Cookies!"

With the recipe and inscription side by side, we donned our reading glasses and stared.

"It's not kind of close or maybe close!" I laughed.

"It's a perfect match!" my wife squealed.

Ayla suddenly appeared, drawn, no doubt, by our boisterous celebration.

"Can I have my book back now?"

I gently closed the book, in awe of our unbelievable find, and handed it to Ayla.

"Time for one of Clara's stories," Ayla quipped. And, with that, she disappeared.

My wife and I stared at each other, still processing the unbelievable thing that had just happened.

"Should we tell her?" my wife asked, breaking the silence.

"Yes," I sighed, "eventually. But Grandma Clara just reached across the years and a thousand miles to connect with her great-granddaughter for the first time. I think she deserves a little alone time with her."

"So do I," my wife agreed. "How about we celebrate?"

"How do we possibly celebrate something so amazingly wonderful?"

"With a batch of Grandma Clara's Caramel Cookies, of course!"

— Dave Bachmann —

The Last African Violet

There is always another layer of awareness,
understanding, and delight to be discovered
through synchronistic and serendipitous events.
~Hannelie Venucia

An unexpected gust of wind knocked the little plant out of my hands. It was my mother's last African violet, and now it had shattered on the pavement. I had promised it to Mom's friend, Gracie, who was ill.

Sitting down on my front steps, I began cleaning up the broken pieces, brushing the remains into the bushes. Suddenly, I felt a hand on my shoulder.

"Don't worry, dearie. We've got this," a soft female voice said.

Where had she come from? A moment ago, there had not been a single soul near me. The mysterious stranger sat down next to me and, with gentle hands, took the broken plant and continued to collect all the bits of green leaves and a couple of violet petals. Then she carefully placed everything into a bag she carried and placed it in my hands.

I started to explain that my mom had left me the plant when she died. She stopped me, saying, "I know. I know."

She told me to take it to a little nursery she knew on Preston Road where they were experts on African violets.

"They can save this for you. Gracie will love it."

"How did you know it's for Gracie? Do you know her? Are you my guardian angel?" I quipped, puzzled.

I'm not sure, but I think she winked. She got up from the steps and was gone as quickly as she had appeared. It gave me an eerie feeling in a pleasant way.

Gracie had been my mother's best friend. They were both in their eighties. They had met at a supermarket when Mother was searching for something, and Gracie helped, saying, "Here it is. On the top shelf."

My mother replied, "Oh, tank you. I never vood have found it."

Noticing mother's accent, Gracie asked, "Where are you from?"

"Czechoslovakia."

Well, that's all that needed to be said. Gracie's family was from the same country.

The two women took their groceries to their cars, drove to my house where my mom also lived, and spent the day together eating Mom's poppy-seed cake and talking all things Czechoslovakian.

After Mom passed away, I kept in touch with Gracie, but not enough. When she was ill, I went to visit her in the hospital. She lay there telling me how she loved my mother's cooking, spending time with her, etc.

"She had such beautiful plants."

And that's how I mentioned to Gracie that my mom had left me seven African violets when she passed away.

"Seven! Goodness gracious, y'all are so lucky."

What could I say? "Would you like one, Gracie?"

"Oh, I couldn't," Gracie replied in her delightful East Texas accent. "But since y'all have so many, why yes! I'd love one. I always loved your mom."

I didn't have the heart to tell her that since Mom had died, six of the violets had also died. Not having a green thumb, I had carelessly let them go. Mom had grown plants easily, but I never could. When I realized I had only one plant left, I started taking care of that one seriously, with more love and effort. It was finally thriving, with a few purple petals. And here I was promising it to Gracie.

Although Gracie had been Mom's close friend, I realized I didn't know much about her. While visiting her during her illness, I got to know her better. I knew that she was a widow and learned that she had an estranged daughter named Willow, whom she hadn't seen in years. Gracie's voice reflected the hurt she felt when she spoke about Willow. But the love in her eyes for her daughter was unmistakable.

I tried to find Willow on social media. My search on her maiden name produced nothing, and even Gracie didn't know her married name.

Meanwhile, I had a plant to resurrect. I took the plastic bag with all its pieces and went searching for the nursery on Preston Road. Timidly, I walked up to the counter and opened the bag full of scraps. The nursery owner looked at me and said, "The trash is over there."

I explained it had been an African violet, and I wanted to save it. He said it was too late for that, but why not buy another plant like an iris or tulip? But when I insisted on an African violet, he said, "We don't have any right now."

One of his employees overheard us. "I can help you," she said.

She took me to a work area and examined the remnants of my pathetic plant.

"I am so heartbroken," I sighed. "It was my mother's, and I promised it to her friend. But I think it's gone!"

The kindhearted woman picked up the tiny fragments of green leaves and showed me little roots trying to peek through.

"See these? We can make it work."

She brought over some soil and a small pot and got to work. She added plant food, rooting solution, and a little water. Soon, I could see a plant emerging. When she brought over another pot, I realized that what I had visualized as one plant, she had seen as two. With loving hands, she had created two enchanting, albeit diminutive, plants.

I stood by watching her work, touched by her expression as she told me how her mother had loved African violets, too.

"Now you'll have one pretty African violet for your mother's friend and one for you," she said when she was done.

I imagined my mom smiling down, happy to know that I did end up with one of her African violets after all.

I was so grateful that my plant had been saved. I paid, thanked the nice lady, and promised to come back soon. Only as I was leaving did I remember to introduce myself. She responded, "It's my pleasure meeting you, Eva. My name is Willow."

Could it be? Yes, it was Willow, Gracie's estranged daughter, now a middle-aged woman. She had straightened out her life and desperately wanted to reconnect with her parents but was ashamed of her chaotic past. She was afraid that her parents could never forgive her for the hurt she had caused them in her youth. Sadly, she didn't even know her dad had died.

I hugged Willow. We picked up the two African violets and went directly to Gracie. Through tears and laughter, a loving reunion took place. Gracie received the African violet she had wished for and, even better, found her long-lost daughter.

Two weeks later, Gracie took her last breath. Those two weeks were a blessing. The past was buried as forgiveness and love prevailed.

I never again saw the stranger who appeared on my front steps and helped me find the way to Willow. But I do believe she was sent from heaven.

— Eva Carter —

The Reunion

*Life is magical, and the synchronicities continue to fill
me with wonder every day!*
~Anita Moorjani

The woman several yards away had dyed blond hair, a patterned shawl, a dog on a leash, and a toddler in the stroller beside her. When I approached the park near the edge of our town's business district, she gave me a friendly nod and struck up a conversation.

"How old is your daughter?"

"Eighteen months," I replied. Samantha's birth seemed both near and far, a whirlwind of craziness that still left me breathless. "And your son?"

"Seventeen months. I guess that means they will be in the same grade."

"Probably." I smiled at the simple awkwardness of a conversation like this. Since the start of the Covid pandemic, there hadn't been many. "That's why we moved here, actually. For the schools."

"Us, too." She nodded at her son. "This is Alexander, by the way."

I cocked my head at the familiar name. Alexander? Hmm... "Well, it's genuinely nice to meet you. This is Samantha."

We exchanged a few other comments about parenting toddlers and the weather before I excused us to get to the local bakery. The chat ended with an affirmation that we'd probably see each other again. Our town was small, and while we lived on the edge of Cincinnati, people's daily lives tended to intersect.

"We should get our kids together," she added. "Since they are almost the same age, they would probably like it."

"We should. That sounds great," I replied just before I walked away.

I got about twenty steps before a strong feeling came over me, heightening every sense in my body and compelling me to turn around.

Don't let this moment pass. Don't let her leave. She doesn't look the same, but maybe...

I called out to her. "I have something I need to ask you." I angled my stroller in her direction. She was still close enough to hear me shout, "Is that okay?"

"Sure, what is it?"

I moved closer before I got the courage to ask the question building in my mind for almost our entire conversation. "You said your son's name was Alexander?"

She nodded, closing the space between us with each breath. "Yes."

"Alexander who was born at thirty weeks?" I blurted. "Alexander who spent two months in the NICU at UC?"

"Oh, my god," she replied. "Is this little Samantha?"

Eighteen months earlier and a world away from that park, I delivered my daughter Samantha three months early at the end of my twenty-sixth week of pregnancy. Over the course of a few hours on that fateful night, I developed a life-threatening case of preeclampsia, one that went from serious to dire in the span of a few breaths. Doctors at the University of Cincinnati Medical Center delivered Samantha via emergency C-section, convinced that neither of us would live if they didn't take definitive action. It was the scariest experience of my life. It opened my eyes to the realities of preeclampsia, which kills thousands of women each year and is one of the leading global causes of pre-term birth.

Samantha weighed one pound, ten ounces on the night she was born.

Miraculously, she was healthy. And UC had a Level III Neonatal Intensive Care Unit capable of taking care of Samantha until she was ready for the real world. Our family was right where we should be, cared for by the best doctors in our region. We had more blessings in our life than we could have asked for—even as we grieved an unexpected end to the pregnancy and the mixed emotions that came with an emergency delivery.

One month after Samantha showed up in that NICU, Alexander arrived on a cold December night, the result of pre-term labor that couldn't be stopped. Nurses placed his incubator next to my daughter. I remembered the pirate stickers on his nameplate and the way he looked so much bigger than Samantha. Those extra four weeks of gestation made a huge difference for him. Alexander was adorable. And, by another miracle, he was healthy, too.

Samantha and Alexander spent the next two months together. They shared the same primary nurse, and I got used to seeing Alex when I visited Sam every day. And while it wasn't my place to focus on his recovery, I found myself attached to the little boy who lay next to my daughter and kept fighting and growing right alongside her. At night before I went to sleep, I prayed Alex would make it another day and keep walking the tightrope that is the reality of a long NICU stay.

My husband and I ran into Alex's family several times over those long weeks. Each time, we exchanged pleasantries and words of cautious hope, but the NICU wasn't exactly the place to strike up a friendship. It was a place to survive. Those pleasant conversations and quick words of encouragement didn't lend themselves to permanent connection. It's hard to make friends when you're just trying to get out of bed every morning and focus on your own child's critical needs. Still, when Alex left the NICU about ten days before Sam's discharge, a feeling of sadness and loss tugged at my heart. I didn't expect to see him ever again, but I hoped he'd have a happy and healthy life.

And now, Alex and his mother stared back at me.

A heady mix of gratitude, heartache, and hope washed over me in the seconds after Joy asked if my daughter was "little Samantha." Fifteen months is a long time, and for the two of us, those months were even longer. We brought our children home from the hospital just weeks before the pandemic began. Even Joy had changed, dyeing her hair and growing it out since I last saw her. Nothing about being a parent looked the way I expected. Nothing.

"I can't believe it." I pulled Joy into one of the deepest hugs that I'd given in fifteen months. "I can't believe this."

"Is Samantha okay?" Joy sobbed into my shoulder for a few long minutes, the gravity of the emotion she'd carried equal to mine. "She's catching up?"

"Yes. And Alex?"

"He's perfect. Healthy."

Once we stopped crying, we whipped out our phones and exchanged contact information, promising that we'd get our children together for a playdate. The following week, Joy and Alex showed up at my house for coffee and breakfast. And it didn't take long for Alex and Sam to show us that, while time had passed, something inside them remained connected. They knew each other in ways few children do, tied together since birth.

Two miracle babies. Two moms. Four lives forever changed by a multitude of blessings, and on the road to healing together.

— Sara Celi —

Kyleybug

Remember that although bodies may pass away, the
energy that connects you to a loved one is everlasting
and can always be felt when you're open to receiving it.
~Doreen Virtue, *Signs from Above*

I was finding it hard to believe that my daughter's milestone thirtieth birthday was rapidly approaching. It was even harder to wrap my mind around the fact that it had been thirteen years since I lost her in a car accident down the street from my home. Ky was buried on her seventeenth birthday, two days before Christmas.

Knowing I would be facing these days alone for the first time following a difficult divorce, a sympathetic new friend extended an invitation for me to spend five days with her family in Colorado. I arrived at Lisa's home on December nineteenth and planned to return home to Texas four days later, on Kyley's thirtieth birthday.

As my time away from home was nearing an end, Lisa suggested we have dinner with some of her extended family. I learned her daughter and son-in-law, Michael, would be joining us. Someone mentioned Michael's upcoming birthday, which immediately piqued my interest.

"He has a birthday coming up?" I asked. "When?"

"Tomorrow, on the twenty-third," a family member offered.

I smiled and quickly shared that it was also my daughter's birthday. The conversation soon turned to other things, but my heart and mind lingered on Kyley. I thought I would have received some type of sign by then — something to reassure me that she was still with me in spirit — but I had received nothing in the days leading up to the anniversary. Tomorrow was a special day: Ky's birthday. The day I buried my daughter. The day I ceremoniously gave her back to God. I never asked for signs anymore. It had been years since I'd received one, but I wanted a ladybug this year. I needed a ladybug.

When Kyley was a little girl, her grandmother began calling her Kyleybug. Ladybugs had become a sweet reminder of my girl. The family had even taken to calling them "kyleybugs." Now, as I half-heartedly listened to the excited chatter filling the room, I desperately begged God for a sign.

On the drive to the restaurant, my thoughts returned to my daughter. What would my seventeen-year-old girl look like as a thirty-year-old woman? Would she have children? Be married? Would she have a career? Would she still talk very loudly? Would she make friends with every person she met as she did when she was a teenager? Would we be best friends as I had always planned?

I imagined what our dinner that night might look like if she were there with us, and an incredible longing overtook me.

"Lord, please, I need a kyleybug. I need something… anything. Please, God."

I felt no sense of peace following my plea. There was no hint of action on God's part, no calm in my spirit, and nothing suggesting He had anything in the works.

The restaurant was crowded, and by the time our party of eight was finally seated, we were eager to order our food. We sat with our noses buried in the menus, calling out to one another with our meal selections and a chorus of "pass the rolls." Nobody even noticed, much less looked up, when the young woman approached our table.

"Hi, my name is Kyley, and I'll be your server tonight."

I believe she asked for our drink order, but nobody said a word. We all just sat there in stunned silence, staring at the poor girl.

"Umm, is everything okay?" she asked.

"Everything is fine. We just know a very special girl with your same name," a member of our party answered as all eyes turned to me.

I didn't get a kyleybug on my daughter's birthday, but I did get a Kyley. What a wonderful gift indeed.

— Melissa Bender —

The Brick

Deeply, I know this, that love triumphs over death.
My father continues to be loved,
and therefore he remains by my side.
~Jennifer Williamson

My dad passed away last year. Ironically, he passed on Father's Day. It was as if he had us all gathered one last time, and then he slipped away when no one was watching.

He lived a long, amazing life filled with love, laughter, family, and friendships.

As his health declined, the last couple of months were difficult. At the end, he seemed to slowly fade away. When he finally passed, it was a relief as much as anything that he was at peace and could move on. But the loss was still great.

Every summer, my extended family gathers at the family cottage on Lake Huron in Michigan for a long weekend. This year would be the first gathering of family since the funeral. Nieces, nephews and significant others started arriving on Friday night. We came in carrying armloads of food, drinks and luggage. Claims were quickly made on bedrooms and couches for sleeping.

The following days were spent swimming in the lake, on the boat or riding the Jet Ski. We had our normal cookout for dinner, and then we headed into town for ice cream before coming back and building a bonfire on the beach. Stories were told, and although most were repeats from previous years, nobody seemed to mind. They get better with each re-telling. This year, more than one story was about my dad, and they all ended with laughter, which was entirely appropriate as my dad loved a good story.

On my dad's summer vacations from college, he worked on the freighters that sail the Great Lakes. He would sit for hours on the deck of the cottage looking out over the lake and watching the freighters pass by. He could spot a freighter on the horizon, way out in the lake, and identify it by its shape. We knew better than to question his knowledge, and soon the freighter would be close enough to see the name with binoculars. Most times, he was right.

I was walking along the beach on the second morning when an odd-shaped rock caught my attention. It was half-buried in the sand, and the waves were obscuring its true shape. I pried it out and discovered it wasn't a rock at all. It was a brick, well-worn, with one broken corner. I turned it over and was shocked. Stamped into the brick were three letters — FJD — my father's initials.

I stood there stunned, and turning it over numerous times I looked up to the heavens as if the brick had dropped from the sky to this very spot. I knelt down and washed the brick and then carried it back to the cottage to show the family. Everyone was stunned and speechless. Mom started crying.

We passed around the brick. Each person held it and felt my father's presence. It was as if my father had once again gathered with us, not wanting to be left out.

Each of us had been dealing with the loss of my father in their own way, and yet the brick was a sign that my father was still with us, watching over us, and always would be. The comfort of that knowledge was immeasurable.

We placed the brick on the fireplace mantel by the window overlooking the lake. We placed the binoculars next to it so my dad could always look out over his beloved lake as the freighters pass by.

— John Danko —

Just in Time

And, when you want something, all the universe
conspires in helping you to achieve it.
~Paulo Coelho, The Alchemist

When I was four years old, my mother sat me down and explained that I'd been adopted when I was a baby. I didn't quite understand what she was saying, but as I got older, I appreciated how up-front she'd been about my past and our family. This gave me the chance to place a high value on the family that raised me. While I was always curious about my biological parents, I never felt compelled to ask more questions or search for them.

That all changed in my early twenties when I began developing a number of very serious allergies to foods I'd always loved. Doctors provided few details, and most told me to check with my family to determine if there was a pattern of allergies or other immune-system issues to help with figuring out what might be wrong. Not knowing where to turn, I asked my parents to tell me everything they knew about where I came from. Mine was a closed adoption, so they only had very basic information about my birth mother and no information about my birth father.

Searching for more, I met with a counselor at the adoption agency who was able to find copies of the original records that listed redacted information about my birth mother. Finally, I had a few missing pieces to this puzzle. All it really told me was that I'd been born in the same city where I currently resided to a seventeen-year-old who had very little information filled out under the "family medical history" section. Figuring I'd hit a dead end, I thanked the counselor for her help and accepted that my past would forever remain a mystery.

Curious about what other adopted adults do in situations like this, I searched online for adoption forums. This was in the early 2000s, so there weren't as many options online for finding long-lost relatives, and I had no idea where to look. I stumbled on a forum simply named adoption.com where I saw post after post of adoptees and birth parents searching for one another.

As I looked, panic began to set in, and I had to step away from my computer. Until now, I'd never even considered looking for my birth mother. I'd told myself that she was young, a child herself when she gave me up for adoption, and there was no way she'd consider reconnecting after all this time. And what would I say if she was actually looking for me? "Oh, hi. I'm your birth daughter, I guess. I'm twenty-three now, and life is going okay. I do have a lot of weird new allergies, and my doctors thought it would be helpful to know family medical history stuff, so here I am. How are you?" The anxious thoughts and questions swirled through my mind for the rest of the evening.

The next morning, I dragged myself from bed and went back to the forum. My hands shook as I began typing things into the search box, trying to find any posts about my city or birth date. I came across several from my city and a few baby girls who were born on the same day as me, but nothing seemed relevant.

After spending the rest of the day agonizing, I decided to write my own post. I titled it "Searching for birth mother" and described my birth date, the city, and the small pieces of information I knew from my redacted file. I read and re-read my post before finally taking a deep breath and hitting the submit button. My eyes welled with tears as I saw my listing pop up in the feed, and I stepped away from the computer, certain that I'd just sent a plea into the void.

Telling myself I'd done everything I could, I vowed to avoid checking the forum for the rest of the day. The next morning, I opened the page again and felt my blood run cold as the little envelope on the page blazed in red with a tiny "1" over it. Telling myself to take a breath, I clicked to open the response I'd received on my post, which simply stated: "I think I might be your biological mother," followed by details about the birth and hospital that matched information I had not included in my original post.

Standing away from the computer, I burst into tears as my head swam with feelings of relief, joy, anguish, and confusion. She told me she'd been looking for me and gave me her e-mail. Only after we finally started talking to one another did she share that the day I posted on the forum was the first time she'd ever been on it. In fact, she was beginning to write her own post when she saw mine pop onto the feed. Without my allergies, I likely wouldn't have started searching. Without dead ends from my family and the adoption agency, I likely wouldn't have gone online. And despite there being several adoption forums just like that one, we both found our way there on the same day with the same plan.

Connecting proved to be very powerful. I was able to reconnect with her, my birth father, siblings, and other family members. Lifelong questions have been answered, and we've been able to create a relationship I never dreamed was possible.

— Charlie Morrow —

Betty's Lemonade

Don't grieve. Anything you lose
comes round in another form.
~Rumi

I entered the enchanted garden of this hidden backyard oasis and felt the breeze at my back as the sunlight gently warmed my skin. There were spectacular fountains covered in flowering vines, and plants bursting with blooms filled the air with delightful scents. A canopy of towering trees provided shade and surprising comfort, and I felt embraced by the natural wonder all around me.

I felt a calming presence in that middle-of-the-city back yard. It brought a certain grounded feeling to what felt like a surreal morning. Soon, the proceedings would begin, and the finality and weight of the day would be felt by all those assembled there for the memorial gathering for my extraordinary friend, Betty.

The testimonials and stories took my breath away. Many spoke of her magnificent accomplishments, her explorations, adventures, and contributions. Her circle of friends wrapped around many different parts of the community, for Betty was passionate about life. She was a mover and shaker, a doer, a constant student eager to try new things, a motivator, a generous benefactor with an amazing sense of mission, and a gracious grande dame.

After the more formal part of the memorial concluded, we sat down to a buffet of Betty's favorite foods. The mood was jovial as the guests shared experiences they had with Betty over the years, one more remarkable than the next. I talked about the many opera performances I had attended with Betty.

We had been told to bring something by which to remember Betty in some way. Since I had no idea what to bring, I had gone to the store hoping to be struck with inspiration. Although I had no plan, an amazing synchronicity came about during my shopping expedition. A display of T-shirts beckoned to me with such insistence that I dared not refuse. I began to sift through all the merchandise and magically came across a T-shirt in Betty's favorite shade of yellow with a design of a lemonade stand on the front. Not only that, it had written under the drawing, "Betty's Lemonade Stand"!

Why did this matter? Well, lemons were one of Betty's absolute favorite foods. She began every day with a tall glass of lemon water — an unsweetened lemonade. She had determined it to be her elixir of youth and wellbeing. It was always freshly squeezed with lemons from her own lemon tree or that of her neighbor.

I grabbed the shirt and rushed over to the cashier, eagerly telling her of this remarkable coincidence. The clerk began to check me out but noticed there was no price tag on the garment. She went over to find another one to establish the price, but there was no other T-shirt like it. The clerk even tried calling another store to do a price check, but she was told they had never heard of anything like it.

A supervisor arrived to help. When she heard the story of Betty and her lemons, she threw her arms up in the air and declared, "The shirt is obviously meant to go home with you. It's yours — no charge!" Betty was clearly in charge.

I arrived at that garden party wearing that special T-shirt bearing witness to the heartwarming miracle that brought it into my life. Betty left this Earth quite suddenly but without suffering. We were told she had been out of town attending the wedding of a family member, had danced with gusto at the party following the ceremony, and had then returned to her hotel room. She apparently collapsed to the floor shortly thereafter and expired. I think she regretted not being able to say farewell to her friends and found a way through that T-shirt to have one last, definitive communication. What a wonderful goodbye and hello all at once!

—Suzanne Weiss Morgen—

For Anna, Always

Sons are the anchors of a mother's life.
~Sophocles

I awoke on July 1, 2021 to find a message on my phone from a dear friend. She was offering comfort, as it was the third anniversary of my son's memorial service. Her son had been a loyal friend of Nick's and had read a special scripture at the service.

There are so many hard days when you're grieving your child, days when it's even more painfully obvious that your family of four is now only three: the dates that marked the months and years since Nick's death, such as birthdays and holidays, and the anniversaries of his death itself. I'd let the date of the memorial service slip into the background, so my friend's reminder was bittersweet.

Later that morning, I received a message from another dear friend. Kathryn wanted to know if we could meet for coffee that afternoon. This was unusual as we normally had to plan our time together days or even weeks in advance. A spontaneous meet-up never happened. But, on this day, when I suddenly needed special comfort, it did.

Kathryn had lost her husband several months before, so our time together was often filled with sharing about our grief and fond memories. Kathryn and I are both artists and writers, and we can spend hours talking about creative endeavors and how emotionally necessary they are for us, especially in grieving. She had even given me a box of art materials at Nick's memorial service, which launched a season of healing for me. Between our in-person visits, we would message each other words of encouragement or photos of things that we felt were signs from beyond.

A few weeks prior to this particular day Kathryn had sent me a photo of a bracelet she'd found buried in the sand while walking the beach on Anna Maria Island. Kathryn's parents owned a beach house there, where she would spend days when times were emotionally difficult. The island is also a place where our family had vacationed, both with Nick and after he left us. It was precious to us, especially to my daughter, Anna, who loved that the island shared her name. The bracelet Kathryn found was a leather cord holding a metal bar engraved with "Nick Always." She'd said she would give the bracelet to me the next time she saw me.

This had to be more than coincidence: a bracelet engraved with my son's name, found on a beach that is meaningful to both her and my family, and presented to me on the anniversary of Nick's memorial service where Kathryn had also given me a meaningful gift.

Our meeting went as usual, and she handed me the bracelet as soon as we sat down. I could barely contain my tears at seeing those engraved words. Nick was letting me know he would be there always.

And yet, something didn't feel right.

The bracelet fit, but it didn't. It felt out of place on my arm. I wondered if maybe it was from guilt. The bracelet obviously had been a special gift to someone else at some time. Was I supposed to find who it originally belonged to? Was that even possible? Even in this day of internet connectivity, I knew there was no way I could ever track down the original owner. And, despite my discomfort, I couldn't shake the feeling it had truly been sent by Nick. I just felt that there was more, that it had another purpose.

For a couple of days, I wore the bracelet, wondering what to do. Should I leave it somewhere to be found, as it had been left behind for Kathryn to find? Should I hold on to it and wait for God to lead someone into my life who had lost a Nick of their own?

The answer arrived when my daughter Anna came to me in tears. Grief over the loss of her brother had been weighing heavily on her. She had reached the stage of life that Nick had hit when his life ended, and she was feeling lost and lonely, missing the guidance of her older brother. We talked, and I offered her all the words of comfort and understanding that I could, but she seemed to need something tangible to hold onto.

I took off the bracelet and handed it to her.

"I think this was meant for you, not me," I said.

She put on the bracelet, and her tears immediately dried. And the uncomfortable feeling I'd been struggling with immediately disappeared. Since that moment, not a day has passed without the bracelet encircling her wrist. All of this had come together to bring Anna a much-needed message: Nick is with her. Always.

— Kat Heckenbach —

Room 241

*When you live your life with an appreciation
of coincidences and their meanings, you connect
with the underlying field of infinite possibilities.*
~Deepak Chopra

"I'll see you tomorrow here at the nursing home," I said as I kissed Dad's forehead. He nodded and mumbled a few unintelligible words.

It had been a long day full of visitors, and I was headed home. Dad had been transferred from the hospital to the nursing home only two days earlier. After a surgery and a brief stay in the intensive care unit, it became obvious that Dad wasn't going to recover. His congestive heart failure, COPD, and breast cancer had taken a toll. The hospice nurse wasn't sure how long he had left, but she said it would likely be several days.

When Dad moved into the nursing home, we were all in shock. I stood in the hallway and took a picture of his room number. When communicating with people who wanted to visit or send cards, I wanted to make sure I had the correct information. He was in Room 241.

That evening, a few hours after I left Dad's room, a nurse called to tell me that Dad was gone. Mom had been with him in his private room, resting on the couch nearby. Everyone was surprised that he had passed so quickly, especially Mom, who was too overwhelmed with emotion to make the phone call.

After Dad died, it was difficult for Mom to live alone, although she was certainly capable of doing so. They had been married forty-eight years. Her biggest complaint was about persistent back pain that never improved despite chiropractic adjustments and massages.

I urged her to go to the doctor and met her there. After a radiologist read her MRI results, Mom was diagnosed with terminal cancer. The scan showed tumors throughout her body and on her spine. I couldn't believe it. Dad had only been gone five months.

As Mom's illness progressed, she ultimately left her home and moved into the Hospice House, run by our local hospice agency. Most people don't ever leave the Hospice House, but she did. Due to Medicare regulations and her health, she had to be transported elsewhere. It broke my heart to move her, especially because she didn't want to leave that facility.

The hospice social worker recommended a small nursing home in a surrounding community. Unfortunately, the only room available was one that Mom would be required to share with another resident.

Mom didn't want a roommate. Heck, I wouldn't either, especially if I were dying. The roommate would likely be a stranger. We needed to find another option quickly.

Later, the social worker called me with an update. "Now there's an opening at a different nursing home about twenty miles from here. Your mom could have her own room if you wanted to proceed," she said. It was, without a doubt, the best option for Mom.

I will never forget the nurse at the Hospice House who wrapped Mom in a quilt and kissed her on the cheek as Mom was transported from the facility. I stood there in tears, knowing Mom had the best care in the world. The nurse hugged me, too. What would Mom find at the next location?

I met the hospice social worker in the nursing home's parking lot as we waited for Mom to arrive. It was a cold winter day. "Have you ever been here before?" she asked. I told her it was the same place where my dad had stayed before he passed away.

"I wasn't aware of that," she said, with a surprised look. She smiled at me with her kind eyes. I think she was sorry she had asked.

Eventually, the social worker brought me to Mom's room on the second floor. It seemed to take forever. I was relieved Mom had gotten there in one piece.

The first day Mom was there, I repositioned her pillows as she struggled to get comfortable. "I think this is the same room where Dad stayed. It seems familiar," I said, looking around the room.

"No, I don't think so," Mom replied.

The nursing home complex was big with multiple buildings on a sprawling campus. Every building had multiple floors. What were the chances my parents would both be in the same room as they transitioned from this world to the next?

I began to doubt it myself until I reached for my phone. I scrolled past dozens of pictures until I finally found what I was looking for. When Dad moved in nine months earlier, I had taken a picture of his room number. He had stayed in Room 241.

I walked into the hallway to take a picture of Mom's room number. Was I seeing things? I needed photographic evidence. Mom was staying in Room 241, too. Was this a dream? Suddenly, I felt like everything was going to be okay. Peace seemed to wash over me. I don't really believe in coincidences. This was a sign.

"You're kidding me!" Mom said, shaking her head.

A few hours later, an employee knocked on the door to see if we needed anything. She was there when Mom moved in. She might have been there when Dad moved in, too. I told her about my parents sharing the same room nine months apart. She looked stunned.

"Oh, my goodness," she said. "I'm sure we can move your mom to another room. I'm sorry. This is probably upsetting to your family."

I told her it wasn't upsetting at all. Instead, it felt like a sign from above. It seemed like Dad was there, too. As crazy as it sounds, there was a sense of peace knowing Mom and Dad would leave this world in the same room. Mom loved this sign of Dad's presence. She and I felt like Dad had a hand in making it happen somehow.

"Is this a hospice room?" I asked.

"No, not at all," she said. "We don't have any rooms designated for hospice patients. This room just happened to be available when your mom needed it."

I nodded and wiped away a few tears. I was speechless.

Because I was there every day and most evenings, I grew fond of the nursing staff. They treated Mom with great care and concern. They treated me with kindness, too. One evening, I told the nurses on duty that my parents had shared the same room.

"I thought you and your mom looked familiar," a nurse said. "Now I know why! I was there when your dad died. I felt bad making that call to you. He had just moved in."

"That was you?" I asked. "It must have been hard for you as well. You handled it beautifully." We decided that life unfolds in mysterious ways.

Mom lingered in the nursing home for two long weeks. It was the best place for her because Dad seemed to be there, too.

Mom took her last breath on a sunny February morning while I sat at her bedside. She was ready to go. It was finally time for her to leave. I like to think that Dad was waiting for her on the other side after having orchestrated the perfect place for her departure.

— Tyann Sheldon Rouw —

The Secret

To her, the name of father was another name for love.
~Fanny Fern

A soft drizzle fell as I pulled into the driveway after my weekly grocery-shopping trip. Usually my husband Tom was my enthusiastic assistant for these shopping excursions; his exuberant personality made even mundane outings an adventure. That morning, however, he had forgone our weekly errand. The older of our two daughters, Molly, was to be married in a few weeks, and he had a to-do list in progress. He was excited about the celebration and determined that it would go off without a hitch, so I left him in peace. Thus, I found myself gathering an armload of bags in the rain and nudging the back door open with my knee.

Tom was seated at his computer desk in the kitchen, wearing headphones. I patted his shoulder as I trudged past with the wet bags. Startled, he turned to look, and then he broke into his twinkling smile and removed his headphones.

"Honey, I've got it! The song for the father-daughter dance. Listen!"

He began to play an Irish ballad we had both long loved about a father's pride at his daughter's wedding. I was touched by the sentiment, but my mind raced. How could I tell him that the choice of music for the father-daughter dance is made by the bride?

"She'll be so surprised," he beamed.

There was nothing else for it: I enthusiastically agreed and then slipped away to telephone the bride. Molly laughed affectionately at my description of her dad's plan. "Well, I certainly will be surprised!" she agreed, and the matter was settled.

On the big day, the reception was in full swing. Finally, the lights lowered, and the first chords of the ballad began. Molly recognized the lovely tune immediately, and hers were not the only tear-filled eyes in the ballroom. When he returned Molly to her new husband, Tom found me watching with our younger daughter, Kathleen, who had had the foresight to bring tissues.

"Do you think Molly knew what I was trying to say?" he asked quietly.

I could only smile and hug him. "She knew."

More than once over the next few weeks, Tom reminisced about the success of his surprise, to everyone's amusement. Kathleen was working at home for the summer, and her sunny presence helped us adjust to Molly's departure. However, one day after Kathleen had breezed out the door, her father's affectionate smile faded. To my shock, it was replaced with an uncharacteristic look of deep concern. My face must have betrayed my surprise because Tom turned to me.

"I just realized," he said slowly. "What about Kathleen? She will get married, too, one day."

I was so relieved that I laughed. "Kathleen is only in college and not even engaged. You have plenty of time to worry about your father-daughter dance!" But he wasn't convinced. "I want to find the perfect song for Kathleen, too," he insisted. "One that shows her exactly how I feel." Single-mindedly, Tom moved his CD collection to his desk and spent the next days glued to the chair with his headphones on, shuffling CDs. Finally, the headphones came off with a flourish, and the twinkling smile broke out again. "I have it!" he exclaimed. "It's perfect!"

"What song is it?" I asked curiously. Tom chuckled.

"This time, I'm going to surprise everyone, even you!" After a moment's reflection, though, he decided that it would be wiser to share this important information with someone. So, I was sworn to absolute secrecy. The song was a less popular one from decades earlier; in fact, I had heard it only on the album, never on the radio. It was a poignant lullaby from father to daughter, and as we listened, Tom said quietly, "Kathleen will know. She will understand what I'm saying to her." I wrote on the case that the song had been chosen by her father and was to be played at Kathleen's wedding. I placed the CD in the folder containing our wills. Tom was again bursting with pride and excitement.

The CD was still in the folder and the vow of silence still unbroken nineteen months later as Tom lay dying. The devastated children had said their goodbyes. Shattered, I was going alone to the hospital to carry out my final privilege of holding Tom's hand as his life support was removed. I carried a CD player and some of our old favorites that held so many memories, hoping to comfort him as he made this final journey. Lastly, I added the wedding CD. So it was that Tom was eased out of this world with the song he had so lovingly chosen for himself and his daughter. After his funeral, I returned the CD to the folder, now a sacred secret.

The day eventually came when a wonderful young man called to ask my blessing to propose marriage to Kathleen. I was overjoyed, happily anticipating the festive wedding celebration, which was scheduled for a few days before Christmas. I knew Tom's absence — his larger-than-life personality — would leave a painful void. But I did have the secret: the special piece of music that Tom had chosen with such care. I wistfully recalled Tom's excitement and anticipation, his certainty that Kathleen would understand the message he was sending by the song. The ache in my heart was overwhelming. He would never have missed this day, I knew.

Soon, it was December, and the ceremony was only days away. One of the last remaining details was the final dress fitting. Kathleen, the seamstress and I were very merry in the fitting room, listening to carols on the sound system as seams were pinned and darts tweaked. At last, the seamstress stood back to observe. "I think it's perfect," she decided. "Let's see the full effect with the veil!" I fondly watched the bride in her rustling gown step onto the dressmaker's pedestal while the seamstress reached for the veil. Suddenly, I realized that the Christmas music was no longer playing, and the room had gone silent. Then, across the sound system came the introductory bars to an older song, a lullaby, one that I had never before heard on the radio.

So it was that while the seamstress gently placed the veil, and a stunningly beautiful bride-to-be smiled shyly into the mirror, turning from side to side, the poignant music and lyrics that her father had so carefully chosen for their special dance floated through the air. And with an enveloping sense of peace, I knew with certainty that Tom was there with us after all, sending his love and blessing to his beloved daughter.

Yes, honey, I thought, smiling through tears at our unsuspecting daughter, *I'll tell her you were here. She'll understand.*

Days later, at the reception, I introduced the father-daughter number. I told Kathleen and the assembled guests the story of how Tom had carefully chosen the music years ago. As the sweet song filled the room, and Tom's son circled the floor in his father's stead with the beautiful bride on his arm, again mine were not the only tear-filled eyes in the ballroom. Tom's secret message of love from across the years was safely delivered at last.

— Loreen Martin Broderick —

11

A Passport Photo on TV

The most beautiful thing we can experience
is the mysterious.
~Albert Einstein

*E*ithne was on the plane that went down. This message flashed in a text after an acupuncture appointment in Manhattan. Half-dressed, I froze, staring at the message from our former *Riverdance* colleague. Our twenty-eight-year-old friend was dead.

Hours into the early morning flight on June 1, 2009, Air France 447 had disappeared without a trace somewhere between Rio de Janeiro and Paris. Two hundred and twenty-eight people were onboard. Three were Irish doctors, one of whom was my friend Eithne Walls. No distress call was ever made. The plane simply vanished. The Arrivals board at Charles de Gaulle Airport flashed, "Delayed." Had the plane plummeted into the Atlantic, lost its signal, or been taken over by terrorists? No one knew.

Nine years earlier, Eithne and I first met during rehearsals for our Broadway debuts in *Riverdance*. In a windowless studio, the dance captain instructed us to stand in a line and cued up the music. Then, side by side, we beat our feet against the wood floor, tapping out each rhythmic step until we moved in perfect sync. Upon finishing, I dropped to the ground and bent over my achy legs, worried that, at twenty-four, I was too old to still perform.

With a distinct brogue, the fair-skinned beauty introduced herself.

"Where are you from?" she asked.

"Missouri."

We soon discovered that our families were from neighboring counties in Ireland, but Eithne didn't know my mom's Tyrone clan. I rattled off other names, and we found a connection — the "lad" who'd carpooled with Eithne to dance lessons had gotten me into my prior show, Michael Flatley's *Lord of the Dance*.

"It's brilliant you were in *Lord*. Why did you leave?" Eithne asked.

"I had to go back to law school. I just finished my first-year exams."

"My sister's going to be a barrister, too. I'm going to be a doctor like my brother," she said.

In an instant, we were friends, the two nerds in the cast.

After *Riverdance* closed, an ocean separated us, but Eithne remained my most trusted friend. She traveled to Manhattan often, making her a more frequent visitor than my school friends, and the only one who left thank-you gifts and handwritten cards. When Eithne questioned pursuing a career as an eye surgeon, I assured her that if I could thrive as a lawyer on the male-dominated Wall Street, she could excel in a testosterone-filled field. She was working at Royal Victoria Eye and Ear Hospital in Dublin when she'd flown to Brazil and had e-mailed that she would visit in November.

Standing in front of a candle and photo of Eithne a day after the crash, ingrained Catholic prayers that I'd abandoned jumbled in my head as I worried about Eithne, hoping she'd be found but feeling she was dead. I feared she could be trapped between worlds in some way from such a horrific death. I began shaking. "Ettie, let me know you're okay," I screamed.

My phone buzzed with a new text: *Turn on Channel 4. Eithne's on TV.*

I raced to the television. Eithne's passport photo filled the screen. Without any make-up and with her hair tied in a ponytail, Eithne smiled on-camera.

I stared at my text. I looked at the TV. A light breeze blew over me from my right side, although my windows were shut. All the hairs on my arm rose. Goose bumps ran across my skin. Calm and quiet surrounded me, and somehow I felt connected to Eithne. I wasn't alone, and she was letting me know she was indeed okay.

— Tess Clarkson —

12

A Date with Destiny

The probability of a certain set of circumstances
coming together in a meaningful (or tragic)
way is so low that it simply cannot be
considered mere coincidence.
~V.C. King

My friend Carla was born with an inquisitive mind. She loved to people-watch. As a young girl, she would make up stories about individuals whom she had encountered. Despite being gifted, though, she hadn't pursued her interest in storytelling. At the age of forty, she'd resolved herself to being a dedicated wife and mother.

Yet something stirred deep within her as she sat in the local Friendly's restaurant one Friday night. Her toddler daughter was seated across from her, dissecting her ice-cream sundae. Carla's eyes kept wandering to the diners seated at the nearby tables.

Families were sharing desserts, some middle-aged girlfriends were engrossed in lively conversation, and a few couples were snuggled together. Nothing caught her attention until she noticed two young girls who looked to be around twelve. It appeared that it might be their first time dining out without parents. The newness of their experience was evident. They beamed with pride at their adult behavior.

Something about the friends intrigued her. She watched with interest as they ordered. The girls giggled while they waited patiently for their food. They politely thanked the waitress once she placed their dishes before them.

Carla was touched by their friendship. She wondered what they were discussing. Their connection took her back in time. She could still remember sitting with her best friend and showing her the ring that her first boyfriend had bought her. He was so proud to be able to give her a token of his affection. He promised her that he would always love her, and she believed him.

Simple, Carla thought to herself. *Back then, life was so uncomplicated, and love was so innocent.* There was no sex involved, just kissing. Being admired by a handsome preteen boy had made her feel beautiful.

She often wondered what had happened to Joey. His family had moved away in the ninth grade. For a while, they had continued to communicate, but life took them each on different paths over the years. They eventually lost contact.

She'd experienced so many changes since that moment in her life. She'd gone to college, gotten married, had two children, and moved away from her hometown. It was unfathomable to think that she hadn't seen Joey in close to thirty years. She often wondered what had become of him.

"Mommy, Mommy, do you want some?" her daughter pleaded, disrupting her introspection.

"Sure, honey," Carla answered, dipping the tip of her spoon into the vanilla ice cream. Her daughter smiled appreciatively at her.

Carla was trying to focus on her daughter, but her attention kept drifting to the two girls across the way. She had no explanation for her fascination.

The girls devoured their food and were attempting to get the waitress's attention. They were ready for the check. Carla's first inclination was to wave down the unobservant waitress, but she feared that her interaction would only embarrass them. She didn't want to defeat any confidence that the girls had earned from mastering their outing.

The server finally returned. Carla watched protectively as the taller girl reached for the check. The waitress plopped down the bill and quickly returned to her other tables.

The dark-haired girl flipped over the bill. She whispered the price to her friend. Her friends' eyes seemed to pop out in shock. Carla could decipher the words she had mouthed: "Oh, my God!"

At first, they laughed at their miscalculation. Then, Carla saw the anxiety rise in them as the reality hit that they did not have enough money. The girls panicked.

Carla couldn't bear to see them in such distress. She had become attached to the duo, especially the raven-haired girl. She rushed over to their table.

"Girls," she offered in a soft tone so as not to bring attention to the situation. "I saw what happened, and you remind me of myself at your age. Can I help you out?" she offered, displaying her wallet.

The girls did exactly what they were probably taught to do if a stranger approached them: They politely refused her offer.

"Are you sure?" Carla insisted. "It's okay. I have a daughter of my own, Julie. See her over there?" She was trying to reassure them that she was a safe adult. "I'd want someone to help her out if she had miscalculated."

"No, thank you. I'll call my dad!" the girl who reminded her of herself insisted. "But thank you, it was so nice of you to offer."

Carla was impressed with the girl's social skills.

"Okay, I get it that you're not supposed to take anything from people you don't know, but I'm right over there if you change your mind," she reiterated in a motherly tone.

"Thank you again!" the girl responded. She seemed to be relieved at the sight of Carla's four-year-old daughter waving to them.

The girls handled the situation impeccably. They made a phone call, and shortly after that one of the girls ran out and returned clasping a fistful of bills. Apparently, a parent had come to the rescue.

Carla waited protectively until the girls gathered their things and exited. She clasped her daughter's hand and followed them outside. She had no explanation for her interest.

The girls scurried to a large, late-model SUV. It was apparent that their lack of money wasn't due to neediness. Carla watched as they climbed into the back seat of the vehicle. She turned to leave when suddenly she heard a voice from the driver's seat.

"Carla, Carla, is that you?" the driver said. She recognized that voice, but she couldn't place it. She turned to see who it was.

"Oh, my God!" she gasped. "Joey, is that you?"

"The one and only!" he joked, as he exited the van to embrace her. "This is really odd. I was just telling my daughter about you because she just turned twelve, and I thought about you and me at that age. Then, wham, here you are miles away from our hometown! Wow, I've thought of you so many times and wondered how your life turned out."

"That's your daughter?" Carla exclaimed. She was astonished. "I was ready to leave ten minutes ago, but I hung around to make sure the girls were alright."

"Yeah, she told me how nice you were."

Carla couldn't process it all. The child who fascinated her was the offspring of her first love. She hadn't seen him in over three decades.

"Can you believe this?" Joey exclaimed. "It's wild."

The two old friends exchanged phone numbers and agreed to meet at a later date. They were both married now, but it would be fun to reminisce. After thirty years, they would never have to wonder about each other again. A set of strange circumstances had reunited the childhood friends after all those years.

— Patricia Senkiw-Rudowsky —

Chapter 2

Touched by an Angel

13

Butterfly Love

*Pay attention to your dreams — God's angels often
speak directly to our hearts when we are asleep.*
~Eileen Elias Freeman,
The Angels' Little Instruction Book

I rarely remember my dreams, but I recalled all the details of this one. The vivid images seemed more like a memory than a dream. I'd heard of visitation dreams — my sister had one the night our dad died. But I'd never experienced one myself until a few years ago.

In the dream, my husband and I faced a white, three-story house in a Chicago neighborhood. It looked familiar, but I couldn't place it. Cars lined both sides of a narrow street. A young couple, dressed in black, walked ahead of us.

"Why are we here?" I asked.

My husband didn't answer me. Instead, he set his hand on my lower back and nudged me toward the house. We wove around strangers on the steps and stopped on the back porch. With a somber smile, my husband nodded his head toward the door.

I stepped into a crowded kitchen. All the guests stopped their conversations and moved apart to make a path for me. An older woman motioned for me to join her in front of a closed door just past the kitchen. At first, I hesitated, but then my body floated toward her.

"Why am I here?" I asked.

"He's been waiting for you," she said. She opened the door and escorted me into a dim bedroom.

And I saw him.

Rob leaned back against the headboard of a king-sized bed with puffy pillows framing his face. He looked like the energetic man I had dated twenty years ago before we broke up and went our separate ways. A bedside lamp cast a soft, yellow glow on his wavy, blond hair. He wore a light-gray T-shirt. A cream-colored comforter covered him from the waist down.

Rob's mom stood to his right, her eyes moist with tears. To his left, his wife sat in a chair with her eyes downcast. They didn't notice me, but Rob did. He welcomed me with a boyish smile and mischievous blue eyes. As I walked toward the bed, he seemed to relish my surprise.

I stopped a few feet from him. Unsure of how to act or what to say, I glanced at the three other women in the room for guidance, but they were lost in their thoughts and oblivious to my presence.

I frowned at Rob and shook my head, confused.

"I don't get it. I'm not supposed to be here. You didn't love me like that…. I was just one of many."

Rob gazed into my eyes. I couldn't look away. His lips didn't move, but I heard his soft voice.

You belong here. You always did.

He reached his hand out to me. I tripped backward. Then, I woke up.

Too rattled to fall back to sleep, I crept downstairs, but the odd dream replayed in my head. When I reached the bottom of the staircase, my stomach dropped.

A year before, Rob had announced his cancer diagnosis on Facebook. I quickly grabbed my phone and checked Rob's page. It had been a few weeks since anyone posted any updates on his page. I assumed no news was good news and dismissed the dream.

Later that morning, Rob's and my song played on my car radio. An eerie feeling came over me to check Rob's Facebook page again. I pulled into a nearby parking lot, took a deep breath, and clicked on his profile. And that's when I saw the post announcing that he had died early that morning. It occurred to me that he had died while I was having that dream.

I called my sister, Mary, and told her what happened. Before she had a chance to respond, I blasted her with questions.

"This doesn't make any sense. Was it him? Why me?"

"He cared a lot about you," she told me gently. "Maybe more than you realized. He wanted to say goodbye."

This did not jibe with the Rob I'd known. I always thought that Rob loved like a butterfly. One day, he picked a zinnia, the next a milkweed.

The last time I saw him, we ran into each other in downtown Chicago. Rob was headed to the commuter train, and my niece and I were on our way to see a Broadway show. As we approached each other on the busy sidewalk, we recognized each other immediately.

After a quick hug, I told Rob about my husband and eight-month-old son, and he showed me his new wedding ring. He gave me a playful shoulder punch, and we teased each other like the first day we met. Later, my niece told me it was like watching two fifth graders flirt. Awkward.

I'll never know why Rob appeared in my dream the night he died, but I've learned to accept it as a gift. Some believe that people appear in visitation dreams to offer peace and love. For years, I dismissed Rob's and my relationship as merely physical and lacking depth. But my dream made me rethink my conclusions about our relationship.

He came into my life for a reason: to teach me about what I wanted — and didn't want — in a healthy relationship. Rob expanded my worldview. I'm from a small town and led a sheltered life. We dined at exotic restaurants, visited art exhibits, and hiked up mountains. I'm grateful for those experiences.

But he also held narrow-minded beliefs that led to frequent arguments. He jumped from girlfriend to girlfriend, so I thought it was just a matter of time until he got bored with me. I felt insecure with him. I played the role of a jealous girlfriend and hated myself for it.

I had always placed great importance on physical chemistry, especially with Rob, but I realized I wanted friendship and a shared set of values in my next relationship. I'm grateful that I found these qualities with my husband.

This visitation dream helped me appreciate the good and bad parts of my relationship with Rob. Weirdly, he helped me be a better wife, mother, and friend. Maybe he felt the same and wanted to thank me for helping him be a better person. To tell me he has no regrets. To assure me that he's at peace. To tell me that someday we'll cross paths again and he'll greet me with a playful punch to the arm.

—Adrienne Parkhurst—

14

Tanner's Best Night Ever

Sometimes, our grandmas and grandpas
are like grand-angels.
~Lexie Saige

When my oldest grandson, Tanner, was around three years old, his great-grandfather passed away. Tanner had a special bond with his great-grandfather and was my only grandchild who got to know his Papa Byrd. My daddy was a special man, and I'm so happy Tanner was able to know him, even if it was for a short period of time. He often visited Papa in the nursing home. He loved spending time with him, "reading" him stories and pushing him around in his wheelchair. Those visits from Tanner were the highlights of my father's last days. They had a special bond.

After Daddy's passing, Tanner was confused about why he could not visit Papa Byrd any longer. It's hard to explain to a three-year-old why someone is no longer around for them. It broke my heart to see Tanner asking to go see Papa. The child was sad and confused.

About a month after the death of my father, Tanner's mother, Kensey, was awakened in the middle of the night to laughter. At first, she thought she was dreaming, but she suddenly realized that Tanner was in the hallway. She lay there quietly thinking, *If I say anything, he's going to want to get in bed with me.* She thought he'd soon lie back down and go to sleep. As she lay there, she was shocked to hear him running around, laughing and talking to someone. She had no clue what was going on.

She jumped out of bed and shouted out to Tanner, "What are you doing?"

Tanner happily replied, "I'm playing with Papa Byrd."

Kensey said there was so much excitement in his voice that she just stood there a moment wondering what was happening. She hesitated about going into the hallway — she was a little scared of seeing her Papa. Tanner had never shown this kind of behavior during the night, and a chill came over Kensey. She stood there frozen as Tanner ran around giggling, playing and talking with Papa.

After regaining her composure but still not entering the hallway, she said, "Tanner, tell Papa you have to go back to bed."

"No!" Tanner cried. "I haven't seen Papa in a long time, and we are having fun." Kensey was floored and realized that Tanner was having some kind of experience that she couldn't explain. This child was happy, having a blast with his Papa in the middle of the night. She even began to question her sanity. Was this really happening? She couldn't bring herself to look into the hallway. After a few minutes, Tanner willingly went back to bed and slept soundly the rest of the night. Needless to say, his mother did not.

The next morning, as Kensey hugged and kissed Tanner good morning, she asked, "Tanner, did you have a good night?"

He replied, "Yes, the best night ever!"

"What made it the best night ever, Tanner?" she asked.

He smiled and replied, "Papa came and played with me!"

Kensey knew at that moment that it was real. She sat there with tears streaming down her cheeks as Tanner ran off and played. Then she smiled up at Papa and said, "Thank you."

Tanner is now ten years old and remembers that encounter with Papa. His best night ever, he still proclaims. There has never been a doubt in our minds that Papa did visit Tanner that night to let him know he was there and would always be with him. Today, Tanner enjoys ragging his cousins about how he knew Papa Byrd and they didn't.

— Teresa B. Hovatter —

15

Held by an Angel

Angels descending, bring from above,
Echoes of mercy, whispers of love.
~Fanny J. Crosby

I sat by Andrew's hospital bed watching him sleep, grateful that my oldest grandson had a temporary respite from pain. I gazed at the metal cage holding multiple skeletal pins protruding from his right leg; the staff referred to it as an external fixator. He had a full-length immobilizer on his left leg, and his torso was encased in a complicated brace.

I recalled a conversation my husband and I had had with Andrew only five nights before. He was excited about his new job working for a roofer and the prospect of making enough money to support himself. I couldn't help but voice my concern about being on rooftops. He assured me that they'd be training him and providing safety gear. I was still not convinced and had an ominous feeling about his new occupation.

That day, November 16th, was already not good. It had been raining for days, and now the temperature had dropped. My cellphone rang. I saw Andrew's picture pop up on the screen and wondered if the wet weather had kept him home from his roofing job.

I put my cup of tea on the table and swiped the phone.

"Hi, Andrew," I said.

"Andrew's fallen off the roof, and he's hurt," I heard.

"Andrew, it's not nice to scare your grandma like this, so knock it off."

"Ma'am, this isn't Andrew," the voice said.

"Who is this?"

"I'm Jason. I work with Andrew."

Just then, I heard a scream of pain in the background. It was unmistakably my grandson's voice. He screamed again. I asked Jason, "Oh, my gosh, that's Andrew. How bad is he hurt?"

"Bad. One leg is about six inches shorter than the other. The paramedics are here, and they're trying to get his boot off. He told me to call you."

After learning their destination was the Level 1 trauma center in town, I said, "Tell him I'll come to the hospital as soon as I get dressed."

Andrew's mother was in California on business. My husband and I were the adults he and his younger sister called if a problem arose when their mom was out of town.

I threw on some clothes, grabbed my purse, and left for the hospital.

Arriving at the trauma center, I checked in and sat anxiously in the waiting room. No one allowed me into the trauma room or gave me any idea about Andrew's condition. I didn't know that he was having the first of three orthopedic procedures to save his right leg.

Finally, I was paged to enter through the automatic doors. I met a nurse in the hallway pushing my grandson's bed to a room. I followed along. Andrew was groggy from pain medication but managed to smile and lift his hand when he saw me.

Once settled in his room, Andrew slept as I sat by his bed. A nurse came in to check his vital signs and surgical sites. After learning that I was a retired RN, she confirmed what I had gathered from the conversation in the elevator. In addition to the multiple crush fractures in his right leg, Andrew's left leg was broken with multiple ligament injuries to the knee. He would need more leg surgery after the broken vertebrae in his back had been resolved.

As he awakened, he grimaced in pain. I squeezed his hand.

"God sure loves you," I said. "From what I've heard this morning, you fell three stories. You surely must have a guardian angel."

Andrew was silent for several minutes. "Grandma, I do have a guardian angel. I felt her holding me as I fell."

He paused. "The paramedic told me that I missed hitting the wooden deck and the cement patio by inches either way. If I had hit them, I wouldn't be here talking to you."

— Nancy Emmick Panko —

16

Look at Us Now

Sweet is the memory of distant friends! Like the mellow
rays of the departing sun, it falls tenderly,
yet sadly, on the heart.
~Washington Irving

C ynthia was the star of my eighth-grade math class. At thirteen, she was already a celebrity amongst us. While my classmates opted for preppy trends, Cynthia wore party dresses from the 1950s and chic couture from the 1960s to school, appearing to us like a cross between the lead singer of a girl group and a junior version of Jackie Kennedy. Aside from her status as a young fashionista, Cynthia was quick-witted and charming, and she always rooted for the underdog. Being gay, I was labeled a misfit, a moniker I wore with pride. Cynthia was one of the few people who told me to just be myself, something she did daily by example.

Over the years, I remembered her fondly, with awe and nostalgic reverence. I often wondered what she was up to, where life had taken her.

To our shared surprise, Cynthia and I reconnected in an airport terminal. Although more than a decade had passed, we recognized each other immediately.

The hour was late. I was flying back to college in Chicago after being home for the first time since leaving for school almost a year earlier. Cynthia's flight was canceled so she was waiting out the long night in the airport, convinced the airline would have a seat for her on the first flight out in the morning.

Over the next hour, we sat in the ghost town of an airport in seats facing a window where we watched the last arrivals and departures of the day. We drank coffee and tea from paper cups. We laughed. We caught up, filling in the gaps of the years since we'd last seen each other.

Cynthia was now a successful lo-fi musician, singer, and photographer. She had a devoted following of fans, and critics seemed to love her. Yet, from our conversation, I learned that the constant climb to the top was exhausting. She was grateful but seemed lonely. In return, I openly shared the struggles I was experiencing being far away from home, living the humble existence of a college student, and carrying the sense of dread that my recent writing success would be short-lived.

As I stood to leave and board my red-eye flight back to Chicago, Cynthia made me take pause with her words of encouragement. She reminded me, "We were always the different ones, you and me. But look at us now."

"Yes," I replied. "Look at us now."

I thought about that night and our conversation a few times over the next decade. I followed Cynthia's career from afar. She released two albums to acclaim. Her photography was on the cover of magazines. She seemed to be living a creative life of adventure and fame.

When word reached me that Cynthia had died in her sleep, I was stuck in traffic in Atlanta, trying to get to a literary festival where I was a guest author. I had just published my third novel, and a film I wrote and directed had been released on DVD earlier that week. My life was full, constant and moving. But, in that moment, when I glanced down at my phone and saw the sad words in a text message that Cynthia was gone, everything suddenly felt very still. I realized how significant our night in the airport had been, how that random reunion would now become the last time we would ever see each other.

A few months later, I found myself back at the same airport and in the same terminal. The weather was bad. I was worried about flying. I just wanted to get home. For weeks leading up to that night, I'd been trying my hardest to shake off a gnawing flicker of sadness that was threatening to explode into full-blown depression. Despite my success as an author, I was exhausted and overwhelmed.

Knowing I had a long flight ahead of me, I grabbed a cup of coffee. As I turned away from the coffee counter to head back to my gate, I stopped in my tracks. I did a double take. In the distance, I could've sworn I saw Cynthia, complete in a 1950s party dress made of shimmering colors one would find in a filled punch bowl. She was moving quickly through the crowd like a blazing enigma in sparkly high heels.

I followed, intrigued and anxious. I allowed myself to forget that Cynthia was gone, that she was dead. All form of reason and rational thought left me. Instead, I was filled with adrenaline and hope. I moved faster, wanting desperately to see my friend again. But, just as quickly as she appeared, she disappeared without a trace. Overwhelmed with a flood of grief I had not given myself permission to feel, I sat down in the first chair I saw, knowing I needed to give in and let my emotions surface.

Wiping away tears, I looked up and saw a sign. It was an advertisement for a product that was unique and clever but had yet to catch on. My eyes focused on the tagline of the ad: *Look at us now.* I stared at the words, and I knew. I wasn't just staring at words on glossy paper; I was looking at a message from my departed friend. It was like a gentle hug from beyond, a silent pep talk. It was the spark I needed to reignite the fire that fueled me for so long.

I stood up. I finished my coffee. I took a deep breath, and when I exhaled, I let a lot of stuff go in a single second. Shaken, I headed back to my gate. On my way there, I stopped for a moment. I looked at the seats in which Cynthia and I once sat more than ten years ago. I smiled at the memory, at a flash in my mind of the two of us sitting in the back of the classroom bonding over our shared hatred for math and our mutual determination to be different, no matter the cost. We were eternal misfits, but look at us now.

As I boarded the plane that would take me home, I whispered a word of thanks for the beautiful music Cynthia had left behind — and the shared words she'd sent me, just when I needed them most.

— David-Matthew Barnes —

17

Angels of Light

He performs wonders that cannot be fathomed,
miracles that cannot be counted.
~Job 5:9 (NIV)

I t was a warm, sunny September afternoon in Vancouver. Dave and I had just arrived home from what would be his last ultrasound appointment. I parked the car in front of the house as it was the shortest way into our home. Dave was exhausted and waited for me to open the passenger-side door for him. In my hurry, I was unintentionally careless when I did so.

I should have noticed Dave leaning against the door. When I opened it, he fell sideways out of the car onto the cement walkway that led into our house. He lay there in a fetal position, unmoving, too weak to raise himself. I tried to lift him, but even after eight months of cancer treatment, he still weighed close to two hundred pounds and was utterly immobile. The slightest bump caused terrible pain, so this fall would have been excruciating for him. He didn't speak, and I wondered if he was unconscious. I looked around in all directions for someone to help us but saw no one.

"I'm going to call 911," I said, and turned to run into the house.

Just then, a man walked toward us pushing a baby carriage. I couldn't understand how he had just materialized when I had seen no one seconds before. He was impeccably dressed in a navy-blue suit with a spotless, white shirt and navy tie. Two children, perhaps ages three and five, walked beside him. The dark-haired, older girl wore a beautiful, pink party dress with black patent-leather Mary Jane shoes. A pink crinoline peeked from beneath the dress's full flowered skirt. The little boy looked adorable in a pale-gray suit and tie. His shoes were polished to a high shine.

The man put the brake on the baby carriage and stepped forward. He looked at Dave on the ground and asked if we needed help. I accepted, of course, adding that my husband was very heavy and unable to move.

"Let me try," he said. With one hand outstretched, he leant over Dave. "Please allow me to help you, sir," he said.

Dave didn't move or speak. The man put his hand under Dave's arm at the shoulder. As if he weighed no more than a feather, he lifted him, and Dave's body unfolded like a rag doll's. The man lifted Dave's arm over his shoulder and put his own arm around Dave's waist to stabilize him.

As I led the way into the house, I heard the man tell the children to wait for him. Then, the two men walked up our front stairs and into our home together. I motioned toward our den, just a few steps from the front hall. The man lowered Dave onto a little sofa. He smiled as Dave tried to thank him and said he was glad to help.

As he turned to go, I thanked him profusely. He just smiled, murmured goodbye, and walked back out to the street where the children stood waiting for him.

I had never seen this man or the children, despite gardening in the front yard for many years, so I wondered who they were and where they were going. I thought it must be a child's birthday party. As they walked up the street, I watched to see if they would turn into one of the houses.

The sun glittered and danced on the chrome of the baby carriage as the little group slowly proceeded. They did not reach the corner or turn into one of the houses. With the sun shining so bright on their path, they disappeared. Right before my eyes, in a twinkle of light, they vanished.

My husband passed away about a month later. I stayed in the house for another five years but never saw the man or his children again. I will always remember them as our miraculous angels of light.

—Darlene G. Peterson—

Garbage in the River

A guardian angel walks with us, sent from up above,
their loving wings surround us and enfold us with love.
~Author Unknown

It wasn't just the cold of the January night that caused me to tremble as I walked to my destination. It was the knowledge of what I planned to do that night that sent shivers through my body, clear through to my soul. But, at that moment, I thought my soul was too far from any kind of redemption. I was going to leap. No one would miss me; of that I was more than certain.

My body quaked almost uncontrollably. I wanted to cry, but I figured I had cried all the tears my body could hold the past three weeks. How did everything get so out of control? I had spent all I had to travel to England to be reunited with my best friend turned boyfriend. Over ten years of love and friendship were torpedoed over a series of choices by both of us that left me feeling alone, unforgiven by God, and hopeless.

During my most recent interaction with my boyfriend, he looked at me and said I wasn't the person he fell in love with anymore. It killed me inside because I would have done anything he wanted of me. I had proved it to him over and over. And the coldness in his eyes as he uttered those words let me know it was all over. There was no going back. There was no way to undo the horrid deed that took me to the bridge that night. Besides, how could God ever love me? I hated myself with a royal passion.

The water below was murky and dark, like my broken heart. "Tell me why I shouldn't do this, God. I'm not worth it anymore." Myriad thoughts filled my head. *Where was God when I needed Him and cried out for His help? Was God even there, or had He abandoned me like everyone else in my life?*

Determined not to waste another second, I put out my foot, ready to leap into the cold waters. Somehow, at that very moment, a piece of garbage tossed away by some unknown soul upriver caught my attention. Suddenly, it was as if someone screamed silently into my heart, mind and soul: "You are NOT a piece of GARBAGE!"

I stood on the ledge of the bridge. My body shook as tears flowed down my cheeks. What was I? I was broken, of that I was 100-percent sure. The only thing that gave me hope during high school, when I was bullied mercilessly, was the friendship with my pen pal, turned best friend, turned lover. And now that was coming to an end, along with shared dreams, future children, and a life in Lancashire with him.

I wrestled in my heart and head. It was mysteriously quiet on that road. It felt as if time had stopped, awaiting my decision to decide who I was in that moment. It was as if the water begged me not to force it to swallow me up in the darkness. I decided to climb down from the bridge.

As I did so, a voice called to me through the darkness: "Oy! You! Are you alright?"

My foot almost touched the sidewalk. I turned around to see a handsome man with blond hair. His car window was down, with his head hanging outside to look at me. His amiable face had concern etched across it.

"Oh, hello," I said.

"Are you alright, luv? If you need, I can take you somewhere."

My back was turned away as I said, "I-I don't know. I-I think I'll be okay."

"Are you sure? Do you wish me to stay?"

My heart warmed to the concern of a stranger. "Oh, thank you. You don't have to take me anywhere. I really appreciate it, though, but I think I'll be okay now." I turned to face him and started to say,

"Thank y —"

He was gone; his car nowhere to be seen. I looked up the road, but there was no sign of any rearview lights. I shivered again. The blond-haired man hadn't had enough time to take off into thin air after talking with me a few seconds prior — at least not in the natural world. I reckoned I had met an angel; it's the only explanation I could give for his sudden appearance and disappearance.

I walked along, feeling like an invisible shield of protection embraced me. Shortly thereafter, my boyfriend arrived and angrily told me to get into the car. We eventually split up, and unfortunately I entered a "self-punishing" mode of my life. However, the memory of that night on the bridge when all of eternity screamed, "You are not a piece of garbage" — and I encountered what I believe to be one of my guardian angels — has helped center me and get me back on track many times.

— Rebecca L. Jones —

19

The Ivy Wall

One thing you can say for guardian angels: they guard.
They give warning when danger approaches.
~Emily Hahn

We prepared for the party all week. The weekend was finally here, and everything looked perfect. We couldn't wait to begin.

I had just accepted a promotion for a new job as the Academic Dean at a university in Europe. I hit the ground running once I got there, so I was really busy at work while still hunting for a house to live in. Finally, we found a great place, and we planned to have my hard-working staff and their families over for a BBQ party as soon as possible. I thought it would be nice to get to know everyone better in a relaxed atmosphere. My husband thought we should invite our new neighbors over as well. The more the merrier.

The house had a large back yard that was made for get-togethers, with a lovely pool, patio and BBQ area. It was surrounded by a nine-foot wall, lusciously covered in beautiful ivy. Stairs through the wall led to a raised back garden with trees and bushes. Beyond that was a wall of trees, a national forest.

Our family of rescue cats and dogs quickly discovered the warm spots on the patio and loved to lie beside the ivy wall. It was sunny there and a good place for a snooze. My husband and I would often join them on lawn chairs after a dip in the pool. It seemed like paradise.

As we fussed with our house over the first few weeks, trying to find the perfect place for this piece of comfy furniture or that antique chair, we noticed that the cats were sunning themselves less than usual by the ivy wall. Instead, they often settled into the chairs in our BBQ area, on the other side of the pool. We didn't think about it much, knowing that they would work things out for themselves. The dogs followed the cats, snuggling up to them on the chairs. We were happy everyone was settling in so well at their new home.

Finally, we picked a date for our big BBQ. It was a Saturday two weeks away. However, to our dismay, it rained for days on end before our date, with bad weather threatening to run right through the party weekend. We began preparations anyway and were lucky enough to have the good weather return just in time. As things dried up, we finished the preparations, hung extra lights for the party, and made the final arrangements.

My university colleagues, our new neighbors, and all their families started arriving around noon for a day of festivities. It was wonderful to see everyone relaxing and enjoying themselves. My husband and I began a whirlwind day of meeting, greeting and entertaining everyone. We stoked up the barbecue and grilled while everyone got acquainted by socializing, swimming, and having a great time.

The place was packed, yet the atmosphere was relaxed. Tray upon tray of appetizers, drinks and barbecued goodies were laid out and consumed. It was hard to figure out who was who, though, and to keep names and faces straight. There were just so many people there.

Finally, as time went on, darkness fell, and our party lights twinkled against the ivy on our outdoor wall. Things began to wind down, with the people who had brought young children leaving first. Our adult guests took turns locating my husband or me to say their goodbyes before leaving, although we didn't always know who they were.

A mysterious, darkly dressed woman approached me, smiling as she quietly congratulated me on my promotion and lovely party. Then, she suddenly gripped my arm, became quite serious, and whispered, "But beware the ivy wall." Then, just as quickly as she had approached me, she was gone into the night, leaving me staring after her.

Needless to say, I was taken aback. But my initial shock was dissipated by the departure of more guests, stopping to say their good-byes. Before we knew it, midnight had arrived, and the last guests finally sauntered out.

We were totally exhausted but also ecstatic that everything had gone well. We decided to wind down a little before going to sleep by having a nightcap in the BBQ area with our cats and dogs.

While we were quietly chatting there, I mentioned the mysterious woman and the strange warning she had given me about our ivy wall. My husband didn't know who I was talking about when I described her, saying that he hadn't noticed anyone in the crowd like that. It wasn't surprising, though, considering the volume of people there, many of whom were still unknown to us.

"The cats and dogs have been avoiding that area lately, though," he said with a chuckle and a wink. Lost in our thoughts, we clinked glasses and quietly enjoyed our nightcaps while looking at our beautifully lit patio area.

Just as we were finishing up, we noticed that the twinkling lights on our ivy wall started to shimmer. Looking at each other and then back at our lights, we couldn't figure out what was going on. The dogs began whining. The cats all quickly got up and slinked away. What was happening? Had we been cursed somehow by the mysterious woman?

In slow motion, our whole back wall seemed to be slowly leaning forward. We continued to stare at it, stupefied as it started to wobble.

Then, the whole thing tipped over, thundering onto the patio and into the pool. Ripping down ivy and crushing everything in its wake, it smashed into a thousand pieces.

Still sitting there, we were hit by a tidal wave of water that was displaced from the pool as we continued to stare in disbelief. The neighborhood lights went on at all the surrounding houses since it sounded like an earthquake was happening, with the epicenter at our place.

Our neighbors came over and gathered in our yard, staring in awe at the rubble in our pool and on our patio. Just a bit earlier, most of them had been there celebrating with us. We would all have been crushed by the wall had we still been on the patio when the ivy wall collapsed.

The insurance adjuster who came to investigate said that the heavy rain had put a lot of pressure on the side of the wall holding back the earth on the elevated section of our yard. Ivy tends to pull downward, too, so the additional lights and a crowd causing vibrations were just enough to tip over the wall. He marveled how a real disaster had been averted by the party ending just in time, and that our pets had alerted us to the danger by whining and astutely sitting on the opposite side of the pool.

Little did he know that a mysterious angel had been there to give us an additional warning. We haven't seen her since but are eternally grateful that she attended our BBQ party. We hope she had a good time.

—Donna L. Roberts—

20

Rita on the Granite Steps

Timing in life is everything.
~Leonard Maltin

I'd lived in L.A. for nearly eight years, but I was leaving. My car was already packed, and before I drove to the office for the final time, I took a walk up Beachwood Canyon to hike some steep granite stairs just as I did most mornings to keep my heart beating strong. That's where I saw her — halfway up, moving slowly, struggling with two bulging bags. Normally, I might have rushed past the small, older woman without thinking or speaking. But this day, I offered to help.

"That would be lovely," she said, smiling as she turned her magnetic eyes toward the light. She said her name was Rita.

I don't recall what Rita asked as we ascended the final twenty-five steps side by side, but I remember telling her that I'd been in L.A. for a while and was about to make a big change. After lunch, I'd be driving cross-country to live alone in the woods. "That sounds like a splendid adventure," she said.

When we reached the top step, Rita invited me to sit and catch my breath on a retaining wall next to what I assumed was her home. That's when I got a good look. Rita wasn't the type of person I usually encountered in Hollywood. She was weathered and earthy. She looked like someone who'd enjoy digging potatoes barefoot on ancestral land much like where I was going.

"Are you hungry?" Rita asked with her peaceful demeanor as she pulled a Hostess cupcake from one of her bags.

I was starving, but my hunger at the moment wasn't for food. My job had become too easy and boring. I wasn't contributing much to the world, and I felt myself dying a little each time I traversed the gray office floors. All I'd thought about the past year was starting a new life on land I'd bought near the French Broad River not far from where I'd grown up.

I told Rita I'd save her cupcake for the trip, but I didn't tell her that I was worried about striking out without much money saved. Or that I was taking this leap because I'd recently chased down thieves and almost been killed. Or how, once I'd mustered the courage to quit my job and do what I planned to do, I'd begun wearing loose-fitting, white clothing to distance myself from the so-called real world in hopes of staying safe. I didn't tell Rita any of this as we sat on that wall — at least, not with words — but I sensed that a deep, silent conversation bubbled between us all the while.

By the time I stood to go, it seemed that Rita knew everything about me she needed to know. "Take care on your journey," she said. "Your mother misses you and wants you safely home."

It caught me by surprise when she said that. If I hadn't had so many loose ends to tie up, I might have lingered to let her words soak in.

Instead, I plunged into my day and got busy with final banking and returning keys and computers. I sort of forgot about Rita's words until two hours into my trip when I stopped at a rest area to lie flat on my back atop a picnic table to breathe as I gazed up at the sky. As I thought back on the morning, I fell into the deepest, most pleasant sleep in years. A half-hour later, I awoke completely refreshed.

As I resumed my long drive, I reflected on the morning again. I realized I hadn't mentioned my mother during the encounter with Rita, or the fact that my mother lived in the town where I was headed, or even that my father was no longer living and that I'd bought the land after I'd scattered his ashes into the river with plans to change my life. So why had Rita said what she'd said?

I didn't eat Rita's cupcake that entire week on the road, fearing that if I did, the magic spell Rita had cast with her kind words and holy presence might subside. Some mornings, I let the cupcake sit on the dashboard as something of a talisman, absorbing the sun's gentle early rays that sustained me, safely, all the way home.

I hadn't told my mother beforehand what I was doing. My return home was a surprise, and the first afternoon I sat in her kitchen, she was pleased. "I've been thinking about you so much lately," she said.

As my mother moved to gaze upon the hummingbird feeder outside her kitchen window, the light caught her eyes in a way I'd never noticed. I marveled at how much she resembled Rita; the two might have been sisters.

Then, I recalled the street address of what I believed to be Rita's home—the house where we'd sat on that wall. The very next day, I sent Rita a postcard saying I'd made it safely, that I'd kept the cupcake she'd given me all the way home for good luck, and that I'd eaten it for my first breakfast in the woods near a stream and ancient granite wall that reminded me of the steps where we'd met. Rita and I had shared such a connection that I'd begun to envision her as a new friend—at the very least, a pen pal. If I ever returned to L.A., she'd be the first person I'd want to see.

But I never heard back from Rita.

In the years since, I've thought of her many times—how that final meeting aided me on my transition to a new life. Sometimes, I've wondered whether Rita was actually there at all.

— Robert McGee —

21

Our Margies

*Not everything we experience can be
explained by logic or science.*
~Linda Westphal

A s a child, I was terrified that my family was part of a vicious cycle that killed off one parent while you were still a kid. I didn't know when it began or why. Had there been some unknowable, malevolent force that fed on my family's DNA? Or perhaps we were being punished for some long-ago misdeed, and soul-snatching was the price my ancient ancestors had negotiated. Or maybe we had just been really unlucky, and we were trying to make sense when there was no sense to be made.

Every generation going back at least five generations, on both sides, had a death in the nuclear family — either a parent or a child. All the losses were due to illnesses or diseases.

Of all the historic losses I learned about as a child, I was most transfixed by my father's. My dad hadn't met his father until he was two years old. My grandfather had been inducted into the U.S. Army shortly after his marriage. He was somewhere in Europe, fighting for the allied forces during World War II, when his first child was born. Meanwhile, his wife Margie held down the fort and took care of their little boy.

When my grandfather returned from the war, he went to work in the coal mines in a rural town in eastern Washington, where his long days ended just in time to read his son a bedtime story.

A few years later, when my father's seventh birthday was near, he learned he was getting a sibling for his birthday! He was hoping for a brother named Teddy. This was March 1950, a year that would go down in weather lore as one of the harshest in the state's history. My dad and grandfather were recovering from colds, but that same shape-shifting virus took a greater toll on my grandmother's pregnant body.

When she spiked a 104-degree fever, my grandfather insisted that the one and only doctor in town come to see her. She had a raging bacterial infection, which ravaged her body. The elderly physician didn't arrive for another twenty-four hours because the weather was so formidable. When he finally arrived, he came without penicillin because he didn't think it was safe to use on a pregnant woman. By the time he arrived, Margie's temperature had reached 107. The doctor told my grandfather he had to prioritize which one to save if both couldn't be saved. My grandfather chose his wife.

Sadly, they lost both Margie and the baby.

The baby had been a boy, Theodore. Teddy.

Throughout my childhood, I wondered if and when the spell would be broken. I routinely asked the universe to protect my small family of four. My sensible mom, never believing in angels or any other heavenly intermediaries, made one exception — and her name was Margie. "Grandma Margie watches over our family. She is our guardian angel."

She'd say, "Honestly, do you think your father would still be alive today if he didn't have someone looking out for him?" On a more tender note, she'd say, "A mother's love transcends death. Until your father is with her again, she will always be tethered to him, wanting to protect him." My mom told us that we were lucky to have Margie, but we should also understand that Margie might ask something of us one day. Maybe we'd need to protect or care for someone when she couldn't. As an angel, there was only so much she could do.

When I gave birth to my daughter at age twenty-four, I realized that my childhood family had escaped the dreaded fate. The spell had been broken, as evidenced by my grown sister and still-alive parents attending my wedding and then welcoming their first grandchild into the world. We had been spared.

I now understood that just because you've stopped looking for the monsters doesn't mean they aren't there.

Fast forward to my own happy family of three. My daughter was sixteen when my husband was diagnosed with stage 4 non-Hodgkin's lymphoma. I wondered where my Margie was. Shouldn't she also protect my husband? Just when my husband's lymphoma went into remission, another cancer attacked — a rare gallbladder cancer that advanced quietly and quickly. He was gone in eight weeks.

How could this happen? How did the curse skip over one generation, only to resurface during the next one?

Four years later, I met the man who became my second husband on Match.com. He was a widower, looking for a widow, and I popped up. We had similar back stories: Both of our spouses had died of cancer, leaving behind heartbroken children. He had three children, ages six, eleven, and fourteen. My daughter was twenty.

We met for dinner at my favorite restaurant and found so many connections: He was Jewish like my late husband. Each had Mordecai as his Hebrew name. We leaned the same way politically. We loved independent films, estate sales, and old-world wines. We both hated arrogance and mayonnaise.

Martin was the first man I could see myself with after my husband's death, but I wasn't sure if I was emotionally equipped to raise three more children.

I agreed to go out on a second date. We were in a wine bar where we continued our conversation. We talked about what we loved most about our kids and shared photos of them. At the end of our date, he gently cupped my face and kissed me softly and lingeringly, which sent tingles up and down my spine.

On our third date, I made dinner for Martin at my house. We talked more about our families, and I realized I'd never asked what his wife's name was.

"Margie," he said.

I watched goose bumps crawl up my arms and then felt them march across my neck. I reached for my glass of wine, and my hands began to shake.

Martin asked if I was okay.

I nodded. My father had died a few months after my husband had, which meant he was back with his mother, Margie.

I finally understood that it was my turn to step up to help with the guardian angel role. My mother had been right. Margie would one day ask for my help, only this Margie was not my father's mother. Rather, this Margie was the first mother of my future children.

I was answering her plea to watch over her children and to love them fiercely. Two years later, I officially became her children's second mother. It hasn't always been easy, but raising children never is. I know that Margie knows it took both of us to raise them. I might be biased, but I think we've done a pretty great job.

—Victoria Lorrekovich-Miller—

22

An Angel Escort

*In their eyes shine stars of wisdom and courage
to guide men to the heavens.*
~Jodie Mitchell

I sat in the worn glider, mindlessly moving the chair back and forth, back and forth. The hospital room was dark except for the dim glow of the bathroom light. Through the window, in the distance, I could see the twinkling lights of the big city.

How many days, how many hours, had I sat in this room watching over my husband? The room was as familiar to me as the back of my hand. The quiet beeps and clicks of the medical equipment were soothing background noise. Outside in the hallway, I could hear the night janitor gathering trash. I had become so familiar with the rhythm of the hospital floor that I found comfort in the sounds.

I brought my gaze back to Scott, who was asleep in the bed. He was dying. The doctor told me two days earlier that he only had three days left. He had fought a long war with cancer, but a virus had gotten into his blood, and he couldn't fight it off in his weakened state. The doctor said his body was shutting down. The kidneys and liver had already shut down, and I could tell by his breathing that his lungs were losing the battle, too. It amazed me how tactical a virus could be. It had started at the bottom, with his kidneys, and worked its way up. It would eventually make its way to his brain, shutting down everything in its path. The doctors knew he could only survive so long. I so wanted them to be wrong.

I sat praying and pleading with God to work a miracle and save my husband's life. I had just hung up from a call from our pastor, who reassured me that our friends and church were praying hard. I was forty-seven with a fourteen-year-old, twelve-year-old, and ten-year-old to raise. I did not want to face the future as a single parent. I needed my husband.

I sat in the dark room and pleaded for a miracle. Around 10:00 P.M., I felt a change in the room. I couldn't place my finger on what was different, but I had the distinct impression I wasn't alone. I couldn't see anyone, but I could *feel* them. It wasn't scary; it was actually very comforting. I thought that, in my tired state, maybe I was just feeling people's prayers.

The nightshift nurse came in and did her check. No change. She gave me a sympathetic smile. I could tell she knew that hope was running out. Yet, she still administered the drugs that could help Scott continue to fight.

Shortly after she left, I felt fluttering in the room, like whoever was with me now had friends. I strained my eyes to peer into the dark corners but could see nothing. I was certain I was not alone in the room. I got up and splashed cold water on my face, thinking that maybe all the stress was getting to me. I could not shake the feeling I was being watched by more than one thing. But I didn't feel threatened, so I figured that whatever or whoever was in that room must be friendly.

Around 2:00 A.M., I felt the need to sing. I am not a singer, and yet I felt that I should sing—not any song, but a song I had just heard for the first time on Sunday: "How Deep the Father's Love for Me." I knew every word to a song I had sung once. I sang it and then hummed it as I sat beside Scott's bed and held his hand. The nurse came in for 5:00 A.M. checks and told me that it was the most beautiful song she had ever heard. I asked her if she felt like there was someone else in the room. She said no, but she said the room felt extremely peaceful to her.

After she exited the room, I felt the fluttering again. This time, I could feel the air moving. There weren't just a couple of us in the room anymore.

More beings arrived. There was a feeling of anticipation, like something big was going to happen, and these beings were all excited. I wished I could see them! There must have been hundreds by now with more coming. The whole room was pulsating with movement.

I continued to sit by Scott's bed, holding his hand and softly talking to him. I reminded him of things we had done, memories we had made, and how much he was loved. I asked him if he could feel all the fluttering and swirling or if he could see something I couldn't see. He didn't respond except for occasionally squeezing my hand. The fluttering seemed to increase in intensity. It was like these beings were almost past the point of containing themselves with excitement. Scott stirred and opened his eyes, looking right at me. The love I saw looking at me was a love like I had never seen before. He gazed at me, and it was like the universe held its breath. I think I held mine. As I held his gaze, I was aware of all the commotion around me like the little beings had reached their pinnacle.

Scott closed his eyes, and, just like that, everything was still. They were gone. Every ounce of my being wanted to follow. I had a glimpse of something I could not see, and everything in me wanted to go there with them. It felt as if someone had placed a hand on my shoulder, and I heard very clearly, "No, not now." I sank into the chair trying to comprehend what I had just felt and seen.

I looked at Scott. He was peacefully resting. It took me minutes to realize he was not breathing. He was gone! He left with them! I sat there trying to grasp what had just happened. I could not comprehend the love radiating from his eyes; it seemed to have seared my soul. At the same time, I also realized I had just been allowed a small glimpse of heaven.

I eventually pressed the call button and told the nurse I would need a doctor. I knew only a doctor could call the time of death. Scott's death caused quite a bit of excitement on the floor. Apparently, certain things happen with blood pressure and such, and it alerts the medical staff that the patient is near death. None of that had happened with Scott. He just left, along with those fluttering beings, those angels.

—Jill Leyda Peterson—

Divine Intervention

23

Our Jake

Never lose hope. Just when you think it's over
... God sends you a miracle.
~Author Unknown

Our oldest son, Curtis, and his wife Karyn had recently been on a trip to Italy. They were at our home showing us the pictures of their holiday. When we got to the very last photo, it was only a picture of a written date. I had no idea what it meant, and it took a few minutes before I realized that it was their way of telling us that we were going to be grandparents!

On May 13, 2011, we got the phone call from Curtis saying that he had taken Karyn to the hospital. The ultrasound Karyn had that day indicated the baby wasn't growing as it should. Curt told us they would give Karyn steroids for two days and then do a C-section to deliver the baby. My heart sank as I realized how tiny this baby would be at only thirty-three weeks along. I told Curtis that his dad and I would be praying for all of them — and, boy, did we pray.

Curt phoned us on May 15 to tell us that Karyn had just given birth to a three-pound, five-ounce baby boy. He sounded like such a proud dad. I could hardly wait to meet our tiny new grandson, Jake.

Curt called us the next day and told me they were going to do genetic testing on Jake because they suspected Down Syndrome. I tried to be calm and reassuring as I spoke to my son, but inside I was a wreck. I could hear the concern in his voice, and I wanted to somehow make it all better. I did the only thing I could think of — I prayed.

Curt called later and said that the test results showed that Jake did have Down Syndrome. His voice was strained, and I could tell that he was having a hard time maintaining his composure as he spoke to me. My heart broke for my son, my daughter-in-law, and the unknown future that lay ahead.

My husband and I went to church as usual that following Sunday. My heart was heavy, and I had so much that I needed to talk to God about. In the row directly in front of us sat a mom, dad, and their two teenage sons. I had never seen this family in church before, and it didn't take long for me to notice that one of the boys had Down Syndrome. I couldn't take my eyes off him. I watched this family interact with the boy and each other.

The service started, and the boy with Down syndrome kept gently poking the other brother, trying to get him to look at something he had drawn on a paper. The older brother looked at the drawing and smiled encouragingly before kindly motioning for him to "shhh." The boy with Down Syndrome smiled and went back to his drawing. A few minutes later, he leaned over and began to whisper something in his brother's ear. The brother listened patiently and chuckled quietly at whatever he said before gently motioning again for him to "shhh." A few minutes passed before the boy with Down Syndrome thought of something else that just "needed" to be shared with his brother. Again, the brother patiently and lovingly responded to him.

At this point, the parents both looked over at the boy, smiled kindly, and made soft "shhh" sounds to him. The boy with Down Syndrome grinned, nodded and proceeded to rest his head on his older brother's shoulder, where it stayed for the rest of the church service.

I realized that God used this family to speak comfort, encouragement and hope to my unsettled spirit and hurting heart. It was going to be okay, and the future looked extremely bright.

I honestly don't believe it was a coincidence that this family, whom we had never seen before and have never seen again, was seated directly in front of us that Sunday morning. I believe that God placed them right where they were so we could see a bit of what the future held and know that it was going to be okay.

Jake has been an absolute joy and blessing to our entire family.

— Maureen Slater —

Recipes from Above

Impossible situations can become possible miracles.
~Robert H. Schuller

My father was a gourmet cook. He loved being in the kitchen. It was the one place in the house where he was happiest. He was always whipping up one concoction or another.

He made the most delicious mashed potatoes that felt like silk and melted on the tongue like butter. He made stews, shepherd's pie, and upside-down cakes. His chicken stew in a white sauce was my favourite dish. I also have lingering memories of his extra-cinnamon homemade applesauce that took hours to make as it simmered on the stove. He said his secret was in using the peels. I never liked applesauce, especially the insipid yellowish commercial purees, but I ate his just plain from a bowl and with everything from yogurt to ice cream.

When he was a student, my dad worked in a big hotel, first washing dishes and then waiting on tables, but always with an eye on the cooks, taking mental notes.

I am not sure my mother knew how lucky she was to have a spouse who could run a kitchen the way my dad did. When she came home from work, the table was always set and dinner was ready. Because my dad was a professor, he spent more time at home than in the classroom, preparing lectures, grading papers, and doing research. This freed up more time for cooking, too.

Unfortunately, I did not inherit my dad's talent. I tried and tried, and read recipes, but most of the time I failed at whipping up a decent meal for anybody. Kraft macaroni and cheese was all I could manage.

I should have watched and learned from him, but being young and restless, I was in and out of the house like the wind. And besides, Dad loved rich foods, and I was more of a carrot nibbler in my teens.

And so the scents and palatable dishes my dad created disappeared forever when he passed away — except for the week after we buried him.

As I've said, my limitations in a kitchen were obvious. But during the week following the funeral, I got up one morning with a craving for Dad's chicken stew. I had never made it before, and yet I went to the store and bought some chicken, small potatoes, celery, tarragon and parsley. I still had no idea what I was going to do with them. I didn't even have a recipe.

At home, I chopped up the chicken — something I would never do as the feel of raw meat is disgusting to me — melted butter in a pan, and added flour, spices, and a little white wine. Before I knew it, I had a white sauce to cook my chicken and potatoes in. I had managed blindly, and without a recipe book, to concoct a creamy and delicate white sauce with just the right amount of flavouring. This was the most savoury dish I had ever made. In the past, whenever I tried, despite using a recipe, I only managed to stir up a lumpy and sticky clump of dough.

I had navigated the kitchen like a pro, like a zombie possessed by a spirit. It almost felt like sleepwalking. It was as if Dad had taken over my body and taste buds.

At supper, my son took one bite, turned to me with eyes wide with surprise — my failure as a cook was no secret — and smacked his lips with delight.

"Mom? You made this? This is sooooo good. Wow, I am impressed, Mom."

"I'll second that," my husband said.

"Well…" I hesitated for a second. "I think your grandfather took over here actually. I didn't really know what I was doing; I just did it."

They both stared at me.

"I am serious. It felt like he was holding my hand and telling me what to do."

"You didn't follow a recipe?" My husband was astonished.

"Nope."

"What's for supper tomorrow?"

And then my son asked for seconds.

The next day, I made my dad's mashed potatoes. The day after that, I made a lasagna. And the day after that, I had a craving for smoked meat, something I normally disliked. I picked up some smoked meat on my way home from work, something I never did. But my craving was like an obsession. My father loved smoked meat.

My son thought he had died and gone to food heaven. However, all this meat that kept landing on the dinner table confused my husband; we had been vegetarians for so long.

Mom was turning into an outstanding cook thanks to Grandpa, who had decided to move into her body.

We hoped anyway.

But no.

The following week, it was all gone. It didn't matter what I tried to cook. I was back to making macaroni salads and grilled cheese.

—Julie de Belle—

25

A Chance to Say Goodbye

You should never feel alone. There's always someone
to turn to. It is the guardian angel
who is watching over you.
~K. Sue

O ne summer, my husband Bob and I purchased a teeny camper in hopes of making memories for our two daughters. Camping had never been near the top of my fun list, but I began to share my family's enthusiasm because I would be sleeping inside instead of on the ground. The girls loved the over-the-cab bed where they could look out at the entire world. We learned how to fit the table and chairs in just the right spot, like puzzle pieces put together. We were able to fill every nook and cranny with what we needed, but my main concern was that we would have no phone for two weeks. (This was before everyone carried cellphones.)

Off we headed for the first leg of our journey from Colorado to Yellowstone National Park. By the time we pulled into the parking lot of Jenny Lake in the Grand Teton National Park, the girls wanted to run around and we grown-ups were eager for a walk.

After a while, we realized we were lost. A passerby heard our conversation and gave us directions to the nearest ranger station.

Upon arriving at the ranger station, we walked single file up the ramp. I was in the lead followed by our two young girls and Bob.

Right before reaching the door, I noticed a chalkboard with names listed. I glanced at it but kept walking and proceeded to yell over my shoulder that I was glad our name was not on it. I quickly entered the ranger station to get warm as it had started to snow.

The girls were hurrying up the ramp when they happened to spot a small bird's nest lodged above the chalkboard. They pointed it out to Bob, which caused him to stop. His eyes were drawn to the writing.

He gasped when he read our name, with instructions to contact a ranger.

It turned out that my aunt Erma (my mom's twin sister) had been trying to reach me for days. She only knew that we were somewhere in the Yellowstone area.

The rangers let me use their phone to call Aunt Erma. She shared that my mom was in the ICU with an unidentified disease. She was not able to speak but was conscious, and Aunt Erma felt I should go home immediately.

I was able to fly out of Wyoming to Denver with a transfer to Sioux City, Iowa in record time. My precious mom made eye contact with me when I entered her room, and we both cried. I clung to her for another hour before she slipped into a coma, not to waken again.

A chance encounter with a passerby, plus a tiny bird's nest in just the right place allowed me to share one last bit of earthly love with my mom.

— Michelle Rahn —

26

Heavenly Message

*Let gratitude be the pillow upon which you kneel to say
your nightly prayer. And let faith be the bridge
you build to overcome evil and welcome good.*
~Maya Angelou

I t was New Year's Eve, and I was dressed to the nines: new dress, special jewelry, and spiky heels. Our six-year-old niece was staying with us while her mom, my sister, recovered from back surgery, so I had to find a babysitter, which I had not done before.

Early in December, I started asking neighbors for sitter recommendations. I knew that babysitters would be in high demand on this date. Luckily, I secured one whose name popped up several times. I liked the idea that she was an older woman — no teens for me!

By the time my husband and I were ready to depart for the New Year's Eve gala, my niece and Mrs. Oliver were enjoying a fast game of *Old Maid*.

Our host had secured a room at a new local hotel. We enjoyed the band, great hors d'oeuvres and the wine bar as we mingled with my husband's co-workers. The big meal was scheduled for midnight.

The evening was still young when I had an overwhelming feeling of dread. I wanted to leave. My husband asked if I could stick it out until after the midnight toast, but I knew I could not. A feeling of panic was overwhelming me. I knew my husband was embarrassed in front of his boss, but I would not give in, so we left.

Fifteen minutes later, we pulled into the driveway and entered our home. We found Mrs. Oliver passed out on the couch. There was a bottle of scotch on the coffee table and an empty glass on the carpet next to a burning cigarette.

For many years when we lived in that house, I looked at the burn mark in the carpet as a reminder of what could have been and thanked God for sending His "heavenly message."

— Mary Grant Dempsey —

A Miraculous Meeting

Be an angel to someone else whenever you can,
as a way of thanking God for the help
your angel has given you.
~Eileen Elias Freeman,
The Angels' Little Instruction Book

As I left my mother's apartment, I glanced at my watch. As usual, we had visited longer than planned as we got caught up in laughing and sharing stories. I treasured these visits with her, especially since my father's death eighteen months earlier. *You truly have to enjoy every moment you can,* I told myself as I entered the elevator.

In the ride down two floors, I thought about the call I had received moments earlier from my friend Brenda. A wicked storm had just passed through the area near my home, more than two hours west of Mom's place, and she wanted to see if I was okay. I wondered about any potential damage or power failures as the elevator doors opened.

However, I was distracted by thoughts of the visit ahead. My brother had a portion of my father's ashes for me to pick up, and I was running out of time to get to his place and then back to our nearby vacation cottage for dinner. I jumped into my car and headed out toward the highway.

Right away, I noticed the sky had turned a strange combination of purple and brown. The wind had picked up, and an eerie feeling came over me. In that moment, I just wanted to get home.

Divine Intervention | 87

"Hey, Bruce," I said into the phone. "I feel like I'm driving into the eye of a storm, so I'm going to turn around. I'll have to swing by another day."

Even as I hung up, the winds accelerated. By the time I had driven back into town, a ferocious storm was battering my car. Trees toppled onto the road, and a tent blew out of nowhere and under my car.

I knew I had to pull over, but where?

I turned left to seek refuge at my niece's home. Getting there was treacherous as I swerved the car around windblown debris. The rain came down so heavily that I could barely see the road, even with my windshield wipers on full speed.

Finally, I arrived at her brick home, but she was not there. "Okay," I told myself aloud. "You're safe as long as you stay in this metal box."

That's when my car door flew open.

Suddenly, a screaming, drenched boy threw himself onto the front seat and slammed the door behind him. He was hysterical with fear to the point where I could barely make out what he was saying.

"Breathe," I told him between his sobs. "You're safe here. It's okay." I was pretty rattled, but I tried to stay calm for his sake.

He kept screaming about his mother. "She's going to think I'm dead!" he yelled. After several minutes, he settled down enough to explain himself.

The little guy had been at a friend's house but left late since they were having so much fun playing a game. When he headed out on his bike to meet his mother on the other side of town, he got caught in the storm. He tried to call her from my car, but she didn't pick up. Now, he feared she had died since she was also traveling by bicycle.

Now, this wasn't just any storm. It was a derecho, a fast-moving group of severe thunderstorms that traveled in a straight line to wipe out trees and power lines. We didn't know it yet, but the electrical grid in this town would be down for a full week.

And this ten-year-old boy had been riding his bike out in the open while I had been huddled in my car!

He was panicking about the state of his beloved bicycle, so when the rain eased up slightly, we found it lying on the curb in a huge puddle. I got drenched while loading it into my hatchback; now we were both soaked to the skin.

Finally, the boy reached his mother. She had tucked her phone into the bottom of her backpack to protect it from the rain. And she was desperate to see him to make sure he was all right.

"I'm in the car with a stranger," he told her with a shaky voice.

"Not a scary stranger," I chimed in, finally finding some humor in this nightmare. "Tell us where you are, and we'll come find you."

As we drove to her location, I noticed that no one else was out on the street. If I hadn't pulled up beside my niece's house, who knows where this child would have gone?

It took us several minutes to get across town since so many streets were blocked by giant trees and fallen power lines. We zigged and zagged until we arrived at the intersection that the distraught mother had described to us.

A look of pure joy and relief lit up her face when she saw her son waving from my car. I had barely pulled over when he bolted from his seat and ran into her arms. It was hard to tell which one of the three of us was crying the hardest. It had been an emotional episode, but the little boy was back in the safety of his mother's arms.

We chatted briefly, but they were chilled and eager to get home and into dry clothes. I returned to my car and marveled at the series of events that had put me in the right place at the right time.

My visit with Mom had run late. I had chosen to change course and forfeit my visit with my brother. If my niece had been home, the boy wouldn't have seen me waiting in my car.

Wow, it was lucky for him that this series of events had unfolded the way it did.

I looked over at the wet seat of my car and said a silent "thank you" to whatever greater power had brought us together that day.

— Lois Tuffin —

28

A Mother's Miracle

The tie which links mother and child is of such pure
and immaculate strength as to be never violated.
~Washington Irving

W hen my mother passed away, her loss caused a pain in my soul that I never expected. She hadn't been around much when I was growing up, but I had words of reconciliation that I had wanted to say. Now it was too late.

By the time a year had passed since her death, I felt like I had the pain under control. And then my husband and I found out that I was pregnant. As overjoyed as I was about the new life growing inside me, it reawakened the pain of losing my mom. As my pregnancy progressed, I could not stop thinking about the fact that my mom wouldn't be there. I couldn't tell her I was pregnant and watch her get excited; I couldn't share my fears and have them eased. Mom would never hold my baby or help me learn to be a mother.

One night, about six months into my pregnancy, I was kept awake with worry and fear about becoming a mother, and I fell asleep in tears, wishing my mom was alive to ask for advice. The following morning as I was working at home, my cellphone rang. Glancing at it, I could see it was my OB-GYN office calling. "Just an appointment confirmation call," I assumed, and I ignored the call.

A few minutes later, my phone predictably notified me of a voice-mail. Wanting to delete it, I dialed into my voicemail and listened to the message. But I was shocked to hear not my doctor's voice but my mother's.

I sat frozen as the voice of my mother played, telling me she was sorry she had missed me at Christmas. That she was thinking about me. That she loved me. And, most importantly, that she was proud of me, and I was one of her heroes. "I love you, baby girl" were the last words on the message. But before they were even said, I was crying hysterically, calling out, "Mommy! Mommy!"

My brain struggled to understand what had just happened. The call had been received in November; Christmas hadn't come yet. And then I realized what miracle had just taken place.

Somehow, a voicemail that my mother had left me over a year ago had never been delivered... until now. God had seen my pain and fear the previous night and given me the gift of an answer from my mother, who was telling me she was proud of me, and I was one of her heroes. I didn't need to feel afraid to be a mother. Mom was telling me I would do great.

I fell to my knees. I said, "Mommy, I know you're up there. Thank you, Mama, and I love you, too." I wish I could say that was the last time I ever felt fear during my pregnancy, but it wasn't. However, any time I felt afraid from then on, I would replay that voicemail (which I saved) to remind myself that my mom believed in me.

— Kimberly Ellenwood —

29

Close Encounters of the Angelic Kind

Now faith is confidence in what we hope for and
assurance about what we do not see.
~Hebrews 11:1 (NIV)

Unexplainable? Two close encounters with imminent disasters from which I escaped could be none other than angelic intervention.

As a practicing attorney providing legal services in Oklahoma, I am fully aware of the ramifications of telling lies. No attorney will jeopardize his practice by telling things that are not true. A dear friend asked me to share these too-amazing-to-be-true rescues, and I am willing, regardless of the skepticism that may certainly follow.

The first event happened before I married my loving wife, G.K., who is also a practicing attorney and now shares my law office, Powers at Law, LLC in Edmond, Oklahoma.

I had just said goodnight to my then-fiancée and was driving back to my apartment several miles away. It was raining hard, and visibility was low along the darkened, rain-drenched and windswept highway.

I had a long stretch of straight, fairly level road at one point. I was traveling south toward an intersection where I needed to make a left turn. Every driver knows that a left turn into oncoming traffic requires extra caution.

I could see only one oncoming vehicle on the road headed north.

Under the conditions, it appeared to be a comfortable distance from the intersection. So, I turned in front of it. That is when I knew I was going to be T-boned by an oncoming car I had not seen. Too late to avoid collision, I just shut my eyes and waited for the inevitable crash, which I assumed the other driver was doing as well.

A second later, I opened my eyes, and I was heading safely past the intersection. I saw the other vehicle in my rearview mirror, moving safely north through the intersection. That driver must have been as stunned as I was.

Wait a minute! The physics of this is all wrong! Two objects cannot occupy the same space at the same time.

The inside of my car had been fully lit by the headlights of the oncoming car. The beam of its lights had even lit up the passenger compartment, absolutely too close not to hit me.

After my startled brain tried to process this, I began to pray and thank God for His protection on that rain-drenched night. Then I heard the small, quiet voice that will occasionally speak inside our souls. The voice said, "Sometimes you benefit from what I do for others."

Then I knew that I had been saved only by His amazing love. I could just as easily have wound up in a single-car crash while He protected the other driver.

On another "dark and stormy night," some friends asked that I attend a community meeting. My first thought was that it would be a lot of trouble. Nevertheless, because they pressed, and because I thought that I could be of assistance, I decided to go.

The meeting was about eighty miles away from home. The exit for the city of Chickasha is easy to miss, even in good weather. If you miss it, you wind up on a restricted-access turnpike and can't turn around for about twenty miles or more of added travel.

You guessed it: I missed the turn.

I continued until I found the first highway-patrol turnaround. It was at the bottom of a two-mile stretch along a valley. I did not want to take the time to drive an extra twenty miles on a night like that.

I positioned my car to shoot directly through the officer's gap once traffic was clear. I could see traffic in both lanes from this position, or so I thought.

From what I could see through the rain-splattered driver's side pane, there was no traffic in the northbound lane, and three trucks in the southbound lane were headed toward my position. Two eighteen-wheelers were running side by side, and another was slightly back in the outside lane closest to me, just behind the other trucks.

My plan, if there was no northbound traffic, was to wait for these trucks to clear my position and then start across immediately after the third truck passed.

The plan worked perfectly, even with the heavy downpour and the wind, lightning, and buffeting from the passing trucks. I accelerated across the first lane of traffic. At that point, my plan failed.

In the area screened from my view by the last truck, there was a fourth truck! I was well-lit by his headlights and moving directly in front of him. He hit his horn, which I heard as he went by. I did not see much, but the spray from this passing was like a rushing waterfall hitting a shield of glass in front of my vehicle — not the windshield of my SUV but actually in front of the hood, as if an invisible shield was positioned there.

While this watery spray was sluicing before me, I felt my body jolted forward by my SUV coming to an abrupt halt. Only then did I feel my foot hit the brake, which was already activated.

Let me say that again. My foot hit the brake pedal of my vehicle *after* it had already been stopped. Not a drop of the enormous spray from the eighteen-wheeler even touched my windshield. This defies the laws of physics.

I pulled quickly off the traffic lanes and just sat there thinking about what had happened. I needed to collect myself. I began to offer up thanksgiving to the Creator of all things, including physics, for keeping me safe in the palm of his hand. Psalm 3:3 (KJV) came to mind, "But thou, O Lord, art a shield for me."

My next crossing was uneventful, and I attended the meeting and went home. When I told my wife what had happened, she told me that she had been praying for my safe return.

I think most people would comment that I should probably not drive in the rain, but then that is missing the whole point.

I know the words of Psalm 91:11 (KJV) are true: "For He shall give His angels charge over thee, to keep thee in all thy ways." I have no doubt His angels are traveling with me.

—Don Powers—

30

A Gift from Heaven

*Always give without remembering and
always receive without forgetting.*
~Brian Tracy

ears welled in the corners of my eyes as I slowly tore open the
envelope. Whatever was inside was the last gift my Grandpa
Clem would ever give to me. He passed away less than two
weeks before my seventeenth birthday. I hadn't known what
it was to lose someone before. My heart ached worse than anything
I'd ever felt.

I carefully pulled the card out of the envelope. "Happy Birthday,
Granddaughter," it said. Hot tears rolled down my cheeks and blurred
my vision.

As I opened the card, a twenty-dollar bill fell onto my lap. Twenty
dollars? My tears paused for a minute as a bit of excitement crept in.
In previous years, I could expect to find no more than a ten tucked
away in a birthday card from my grandpa. Without having my own
job, money was scarce to me. Holding the bill tight between my
fingers, the thought played over and over in my head. Twenty whole
dollars. From Grandpa. The last gift he would ever give me. The very
last piece of him.

A week later, I sat alone in my room, the twenty-dollar bill pinched
between my fingers as I puzzled over what to buy with it. Clothes,
maybe? No, that's not something special. Art supplies, perhaps?

Every interest and hobby I had swam through my head. No, no, and no. I couldn't bring myself to buy any of it. None of these things were anything I could look at for the rest of my life and know that it was Grandpa's last gift to me. This money had my heart attached to it. It had a piece of Grandpa's soul attached to it. It couldn't be spent on just anything.

After days of thinking it over, I knew what I had to do.

My body trembled with anxiety as I walked into church the following Wednesday for youth group. Was I sure I wanted to do this? Give away twenty whole dollars?

Yes, I was sure. It was the only thing to do with money that came with so much love.

My eyes scanned the room until I found the person I was looking for. I pulled Pastor Zach to the side.

"What's up?" he asked.

I took a deep breath and pulled the twenty out of my pocket. "I got this money from my grandpa. He died right before my birthday. There's nothing I can buy with this that feels special enough, so I want to give it to missions. If I give this to you, do you promise the church will use it to help someone?"

Pastor Zach gave me a comforting smile. "Yes, of course! I promise this will go to missions. We won't use it to keep our lights on."

I handed him the bill, and he walked away to prepare for the service.

Tears once again spilled down my cheeks. This time, they were tears of happiness and love. The money was gone, but my heart swelled with the thought of helping someone in need. I was in no way an overly generous person, but nevertheless, something compelled me to do this act of kindness.

The act of giving felt so amazing on that particular evening that I also decided to slip a one-dollar bill into the offering. I had never done so before.

The following Sunday, I strolled happily through the mall after begging my mom to take me there after church. I didn't have any money to spend, but that was okay. I was used to it. If I saw something I wanted, I would add it to the list of things I could buy when I actually had some money.

I turned the corner of the hallway, and for some reason I decided to look down. The green paper must have caught my eye. There, at my feet, was a wad of cash.

Eyes wide and alert, I slowly bent down to retrieve it from the floor. This wasn't just one little bill. Somebody must be missing this. But who?

I turned my head to the left. Then to the right. The hallway was mostly empty except for a family with two small children sitting on a bench, and an elderly man about to walk out the door. To my right, an employee of one of the stores stood in the entryway to greet guests. She caught my gaze.

"Did you see who dropped this?" I asked.

She walked over to me, saw the cash in my hands and swiveled her head like I had. Just as I had, she noticed the old man, now only a few feet from the door.

The employee grabbed the cash out of my hand and ran to meet the man before he escaped the building. I watched them talk, then slowly turn and walk in opposite directions. The employee skipped back over to me and handed me the money.

"It's not his," she announced. "Congratulations, it's your lucky day!" A smile on her face, she disappeared back into her store.

Carefully, I unwrapped the wad. There was a ten. A five. Another five. And a one. My breath caught in my throat. My hands began to shake as the realization hit. I was holding twenty-one dollars.

I donated twenty-one dollars to the church only four days ago, and now here was twenty-one dollars laid out at my feet. There was no way it could be a coincidence. There was just no way. This was a gift from heaven. A gift from God. Maybe another gift from Grandpa. Maybe both.

"Thank you for your sacrifice," it seemed to say. "Here is some money in return, money without guilt attached."

For the third time, my eyes were glassy with tears. Grandpa was gone, but in that moment I knew he was still watching over me.

Through the tears, a smile spread across my face. Everything was going to be okay.

—Julia Wachuta—

31

A Sudden Fear

He will command his angels concerning
you to guard you carefully.
~Luke 4:10 (NIV)

The junior high school I attended was about a mile from my home, and I walked there and back every day. It was always during daylight hours, while chatting and laughing with friends, so I never put much thought into my surroundings or what was going on around me.

One day in class, we were given a special assignment that was to be completed before the end of the week. We were assigned a partner and told to work on it together. The partner I was assigned was a girl with whom I never hung out. I didn't feel comfortable around her. Patty was one of the "cool" girls, who had little time for any of us "less than cool" girls. She reluctantly approached and suggested I come to her home at 7:00 that evening. Her home was right across from the huge schoolyard and would be easy to find.

It was late fall, and no longer daylight savings time, which meant it was completely dark by 7:00. My dad, who didn't want me walking to her house on my own in the dark, insisted on driving me. I was a little embarrassed about needing to be driven by my dad, but he wasn't taking no for an answer. Upon arrival at Patty's home, I hopped out of the car, hoping she didn't notice that my father had driven me. I nervously approached and rang the bell. The girl who greeted me at the door was nothing like the girl I knew from school. This one smiled warmly and welcomed me in. She was completely different when she wasn't hanging around with her group of cool friends. We quickly got down to work, and the assignment was completed in no time. We were pleased with our combined effort.

My dad had instructed me to call him when I was ready to come home, but I hated to bother him. I also didn't think it was particularly "cool" to have my father come to pick me up. I was, after all, twelve years old, and not the least bit nervous about walking home. I said goodbye to Patty and started off down the street. I passed by the dark schoolyard and the vacant church, feeling completely safe and confident. I didn't feel I had anything to worry about and was not the least bit uneasy.

For no reason and without warning, I was suddenly overcome with a feeling of absolute dread and fear. My heart pounded so fast that I had trouble catching my breath. I was terrified and didn't know what was happening! I didn't know what to do or where to go, but I knew I needed to get away. I quickly turned back toward Patty's house and ran straight to her door.

I rang the doorbell and was relieved when she answered. I told her I had forgotten that my dad was supposed to pick me up, and I needed to use her phone to call. She didn't mind at all and didn't seem to notice that I was scared out of my wits. I phoned my dad and waited outside for him to arrive. I was so glad to see him. I didn't mention anything to my dad about what had happened as I didn't understand it myself.

At school the next day, I heard kids talking about some girl who was viciously raped in the lane by the church the evening before. Nobody knew any of the details or who she was, but it sounded horrible. I had walked right past that very lane on my way home from Patty's house. It was there that I had become so unexplainably terrified and turned and went right back to her home. Something made me stop walking and turn around, but as a twelve-year-old kid, I couldn't make any sense of it and never told anyone about it.

As an adult, I often think about that evening. I am taken back again and again to the mystery surrounding it. I have no explanation, but I am positive that something beyond my human comprehension occurred. I wonder if I had a guardian angel looking out for me, making me more fearful than I have ever been in my entire life. There was absolutely no reason at all for me to be so terrified, but something made me run back to the house to call my dad and ask him to pick me up.

I will never forget what happened that day. Whatever it was has made me a little more discerning and perceptive. I certainly don't understand the hand of God or His use of angels on this side of Heaven, but I am absolutely certain they are real.

— Maureen Slater —

32

No Other Way to Explain It

*The most glorious moment you will ever experience in
your life is when you look back and see how God
was protecting you all this time.*
~Shannon L. Alder

I t was a beautiful May morning. As usual, I decided to start my
day by sitting outside soaking up the fresh air as I read my
Bible and sipped my coffee. Afterwards, there were two things
I was determined to do. First, make sure my husband got our
decorative patio trees down from the attic and, second, take several
bags of clothes, blankets and comforters to the donation center. I had
been faithful in doing that every year, but for whatever reasons, I had
procrastinated, and the bags were now piling up and overflowing.

Starting my reading and meditation, I read Psalm 91 (KJV):
"For He shall give His angels charge over thee." The passage brought
back memories of parochial school, my fourth-grade teacher, and her
strong belief and teachings on angels. I continued with my reading
and meditation, and then I closed my Bible and silently sat for a few
minutes, enjoying a visit from an exceptionally beautiful red cardinal
that brazenly flew around me several times before landing by my feet
and staring at me. When my visitor finally flew away, I went inside to
start my household chores.

Excited about the out-of-state company we were expecting the
following week, I wanted everything inside and out to look perfect. I
went into the bedroom to ask my husband about bringing the patio

trees down. He was asleep so I figured I'd surprise him and get them down by myself.

I went to the garage to access the attic storage and moved our tall metal ladder into place. I had to move the bags of clothing and blankets out of the way and resolved once again to get those to the donation center.

I climbed the ladder, and two steps from the top I was able to reach up and push open the attic hatch. Then, with my feet on the very last step and part of my upper body in the attic, I saw my trees. I awkwardly raised my leg to climb onto the attic floor. Looking down, and then looking up again, I decided that this was actually too much for me. I should wait for my husband to get them.

As I stepped down, my foot missed the shaky ladder's step. With one foot swinging and the other on the top step, I grabbed the attic floorboard and called my husband. Unfortunately, he couldn't hear me. As I went to take another step down, the ladder suddenly came out from under me, loudly crashing onto the concrete garage floor, leaving me dangling from the attic with sweaty hands.

In that split second, which seemed like an eternity, I prayed and then called my husband. With my body swinging in midair and my hands slowly slipping closer to the edge, I yelled out, "Angels take charge of…" Before I could finish the sentence, I fell, but my entire body except my left foot landed on the bags of clothes and comforters that I had just moved! As my foot slammed into the concrete floor, I heard it crack as pain shot from my foot up to my thigh. Lying on the bags, I weakly yelled, "Help me!" My husband came through the garage door and stood for a second looking like a deer in headlights before springing into action, picking me up and taking me to the hospital. As he drove, he nervously bombarded me with questions, "What in the heck were you doing out there?"

"I was trying to get into the attic to bring the patio trees down. The ladder came out from under me, and I fell," I tearfully answered.

He turned and looked at me with tears in his eyes and said, "Thank God you fell on those bags. It's a blessing they were even out there! But how…?" With a puzzled look, he stopped.

Knowing what he was going to ask, I answered, "Angels took charge over me."

He hesitated, and then in an agreeable tone, he softly replied, "They sure did!"

Arriving at the emergency entrance, he ran in, got a wheelchair, and wheeled me in. Images of what happened and what could've happened danced in my head as I tearfully and painfully waited to see the doctor.

My foot was broken in two places. Surgery, a plate and several screws were placed to hold my foot together. After having a cast on for almost seven weeks, a medical boot for three, and then physical therapy for four weeks, I was walking without any signs of ever having a broken foot. The doctor was quite surprised the healing process wasn't much longer for a woman my age. He called me his miracle patient.

That happened four years ago, but I often think about that day. Unbeknownst to me, my procrastination caused me to build a landing pad that possibly saved my life. My husband and I still can't figure out how I ended up on those bags, which were far from where I should have fallen. Was I mysteriously pushed, carried or guided to land on those bags? It certainly felt like it. However I got there, I'm thankful that I did. And how about that red cardinal flying so close around me before landing by my feet and staring at me? They're in our yard all the time, but never has one ever come that close to me before or since. In reading about them, I was surprised to find that "cardinals appear when angels are near." It also stated that their visitations often symbolize good luck or a visitor from heaven. I believe I experienced both.

Was all of this mere coincidence? I don't think so. Everyone says I was lucky that I wasn't injured more than I was. I quickly tell them, yes, it might've been some luck, but I know deep down that it was a miracle, divine intervention that saved me from imminent disaster or even death. The more I think about it, there's just no other way to explain it.

I still sit outside and read my Bible and drink my coffee. And when I see cardinals, I look up and smile because, to me, they're just reminders of angels being near and their helpful presence that's often there for us.

— Francine L. Billingslea —

33

Peter's Miracle

Dogs are miracles with paws.
~Susan Ariel Rainbow Kennedy

At the time of this writing, I have reached the venerable age of 105. As I look back, I think of the many wonderful things that have happened in my long life, many of which have served to strengthen my belief that miracles really do happen. One of these that I recall today happened many years ago but is still as fresh in my mind as if it had happened yesterday.

Peter was a Russian Wolfhound (Borzoi) with the typical tall, long-legged build of the hunter he was supposed to be but never was. He weighed close to eighty-five pounds and had the long nose and narrow head of the Borzoi, so narrow it didn't seem to have much room for brains. In Peter's case, it didn't. He was what might be termed "dim," and he became easily confused, but his gentle nature and sweet disposition more than compensated for his lack of intelligence.

We loved him dearly. When he became confused, he would sit in one spot waiting for one of his humans to come to his rescue. And someone always did.

On the day in question, I had gathered up my canine family of one Old English Sheepdog, one Whippet rescue, one little wolf pup rescue, and Peter. They were all duly settled in my covered pickup truck bed, and I was headed out for our daily exercise, six miles into the country where there was no leash law and they could run free. They were all trained not to chase wild animals, to stay reasonably close, and to come when called.

After I had walked briskly for about ten minutes, I noticed one dog was missing. Peter, of course! It seemed obvious that he had stopped to investigate some irresistible odor, and then, becoming confused, had turned back the way we had just come. He would easily be able to follow our scent, but in the wrong direction. And when a Borzoi runs, he covers a lot of ground in a very short time.

Feeling guilty, knowing I should have kept a closer watch on him, I retraced my steps, calling and whistling, but there was no sign of him. It was winter and would soon be dark. In desperation, I started to pray. "Please God, keep Peter safe."

After about half an hour of intense searching and calling at the top of my voice, I finally decided the best thing to do was to drive the two other dogs and wolf pup home, which would leave me free to come back and hunt for Peter. By that time, I was frantic with worry. The freeway was off to my right, and in the distance, I could hear the endless hum of speeding cars. If Peter, in his confusion, made his way onto the interstate he wouldn't have a chance. Besides that, there were hungry coyotes that ran in packs in that part of the county.

If I couldn't find Peter before dark, I knew the chances of finding him alive were not good. Over and over as I drove the other dogs home — breaking all speed limits on the way — I continued to call upon God, asking Him to have mercy on Peter.

I reached my house in record time and hustled the remaining trio to the front door just as it opened to reveal my husband standing there.

"I've lost Peter," I shouted breathlessly. "I'm going to leave these three with you and go back to look for him."

"Peter is here," he replied calmly. And at that moment, an elegant, long white nose appeared in the doorway beside him. I stared wordlessly, unable to believe what I was seeing. Then, "Thank you, God. Thank you. Thank you," I whispered as my arms encircled Peter, holding him as though I would never let him go.

My sweet, clueless Peter. How did he ever travel the six miles home unharmed?

My husband said, "I heard a knock at the front door and found a man standing there with Peter." My husband hadn't known we had a dog missing, and said he just stared at him in astonishment.

The good Samaritan explained that he'd been driving south down the interstate in heavy traffic when he saw an enormous dog, with long, flowing gold-and-white fur, standing on the median. The dog stood quite still and seemed to be waiting for someone. The man said he couldn't just leave him all alone in such a dangerous situation. He'd tried to pull over to him but found it impossible to stop because of the heavy traffic.

When he came to a place where he could turn around and drive north again, he'd found Peter still patiently waiting on the median. He parked and managed to get across the three northbound lanes by dodging cars. Peter didn't seem frightened and stood quite still while the man searched him for an address and phone number. He found Peter's name there too, and when he called him by name, Peter wagged his tail and licked his hand as though they were old friends.

When he took his collar and led him to his car, Peter climbed right in and settled himself on the back seat. He was so calm, the rescuer said that if Peter could have spoken, he thought he'd say, "I KNEW someone would come for me if I just waited."

Before he left, after profuse thanks, and an offer of a reward which he refused, Peter's wonderful new friend and guardian angel had told my husband, with awe in his voice, "How he managed to get himself across three lanes of a six-lane highway, during rush-hour, I'll never understand. It was nothing short of a miracle."

— Monica Agnew-Kinnaman —

Angels in Disguise

34

Snow Angels

*When we are touched by something, it's as if we're
being brushed by an angel's wings.*
~Rita Dove

Snow flurries fly by my classroom window.

"Snow! It's snowing!" cries one of my first graders.

"I love snow," whispers another.

Like a magnet, the anticipation of more snow pulls over twenty pairs of little feet to my window.

"Two-minute break," I say, sharing in the magic of the snow.

The excitement is palpable as plans for snowmen, snow forts, igloos, sledding, and snowball fights fill the air.

A gust of wind crashes snow against the window. The cold seems to creep through the window frame.

With big eyes, a child exclaims, "I'm making a snow angel."

I smile to myself. I plan on enjoying the snow from the warmth of my home. Definitely no snow angels.

"Ten seconds to say goodbye to the snow and return to your seats," I say.

I close the blinds, and math resumes.

Math passes quickly, and I almost forget about the snow.

The vice principal taps on the door. I turn and see her smile: early dismissal.

"Are we going home early? Are we?" asks my class.

It's not long until names are called over the loudspeaker, and I'm left with an empty classroom.

I zip up my coat and head outside. My feet sink into the snow, and a cold wind whips around me. My car looks like an igloo. I brush off the fluffy outer layer of snow and grab my ice scraper. My teeth chatter.

Once inside, I blast the heat and clutch the steering wheel. The roads are white. I think back to the flurries from earlier. Now, the snow is coming down fast. I turn off my radio and inch my way out of the parking lot.

I drive and focus on the disappearing tire tracks in front of me. I can feel tightness in my neck and shoulders. *Almost home,* I think.

I try to make a left turn, but my car fishtails to the right. The front of my car sticks to last week's un-melted snowbank. I try to reverse. My tires squeal. I keep trying. Now, my car slides farther into the snowbank. I need help. My hands tremble, and tears puddle in my eyes.

"God, I really need your help," I whisper.

The snow is coming down harder and harder. I feel a knot in my stomach.

Tap, tap, tap.

I jump in my seat and look at my passenger window.

A man with gentle eyes and a five o'clock shadow asks, "Ma'am, may I help you?"

I can't believe the timing, moments after my prayer. At a loss for words, I find myself nodding.

"Do you want me to back you out?"

"Please," I say.

I scooch to the passenger seat. He climbs in and, with one smooth reverse, frees my car. I look back at the snowbank printed with tire tracks and the snow on the road. Was it really that easy?

"Thank you," I say, still trying to process how he freed my car.

"Sure thing. Where are you headed?" he asks.

I look at the white incline. I feel my heart catch in my chest. My relief seems short-lived.

He points to a large snow-removal vehicle. Right on cue, a man in the driver's seat waves. How did I miss seeing his vehicle before?

"Hmm, wait here a second. I will be right back."

He walks to the snow-removal vehicle and then back to my car and offers, "If you would like, he can plow the road to your home. I can drive your car behind him."

The tightness in my neck and shoulders fades away, and the knot in my stomach disappears.

"That would be wonderful. Thank you so much," I say.

The car ride passes quietly as I take in the winter wonderland outside my window. Nothing is plowed yet. Waves of snow paint the world in white.

My home comes into view. I thank him again and wave thanks to his friend.

"You're welcome. Stay safe." And, with that, he returns to the snow-removal vehicle.

Once inside, I think about my journey home and call my mom. As I relay the story, she raises some things that get my mind wondering.

My mom asks if I was comfortable having a stranger drive me home. I'm a cautious person, but with the timing of the help offered right after prayer, I felt at peace. She also mentions that it was odd that the snow removal vehicle wasn't plowing the main roads first. I agree. I was turning off a side road into my neighborhood. Then, she inquires how directions to my home were given to the man in the snow-removal vehicle. I'm at a loss. The man driving my car wasn't on the phone with the man driving the snow-removal vehicle.

"Well, I'm glad you made it home safely," says my mom.

As I get off the phone, I take in the world outside coated in white except for the lone road to my home. I think back to my students' plans for the day. I smile when I realize that my afternoon included snow angels too.

— Christina Barr —

35

A Special Ring Returned

Anyone can be an angel.
~Author Unknown

During her final year, before reuniting with my father in heaven, my mother and I were reading aloud from *Angels on Earth*. It's a monthly magazine containing stories about what people believe are visitations by heavenly messengers — men and women (and sometimes animals) who appear in the stories, often mysteriously to remedy or save a situation, and then just as unexplainably leave.

After reading about one heavenly visitor, I was reminded of the experience Mom had about eight years ago.

She was living in her apartment at the time, at a large residence for the elderly. I often joined her at its first-floor restaurant, the Campus Cuisine, during my lunch break from work.

One noontime when I approached the table where she was waiting, I could see she was teary-eyed.

"What's wrong?" I asked. She showed me her left hand, which was bare.

"I lost my ring," she said. It was an elegant, three-diamond setting my dad had presented to her for their twenty-fifth anniversary. She said it had a sizing clasp on it that sometimes came loose.

"I've looked everywhere for it and turned the apartment upside down."

"Did you tell the office here?" I asked.

"Yes, I did."

"What else can you do?" I asked.

She replied, "I'm going to pray to St. Anthony."

Now, for those who may not know, in the Catholic faith St. Anthony is the patron saint of lost objects, and it's my guess that a few of you can tell your own remarkable stories about this phenomenon.

Still, I remember thinking at the time, it was a really expensive ring, and if someone found it, it wasn't likely to be returned.

Several weeks passed, and no ring turned up. I was pretty sure my mother would never see it again.

After about a month, though, on arriving at our usual table at the restaurant for lunch, I found Mom beaming.

I stared at her. She held up her hand — there was the ring.

"You found it?" I asked.

"No, I didn't find it," she said.

And she proceeded to tell me that, the night before, on returning to the residence after playing cards with friends, she was standing in the lobby trying to decide whether to go to the Cuisine for dinner or just have something light in her apartment when she felt a tap on her shoulder.

She turned to see a tall, handsome man with a mustache, wearing a hat and a long wool coat that one doesn't often see these days. He said, "Are you Anita?"

Mom said, "Yes."

"And you've lost your ring?"

"Yes," Mom replied.

Without saying more, the man pulled the ring from his pocket, put it on Mom's finger, and left the building before my mother could get out an astonished "Thank you."

No one had ever seen this man before, and neither Mom nor anyone else ever saw him again.

— Paul E. Baribault —

36

Ice on the Fairway

All God's angels come to us disguised.
~James Russell Lowell

In 2008, I temporarily moved from Florida to Indiana to look after my mother. She had several health issues that required a caregiver. My father had passed away three years earlier, and I am an only child, so it was up to me.

The plan was to stay with Mom from November until the following spring, giving her a chance to regain her strength. Then we would decide if moving to Florida to live with our family would be the next step. It would be hard to be separated from my husband and grown daughter for so long, but frequent visits were possible.

Mom needed my help and comfort to get better. So, I packed my bags and traveled north.

The only thing that made me a little nervous was getting through an Indiana winter. Dad's aerospace job took us to Florida when I was a baby, and it was the only place I'd ever called home.

However, as a descendant of seven generations of Hoosiers, I was determined to prevail. It was only a little ice and snow. If my pioneer ancestors could handle it, so could I.

And this girl was already used to rough weather.

Anyone who has lived in Central Florida during the summer will tell you it's not for the faint of heart. Blinding rain and torrential downpours with deadly cloud-to-ground lightning is commonplace. I'd often driven through hurricane-force winds as power lines dangled, tree branches fell, and trash cans rolled in the street while going to and from work.

But I soon discovered that Midwest winters presented equally hard challenges.

Driving on black ice, the wheels on my car developed a mind of their own. Underpasses, exits, four-way stops. Slipping and sliding.

It was nerve-wracking.

And if there was ice on parking lots, sidewalks and driveways, I had a remarkable ability to locate it and land on it.

Thankfully, my backside was amply padded. Coupled with bulky clothing, I more or less bounced when I hit the pavement, usually suffering a few bruises and some injured pride.

One Saturday morning in early February, I was at the grocery store, ready to tackle a lengthy list. It was freezing but sunny with clear, blue skies — a treat when compared to the usual snowy gloom. The warm rays were glorious. I leaned against the car for a few minutes, letting it penetrate my homesick heart.

Then, back to Earth.

It was time to find a cart. The groceries weren't going to buy themselves.

As I walked toward the door, my feet suddenly slipped out from under me, and I landed face-down in the parking lot.

I tried to scoot onto the sidewalk, but I was unable to do anything but claw at the pavement. I was stranded on an island of ice that had appeared safe because it was hidden by a dusting of snow.

I hollered for help but no one came. I heard talking and laughter in the parking lot, and trunks slamming. Lots of noise, but no one heard.

Then, a large pick-up truck with monster wheels turned the corner, heading right for me.

The more I scrambled to get away, the more I realized that, barring a miracle, I was going to become a human speed bump beneath a gargantuan set of Firestones.

I'd heard people describe how their lives flashed before their eyes as they faced death.

People. Places. Regrets.

My final thoughts consisted of inconsequential things like bills I hadn't paid yet, wondering if I cleaned the litter box and took my jeans out of the dryer. Then, painfully precious things: my mother's trembling hands at breakfast, my handsome husband who was often mistaken for singer Kenny Rogers, and our beautiful, blond daughter whose adult life had just begun.

Soon, I would be lost to them.

"Please, God, help me."

A pair of golf shoes appeared. Looking up, I saw an elderly gentleman with deeply tanned skin and thick white hair, wearing a beige, short-sleeved polo shirt and pleated, olive-green shorts, smiling down at me.

He looked like a Florida retiree fresh from the links. All that was missing was a golf cart and a bag of clubs.

"Looks like you're in a bit of a fix, young lady!"

He reached down and pulled me onto the sidewalk in the nick of time. The truck passed by, and I was safe.

I laid my head on the concrete, my heart thundering, weeping with relief.

"Thank you so much," I whispered.

"Are you alright, ma'am? Let me help you up!"

The voice had changed. I looked up again.

It was one of the young baggers from the store.

"Where is he? Did you see a man in shorts standing here a minute ago?"

I suddenly realized how ridiculous that sounded.

"Let's go inside the office where it's warm while I call the manager."

As I waited, I looked down at my trembling hands. My nails were torn and broken from my frantic efforts to move myself out of the way of the truck.

The manager, James, was full of apologies. After the accident report was completed, he insisted that I go to the emergency room. I assured him that I was okay, only rattled.

What I really needed was the identity of my rescuer. I owed him my life and wanted to thank him.

When James pulled the security footage, we were both shocked to see that two minutes of time were missing. The frame before the rescue showed me lying in the lot. The next frame showed the bagger helping me up from the sidewalk.

This meant that the only person who had seen the man was me.

At that point, I was in no shape to buy groceries.

The store had delivery service, so I handed the list to James, who insisted on walking me to my car.

Smart man. Probably to make sure I didn't end up in more trouble.

Trying to make sense of what had happened, I remembered others telling stories like mine, meeting a stranger only to realize later that he or she was an angel.

My rescuer, an angel if there ever was one, wasn't dressed for winter weather. He popped in, did his thing and popped out again, staying just long enough to make sure I was safe and perhaps zipping back to the course for tee time. And it seemed he was from the tropics, a reminder of home.

What other explanation could there be? If what I learned was true, heavenly hosts can appear as everyday people to anyone, anywhere. We don't always realize we're in danger and in need of saving.

But they do.

I had prayed for protection before the angel appeared.

"Please, God, help me."

And He did.

— Michelle Close Mills —

Shoe Store Angel

If you can heed only one piece of advice from the universe,
make it this... Pay attention. Do this and
everything else will fall into place.
~Bryan E. Wright

"Ouch!" I cried. I woke up with the kind of headache that hurts your face. Swollen eyes, ears and cheeks felt like an impending sinus infection. But I knew it wasn't. My indecision weighed heavily upon me, dragged me down and gnawed at me like hunger pangs that couldn't be satiated. Could I, should I, travel to Russia and adopt a little toddler girl?

When I viewed her video at the adoption agency, her mischievous smile touched my heart. Her dark brown eyes sparkled and even reminded me of my own toddler pictures. The director of the agency warned me, "Take some time to decide but not too long because other moms are looking as well." I nodded. I thought I knew.

And yet, when I arrived home, doubts consumed me. How would I manage as an older single mom? What if I lacked the stamina and energy to parent a young child? What if she didn't like me? Or worse, what if I didn't like her? Through my bedroom window, I watched gray clouds float across a yellow-streaked sky.

Sleep escaped me for days. I lay awake until early morning ruminating about my life. Irreversible decisions terrified me. Maybe that's why the baby bug hadn't bitten until my forties.

The phone startled me. My best friend called and suggested we shop for my big trip. I resisted, because I wasn't sure I was going.

"Come on," she urged. "You'll feel better."

I mumbled, "Okay," and met her at the shoe store. We grew up with this neighborhood shoe store. We had spent hours after high school looking at shoes, boots, purses and accessories. Warm memories flooded my mind as I stood outside and spied a large, chocolate-brown shoulder bag hanging in the window. I wanted to rub my fingers over the rich leather. I had the thought it would be easy to carry. I envisioned it jauntily resting on my shoulder as I walked the streets of Moscow, but I quickly banished the image. I hadn't officially decided I was going.

I walked aimlessly to the back of the store while my friend shopped for herself. As I turned the corner into the small alcove that contained purses and accessories, I came face-to-face with a strange-looking lady. She was short, skinny and disheveled. Stringy hair hung to her shoulders, and her skin appeared red and blotchy. She stared at me; her large, gray eyes bored into mine. She didn't blink as she took stock of me. She wet her dry, blistered lips and whispered, "You're afraid."

"Excuse me?" I asked. What was she saying? Who was she? I glanced behind me. Was she talking to someone else?

"You're afraid," she said again. Her raspy voice strained, "Don't be afraid."

I felt uneasy and nervous, so I picked up a purse, opened it and studied the lining. After a few silent moments, I decided to ask her what she was talking about. But when I looked up, she wasn't there. I walked to the front of the store but couldn't find her. I searched the aisles. She was gone.

That night, I kept thinking about her. Was she just a demented lady who slipped out the door? Had I looked scared, and she was just trying to comfort me? But what if, I argued with myself, this was one of those moments in life that can't be logically explained but is life-changing? What if she was an angel of sorts, sent to relay an important message that would change my life for the better?

I tossed and turned all night. Strands of stringy hair and blistered lips slithered through my dreams along with images of me embracing my baby girl on her Winnie the Pooh rocking chair, smiling at her dark brown eyes until they gently closed, and softly singing my favorite bedtime lullaby.

The next morning, I stumbled out of bed, barely awake. I held a cup of freshly brewed coffee with shaking hands, breathed deeply and decided. I called the adoption agency. I would travel to Russia. I would adopt my little girl.

And I would buy the purse.

— Bari Benjamin —

The Woman in Room 348

How beautiful a day can be
When kindness touches it!
~George Elliston

"I'm sorry, but visiting hours are over," the nurse said apologetically. "You can come back in the morning."

My husband Eric had just gotten out of surgery and was still struggling with nausea from the anesthesia. I really wanted to stay with him until he was more comfortable, but I knew that the hospital's visiting policies were non-negotiable.

"I'll take care of him until you get back, I promise." The nurse handed me a piece of paper. "That's my cell number. You can call or text me anytime tonight if you're worried or just want an update."

I thanked her and then turned to Eric. "Can I do anything for you before I leave?"

He shook his head slightly without opening his eyes, and I could tell he was miserable. "I can't believe I have to leave while you're like this," I said, tears filling my eyes. "I'm so sorry, babe."

He patted my hand and told me he loved me. "I'll be right here in the morning."

I kissed his forehead and headed to my car, still fighting tears. In my head, I knew that Eric wasn't in imminent danger, and he would be physically okay until I returned in the morning, but it still broke my heart that I couldn't be with him when he needed me.

The hospital was a few hours from our house, so I was spending the night in a hotel. When I got to my room, I put on my pajamas and then texted Eric's nurse. She texted back, saying he was still sick to his stomach.

I sighed, feeling the worry rush in. What if getting sick caused his stitches to break open? How much of the pain medicine was still in his system? What if he was nauseated and in pain from his incision?

I turned on the TV to distract myself, but it didn't work. Around midnight, I heard my phone chirp. It was Eric's nurse. "He's fine now. He just fell asleep," it read. "You should get some rest now, too."

I thanked her for her kindness, and although Eric was doing better, I knew I wouldn't be able to sleep. When I'd checked in to the hotel, the clerk had pointed out a cabinet in the lobby. "It's full of books and games," she'd said. "Because of our proximity to the hospital, many of our guests are here because their loved ones are receiving medical care. You're welcome to use anything in the cabinet during your stay."

I threw on my robe and headed to the lobby to find a book or a deck of cards. I was scanning the titles when I heard a sound behind me. I turned and saw an elderly woman sitting at the table next to the game cabinet.

"I hope I didn't startle you," she said.

"How long have you been sitting there?" I asked. I must have walked right by her and didn't even see her.

"Oh, just a few moments," she answered. "I heard you leave your room, and I thought you might need some company."

"Are you staying in the room next to me?"

She nodded. "I'm in Room 348. I have been there for a few weeks now. My husband is at the hospital, too."

"I'm sorry to hear that."

She grabbed the *Scrabble* set from the cabinet and sat back down, nodding at the chair across from her. I didn't really want to play *Scrabble,* but since sleeping wasn't an option, I figured I might as well. I sat down and helped her set up the game.

"I'm Shirley," she said. "My Hank had heart surgery, and the doctors won't let me take him home yet."

I nodded and told her about Eric's surgery. "His condition isn't nearly as serious as Hank's. They'll probably even let us go home tomorrow. But tonight..."

Shirley smiled and played her first word on the *Scrabble* board. "The first night apart is always the hardest."

"I wanted to stay with him at the hospital, but they wouldn't let me," I said. "I came here, even though I knew I wouldn't be able to sleep."

I took my turn, and then Shirley played again. "I don't sleep a lot either," she said. "It's a nice enough hotel, but I don't think many of the guests sleep soundly while they're here."

"This isn't your first late-night game of *Scrabble* at this hotel, is it?" I asked.

She shook her head, smiling slightly. "No, I've sat at this table a time or two, helping new moms and worried wives get through the night, all with a board game and a little conversation."

"Thank you for following me down here," I said. "I didn't realize how badly I needed someone to talk to."

She smiled again. "That's what I'm here for. I visit with Hank during the day, and at night I keep my eyes and ears open for anyone at the hotel who could use a friend."

"I'm grateful," I said.

While we continued with our *Scrabble* game, Shirley asked me about my children and my job. While I talked, she racked up points on the board. She'd just played the word "quiz" on a triple-word-score space when I realized I was exhausted.

"You win, Shirley," I said. We put the game away and walked slowly toward the elevator and back to our rooms.

In front of her door, I hugged her and thanked her again. "I'll be praying for Hank," I said.

"Thank you. I hope I don't see you tomorrow night. I pray you and your husband will be safely back home."

Of course, I wanted to take Eric home, but the thought of not seeing Shirley again made me sad. I hugged her again and said goodnight.

I was asleep within minutes. In the morning, I woke up feeling optimistic that it would be a good day. I wrote a brief note to Shirley to say thank you since I probably wouldn't see her again. I debated leaving the note by her door, but I decided to drop it off at the front desk instead.

I returned my room key to the clerk and handed him the note. "Can you give this to Shirley when you see her?"

He frowned. "Shirley?"

"Oh, sorry, I mean the older lady in Room 348. She's been here for weeks, and she's so friendly. I just assumed you knew her."

He clicked some keys on the computer. "Room 348 is empty."

"Shirley checked out this morning?"

"No, I mean that no one stayed in that room last night."

"How could that be? I saw her use a key to enter that room around 2:00 A.M."

The clerk shrugged. "Maybe you dreamed it." He handed my note back and said, "Is there anything else I can do for you?"

I walked out to my car, still holding the note. Since I couldn't thank Shirley directly, I thanked God, whom I was convinced had sent me one of his angels to comfort me when I needed it most.

— Diane Stark —

39

A Prayer Answered

*Angels assist us in connecting with a powerful
yet gentle force, which encourages us
to live life to its fullest.*
~Denise Linn

It was the day before my wedding. I'd heard about pre-wedding jitters, but this was more. I couldn't even drink tea without spilling twice as much as I consumed. Family and friends came from out of town for the wedding, but I was too distracted to converse. I didn't want anyone to know about the conflicting thoughts flowing through my mind.

After a year-long engagement, the magnitude of my doubt surprised me.

My mother didn't help. "I want you to remember how much we love you," she'd said. "We love you so much that your father and I will call all the people invited to the wedding if you change your mind."

Her declaration of love made me wonder if she had reservations about George. Did her question magnify some of my doubts, or would I have had them anyway? I hoped to find peace and answers through prayer. I knew where I had to go. I made an excuse about an errand I needed to run and drove to find the answers I needed.

I listened to the echo of my footsteps and breathed in the peace of a place I'd come to love: Princeton University Chapel. The university was just a few miles away from Trenton State College, where I earned my teaching degree. I liked to walk through ancient arches under the watchful eyes of the familiar lion statues. After admiring the gardens and architecture, I always wound up in the chapel. Today, the chapel was my first destination. On this Friday afternoon, I was alone in the sacred space.

I believed marriage was a lifelong journey. Was I, at twenty-one, old enough to make a forever commitment? I wondered how marriage would change us and our relationship. George and I hadn't argued much. Was it because we agreed, or was I giving into his strong will? Would we be able to handle conflicts? I was the oldest of four; he was an only child. I was shy; he was outgoing. Did differences matter? Who would we be in twenty years? Would we grow together or apart?

Movement caught my attention and interrupted my reverie. Vibrant light danced on the floor in front of me. My eyes traced the sunbeam to an angel on a nearby stained-glass window. Its knowing expression and calm demeanor beckoned. I took a seat next to the illuminated stained-glass seraph.

Angels have always had a special meaning for me. I smiled at the memory of my four-year-old self blowing kisses to the angels from my bed. I'd worried that I would fall asleep before I kissed each one. Almost by reflex, I recited the words of the guardian-angel prayer I'd learned so long ago. The ending words, "To light, to guard, to rule, to guide," sent a shiver up my spine.

"I could use some of that guidance now," I whispered.

After an hour of prayer and soul-searching, I walked to the door. Even without a clear answer, I felt my prayers had been heard.

Once outside, I paused to let my eyes adjust to the light. A young man with dark, wavy hair and perfect posture approached. "You look like you're carrying a heavy burden," he said. "Would you like to talk to me?"

Startled by the unexpected intrusion, I stepped back and touched my engagement ring. I looked into his deep, violet-blue eyes. His eyes communicated understanding and compassion. They inspired my confidence and trust. I felt a connection with this stranger. He seemed to sense my quandary.

"I'd like that," I said. We gravitated to a nearby bench.

We didn't exchange names, but I felt comfortable with him. There was something familiar about him. I sat in comfortable silence for a few moments.

"I am getting married tomorrow," I began.

"And you're not sure," he said.

"That's right," I said.

My words flowed. I explained my fears and worries. I narrated my love story and the journey that led George and me to the wedding. His words were few, but as he listened, my questions seemed to answer themselves.

It felt like moments later when he stood up and said, "I have to go. I need to be somewhere," he said. Our eyes locked. I returned his gaze and felt like a weight had been removed from my shoulders.

"Have a blessed day tomorrow. You will make the right decision." He turned and started to walk away.

I looked down at my watch. I was surprised we had talked for more than three hours. I said, "Thanks again for taking the time to talk to me. I feel much better now." But the straight path in front of me was empty. I looked around and wondered how he could have disappeared so quickly. I shivered even though I wasn't cold. A violet-blue butterfly landed on the bench where he'd been sitting.

I said a prayer of thanks and drove home feeling peaceful. My jitters were gone. I was married the next day.

—Judy Salcewicz—

40

Heavy Lifting

Come to me, all you who are weary and burdened,
and I will give you rest.
~Matthew 11:28 (NIV)

I couldn't know that night what was in store for our family. I only knew my stress level was too high. The client crises in my social-work job always multiplied during the holidays. This year, the pressure of managing them seemed far too heavy. As I drove through the darkness, my husband Jim's desire for a career change came to mind. While we juggled day-to-day responsibilities, he quietly watched for a new opportunity. Somehow in the midst of all our issues, I needed to shelve my worry and focus on our December events.

I peered between the windshield wipers' fast strokes and groaned. The parking lot was full. A block-long overflow of cars had pulled onto the campus lawn. Everyone in our small Arkansas town must have turned out for the Christmas program.

Our second grader should have joined his class inside the gym by now, but I was running late. I mentally kicked myself. Why hadn't I sent him early with Jim and Michael, our fifth grader? They were warm and dry inside.

While Jon played with a toy in the back seat, I drove once more through the poorly lit parking lot. Surely there was a closer spot to leave our car.

Then I saw it, spotlighted by my headlights through the downpour.

The narrow area of grass between two cars was perfect for our small sedan. What great luck. We would make it inside a few minutes before the program started. I pulled into the spot, nosing forward to line up beside my neighbor.

With a sickening clunk, the front of our new car dropped about a foot and landed on something hard.

I cried out, "Jesus, help us," and stammered some kind of reassurance to Jon.

The windshield view, distorted by wipers and water, didn't reveal what had trapped us. The campus park, completely level, stretched beyond my headlights' glare. Shaking, I gripped the steering wheel and tried to think. Whether I drove forward or reversed, the sedan's undercarriage might be ripped out.

Within seconds of my prayer, someone tapped on the driver-side window.

With a trembling hand, I lowered it. A man stood there, backlit by the headlights of a vehicle parked out in the street. He was slender and of average height. In spite of the cold rain, his white shirt and dark pants looked dry.

Without expression or a greeting, he gave me instructions. "When I walk to the front of the car and lift, put it in reverse and back up."

I suppose I nodded in agreement, still in shock. He moved unhurriedly around to the front of the car and into my headlights.

His white shirt dazzled in the lights. I watched him reach under the bumper. With no apparent strain, he lifted and held the car's front end. I remember staring a moment, and then I put the car in reverse and looked over my shoulder until the front tires rested on the ground again. His help had taken less than a minute. I turned to thank him.

He was gone.

I looked around, searching for our Good Samaritan. How had he moved out of sight so quickly? Maybe he had run to that vehicle whose headlights had lit the scene, but now there was no vehicle on the street.

This time, my headlights revealed not only the campus grass but what had trapped us — a wide, grassy mound covering a concrete culvert, buried except for the open end where we'd dangled. I left the car in its safe spot and got out with one last glance around.

I rushed Jon into the school gym barely in time and settled into my bleacher seat. After a few deep breaths, my heart rate settled back to normal. Jim supervised his high-school video crew documenting the concert. Telling him about my answered prayer would have to wait. Our sons' classes sang their Christmas songs with gusto.

No doubt the other student groups performed well, too, but I was oblivious to them. Instead, I peered from face to face in the audience, sure I would spot the man who had helped us.

I never saw him again.

Still awed by the rescue but puzzled, I asked Jon the next day if he'd noticed where our helper went.

He stopped playing with his toys a moment. "He walked straight out there in the dark, I think."

On a cold, wet night, why would any person walk away from a warm building into the deserted campus park? Unless that average-looking fellow wasn't a person at all…

Much later, I realized our car-lifting angel marked a turning point in our family's direction. Within a couple of months, an opportunity opened for Jim to change careers. We each resigned our jobs and made a leap of faith to graduate school with children, pets, and a shoestring budget. When Jim completed his studies, his new career led our family into opportunities we couldn't have imagined on that cold December night.

In the decades since that evening, life has thrown plenty of difficulties our way. But now, no matter the size of the problem, I remember to ask for help. I don't think I've met another angel, but with each dilemma, God provides the heavy lifting right on time.

— Jetta B. Allen —

41

Angel Therapy

*When someone dies, an angel is there to meet them
at the gates of Heaven to let them know
that their life has just begun.*
~Author Unknown

My dad went into the hospital in November 2014 for a knee replacement. Three days later, he suffered a heart attack and was rushed into the ICU. Doctors discovered that he had congestive heart failure and kidney failure. He needed dialysis to have the necessary triple bypass, but he had decided years ago that he wouldn't do that to prolong his life. And so, he would live out the rest of his life in skilled care at their retirement community under the guidance of hospice.

After four weeks, his heart rate had improved. He was getting stronger and was able to do things for himself. His medications were working and keeping his condition stable. He was released from skilled care and returned to the cottage he and Mom had occupied for seventeen years.

On February 3rd, the head hospice nurse officially released him from hospice care — much to the amazement of the head doctor.

"Are we talking about the same man?" he asked in astonishment, calling it a miracle.

One night, in a rare moment of expressiveness, Dad opened up to Mom. He said that while he was in skilled care, he had a visit from an angel. *A human angel.* She knocked on his door and asked to come in. He had never seen her before, but she seemed to know his precise needs. She held his hand and prayed. Then she disappeared, and he never saw her again.

He said that he felt significant improvement afterward to the point that he could walk the halls. He wasn't totally healed, but he felt like he could go on with his life. He had hope.

Mom knew that Dad had a fascination with angels. He enjoyed reading stories about them. One time, he even shared some stories with a woman whose husband had taken his own life. Dad knew him well — they had worked together at a car auction. He took solace in the knowledge that she had found encouragement in what he shared.

Dad didn't have to convince Mom to believe in angels. Her childhood memories are filled with them. Her mother hung a framed painting on the wall in her bedroom. She can still picture it: A child is walking alone across a perilously constructed bridge. In the background is an angel with wings spread wide.

When her twelve-year-old cousin, Ruth Ella, was taking her last breaths after a long battle with pneumonia, she looked out the window and said, "There's an angel there." And then Ruth Ella was gone. That had a powerful effect on Mom.

But those were paintings and visions. What about angels in human form? Some people believe that Earth Angels are sent to ascertain elements of the human condition and to guide humans on Earth, that they are messengers and protectors, but also are powerful healers who have the capability to restore a person's mind, body and soul.

When Dad told Mom about the angel who had visited him in the form of a woman, he asked her to promise she wouldn't tell anyone else until he was no longer living. He thought people would be skeptical or completely disbelieving.

After he passed away suddenly one morning in 2016, Mom told me the story of the angel, and I included it in my eulogy at his memorial.

We will always be grateful for the angel who helped restore him to health so that we would have that additional time with him.

— Rick Weber —

Chapter
5

Messages from Heaven

42

Diamonds from Heaven

*Mother, the ribbons of your love
are woven around my heart.*
~Author Unknown

I woke up from a deep sleep with the familiar feeling of sadness. I had had that dream again. I'd been having the same dream for over thirty years. There were times when the dream wouldn't occur for several months and sometimes for a couple of years. But it never failed to return.

The dream was so realistic and baffling. I couldn't make sense of it, no matter how much I tried. I'd wake up puzzled and confused. "Mom, what are you trying to tell me?" I'd whisper to myself.

My mom had passed away in 1988, and I'd been having the dream ever since. Although it varied from time to time, my dream always had the same theme. My mom would slowly approach me. It was apparent she was heartbroken. I always asked her why she was sad, but she never answered. She held out her palm as if she was showing me something. But all I could see was a blinding, bright light glowing from her hand. Mom would look down at her hand as if she were about to cry. I felt deep sadness as I hugged her. I could physically feel her hug as I wrapped my arms around her to comfort her.

"Please, don't cry," I would urge her.

At that point, I would wake up in sorrow. The dream always made me feel out of sorts the entire day.

Recently, it would have been my mom's 100th birthday. That

night, on the eve of her birthday, I had my familiar dream again. This time, I didn't wake after our hug. This time, Mom looked at me with pleading eyes and finally spoke. I couldn't make out what she was saying. Her voice was soft and muffled. Her words were drawn out when she repeated what sounded like "yawn" or "urn." After asking her several times what she said, I woke up more troubled than ever. What was she saying?

That morning, my husband Harold was going to visit his mother. I wanted to stay home and have a good cry. I was missing my mom on her birthday, and the dream added to my emotional state. Throughout the years, I had confided to Harold about my recurring dream. Now, I told him how the dream had changed last night. He knew I got sad every year on my mom's birthday, so he suggested I go along for the hour-long drive to his mother's house. "It might do you good to get out of the house today to keep your mind occupied," he encouraged. I knew he was probably right, so I reluctantly agreed to go.

My mother-in-law greeted us with a huge smile as we entered her house. At ninety-two, she is as spry as the day I met her. She immediately sensed there was something bothering me, so she tried to cheer me up with cookies, cake and whatever else she had in her kitchen. "Why the long face?" she finally asked. I didn't tell her about my dream for fear she wouldn't understand. Instead, I only told her it was my mom's birthday and I was missing her a great deal.

"Come with me," my mother-in-law said as she motioned me toward her bedroom. Once again trying to cheer me up, she opened her closet door to reveal an abundance of sweaters she had knitted and crocheted. "Pick whatever you want," she encouraged me. I appreciated her trying to make me feel better, so I went along with picking out a couple of sweaters. It was bittersweet going through all the sweaters since my mom had also been an avid knitter and loved to crochet.

"Get that bag on the bottom of the closet," my mother-in-law instructed, pointing to a black, oversized leather bag in the far back corner. As I pulled it out, I remembered that bag; it was my mother's. I had given it to my mother-in-law after my mom passed away when I cleared out my mother's apartment. The bag was filled with yarn, knitting needles, and crochet hooks. I had kept some for myself and given the rest to my mother-in-law.

"You should keep it," she said as we walked back into the kitchen.

I was surprised to see that the bag still had some of my mom's yarn and needles. Running my hands over the skeins of yarn, I felt a connection with her. Then I felt something hard between the yarns. I pulled out a ball of colorful yarn and something bright caught my eye. The early afternoon sun was streaming through the kitchen window, and a brilliant, blinding light shone on the ball of yarn.

I sat there frozen when I realized this was similar to my dream. The only difference was that I was holding the glowing object. Embedded in the yarn was a beautiful, white-gold ring with an intricate design that included eight tiny diamonds. Then it dawned on me that my mom wasn't saying "yawn" or "urn" in my dream. She was saying "yarn"! She wanted me to find her ring. The ring might have slid off her finger while she was sifting through the bag of yarn, and she hadn't realized it at the time.

That night, while Harold and I were watching TV, I felt myself getting sleepy. Though I tried to stay awake, I eventually dozed off. Within seconds, I was dreaming again, that familiar dream, but now my mom was smiling. She reached for my hand and raised it to look at the ring, and then she smiled at me again. This time, no words were needed. I knew the ring was back where it belonged.

— Dorann Weber —

Recovery Room Visitor

Music is well said to be the speech of angels.
~Thomas Carlyle

I t was early 2020, and my son was desperately ill — but not with Covid. He had been newly diagnosed with a disease that required an immediate transfer to a larger hospital. It was an emergency situation, but, of course, the hospitals were full. After a twelve-day stay in our local hospital and many failed referral requests, they finally found room for him at the University of Virginia Medical Center.

This was the very same hospital where my young uncle had died not so many years before — the same uncle after whom I had named my son: Uncle Jeff.

Of course, my son's health and needed transfer were all that mattered. We said yes to the transfer, and I made the midnight trip following the ambulance that would take my baby where they could make him better. (Mind you, my "baby" was twenty-one years old, but any mother can tell you those numbers do not matter one bit when it comes to a situation like this.)

A few days following this transfer, we learned the extent of his disease. Emergency surgery was needed immediately. The doctors spoke to us of the risks. My son was very ill, and this was definitely not the optimal time for such extreme surgery given his health status; however, not proceeding with the operation was no longer an option. It was his only chance to survive.

So, off to surgery he went.

Sitting in that waiting room, waiting for news of how my son had fared through this extreme surgery, was easily the worst moment of my life. We had already lost his great-uncle Jeff in the same hospital. It couldn't happen again.

Many hours later, I heard that he had made it. He came through the surgery as well as could be expected. Many surgeries and life alterations were to come, but he had survived. That was all that mattered.

In the days that followed, the nurses spent a lot of time teaching us how to care for and maneuver life with my son's new ostomy bag. The portion of his intestine that sat outside his body, called the stoma, was very tender and required delicate care. At one point, a doctor came in and jokingly asked my son if he had named his stoma yet, as some young patients were apt to do. When my son had no answer, the doctor suggested "Garth." The other members of the surgery team laughed, and my son joined in.

I, however, didn't get the joke.

"Did I miss something?" I asked.

The doctor said, "Jeff, you didn't tell your mom about serenading us in the recovery room?" This prompted even more laughter from everyone. His doctor then went on to explain to me that my son had sung the lyrics to "The Dance" by Garth Brooks as he was coming out of anesthesia, and he knew every word.

A chill ran up my spine.

"Jeff, do you even know that song?" I asked. As expected, he told me that he may have heard it a time or two, but he couldn't tell us the lyrics now at all. Everyone passed it off as "strange" that he could know those lyrics so well by heart while under anesthesia but couldn't tell them to us at all days later when he was fully awake.

Everyone thought it was strange, that is, except for me.

Hours away in a little church graveyard sits Uncle Jeff's tombstone. An avid Garth Brooks fan, the following lyrics are printed on his black marble stone:

"I could have missed the pain, but I'd have had to miss the dance." — Garth Brooks

Strange things happen in this world that cannot be explained, but I don't count this as one of them. The explanation is clear. Uncle Jeff made sure that his young namesake made it through what he couldn't. My son was not alone in that recovery room with no family nearby. He had his great-uncle right there by his side through it all.

Coincidence?

I don't think so.

— Melissa Edmondson —

Two U's, one L, and a V

He was a father. That's what a father does. Eases the
burdens of those he loves. Saves the ones he loves from
painful last images that might endure for a lifetime.
~George Saunders

One of the first purchases my dad made when he started his own business during the 1980s was a huge metal lateral filing cabinet. The cabinet held pride of place in every small office my father rented.

As times were often hard, and paying for childcare wasn't really a possibility, I spent much of my childhood in those offices. I read picture books in the corners and took naps under desks — and spent a lot of time playing with the filing cabinet. Its smooth, metal surface was ideal for magnets. In elementary school, I did my spelling lessons with the plastic alphabet magnets my dad bought me. In middle school, he got me several sets of small magnets with whole words, and I started writing poetry instead. In high school, the poetry gave way to a set of scientific magnets one could use to build models of atoms and study the periodic table. By then, all the practice I'd gotten in filing and alphabetizing was instrumental in getting my first job outside the family business — working as an assistant in a doctor's office.

At the age of seventy-eight, my dad suffered a series of strokes. He retired — some might say *"finally* retired" — and devoted the good hours he still had each week to a cause very close to his heart: volunteering at the local elementary school, where he sat for hours listening to kids with learning disabilities read him stories. Having struggled with dyslexia all his life, Dad knew how important it was for kids to have a chance to practice their reading skills with an interested adult, one who would happily listen to whatever kind of story or book they wanted to read and never shamed them for their mistakes.

The filing cabinet was now covered in magnets holding the letters and pictures the kids made for him. There were many more filed inside.

Sadly, my dad's physical health deteriorated quickly after his retirement. When he passed away, the filing cabinet came to me. For years, it moved with me from state to state, finding a spot in every place I called home. When the pandemic began, however, I hit some hard times and had to downsize, moving into a small apartment where much of my furniture simply wouldn't fit. I started listing the large items on Craigslist and Facebook. I managed to sell pretty much everything before I moved—except the filing cabinet. Several people were interested, but something always happened at the last minute that prevented them from making the purchase, from unexpected car repairs to a sudden transfer at work.

I began wondering if my emotional attachment to the cabinet was blocking the sale somehow and starting calling local charities, thinking I'd donate it instead. But the earliest anyone could come to pick up the cabinet was a full five weeks after my moving day. Finally, one day before my move, I received the following message through Facebook:

"Dear Ms. Barney: Is there any chance you might consider donating your file cabinet to a local school? I'm a teacher with the elementary ESL program here in Albuquerque. As I'm sure you know, our budget has been severely cut, and teachers now need to provide most of their classroom materials themselves. Currently, I'm keeping all my students' worksheets and papers in old, cardboard file boxes that are falling apart, so your cabinet would truly be a blessing. Please consider it and let me know. Thank you!"

I didn't have to consider it. I could feel my dad's hand behind this development as clearly as if he was standing in the room with me.

"YES!!!" I texted back. "Can you come get it today?"

From that point on, everything went as smoothly as if it had been supernaturally orchestrated, which I firmly believe it was. The ESL teacher, a wonderful woman, was indeed able to pick up the cabinet that very day. When the two of us weren't strong enough to get the cabinet off my porch to her car, a neighbor I'd never met before saw us struggling and offered the use of his furniture dolly, helping us move the heavy cabinet with ease. At first, all three of us were worried that the cabinet would be too big for the teacher's car, but it went through the back door of her SUV as smoothly as butter, with exactly half an inch of clearance to spare. "Must be meant to be," my dolly-wielding neighbor said in surprise.

Nobody would ever believe me, but I knew my dad had arranged the whole thing. Of course, he'd want the cabinet to go to an elementary school. Not only that, but I felt he was sending me a message. Rather than being upset that I had fallen on hard times and had to get rid of the cabinet, he was telling me it was okay, that he still loved me and would be watching over me in the days to come. That message was worth everything to me, and I fell asleep with a smile on my face.

Dad wasn't done with me, though. A few days later, the teacher texted me again. "When we moved the cabinet into the classroom, the bottom drawer wouldn't close," she wrote. "We couldn't figure out why until we pulled it all the way out and found some old magnets jamming the drawer glide. They must have been stuck to the bottom of the next drawer up and shaken loose during the drive. Would you like them back?" She sent me a picture of four bright plastic alphabet magnets I clearly remembered from my childhood: two U's, an L, and a V.

Once again, I didn't hesitate. "YES!!!" I texted back. And I sent the teacher my new address.

The next week, I found a padded envelope in my new mailbox with the magnets carefully packed inside. I instantly took them out and put them on my refrigerator, spelling out my dad's last message: LUV U.

— Kerrie Barney —

45

Answered Prayers

I believe that prayer is our powerful contact
with the greatest force in the universe.
~Loretta Young

The doorbell rang. We looked at each other. Alison was here. Again. We weren't really surprised. After all, it was September 18th. And, for the past seven years, she had come on this date without fail. It was the date our son, Brian, had died by suicide.

Sometimes, Alison came alone, but more often she came with a sibling or parent. On this day, she came with her mother. We welcomed them in with open arms.

We chatted easily about the events of our lives since we last spoke. The exchange was light and easy, just like always.

Eventually, the conversation turned to memories of Brian. The past few years had been easier than those early years. Back then, I cried just hearing Brian's name. Memories were often painful, and we ended up crying and hugging Alison with mixed emotions. Talk of Brian back then filled me with sorrow and made me miss him even more.

But now, those memories made me smile as we remembered the good times, before Brian got sick. We loved hearing the stories from his friends because they made us feel like he was still a part of our lives and theirs.

We told Alison we were glad that she was able to share these memories with us. After all these years, we still worried about the effect of Brian's death on his friends. It helped us knowing that Brian's friends were okay, as evidenced by Alison's stories.

At one point, Alison's mother said, "Honey, I think you should share the dream you had about Brian with the Todds."

My curiosity was piqued. "Yes, please tell us."

Dreams usually made for very interesting discussions between my husband and me, as we both had dreams about our son. Based on our interpretation of them, we usually felt much closer to Brian after discussing them.

Alison said she had the dream during her last Christmas break nine months earlier. In the dream, all her friends were at her house having fun, just like the night Brian had died. Suddenly, there was a knock on the door, and Brian walked in. Everyone was hooting and hollering and making a commotion because they were glad to see him. Then, the whole room went silent as they all remembered that Brian had died.

That's when Brian spoke. He said, "I can't stay long, but I just wanted to stop and tell you all that 1) I'm okay, 2) I'm in a better place, and 3) I'm doing important things now." And then he was gone.

When Alison finished, I burst into tears, surprising everyone. This dream did not have to be interpreted. It was an answer to my prayers.

I explained my tears to Alison and my husband. "As a mother, I always felt like it was my duty to protect my children. I had to make sure that they were okay. Death did not change that fact. I still needed to be reassured of Brian's wellbeing. For almost seven years, I have prayed for the same three things: 1) Was Brian okay? 2) Was he in a better place? And 3) would God allow him to do substantial things in heaven?"

When the answers to my prayers did not seem to be coming, I even "suggested" to God that if I couldn't receive the answers, perhaps comfort could come to me through someone else's dreams. Never had I shared these prayers with anyone, not even my husband.

Alison had told me exactly what I needed to hear.

— Janet M. Todd —

46

Homecoming

The love game is never called off
on account of darkness.
~Tom Masson

I remember our final exchange as if it were yesterday — the gentle sweetness of the last kiss we shared and the last words spoken. I told him, "Come back to me, my love." Somewhere in my soul, I knew there was a different plan. My words were a simple wish, one that would go unfulfilled — or would it?

In the days and weeks following my husband's death, the kids and I began to notice things that made me wonder if he had fulfilled my request, just not as anticipated. On a quiet evening about two weeks after his passing, my daughter and I were on the couch watching something not worth remembering on the television. My son was situated behind us at the computer. Out of nowhere and for no apparent reason, the dog began whimpering and started looking around the room. I don't recall how much time passed, but in what felt like the blink of an eye, the power went out in the den, and we were enveloped in darkness.

We sat in stunned silence for a time and then began analyzing the situation. "These things are known to happen," I offered. The kids ran through a list of logical possibilities but never settled on a definitive cause. At the same time, I headed to the garage and started flipping breakers. *We've never had any power issues in the past,* I thought as I scanned the panel for the breaker tied to the den. Odd that the only room to lose power was the one we were in. Coincidence or not?

We soon discovered it was not.

The following evening brought a repeat performance, which made me begin to wonder if I should call an electrician, but my mind went somewhere else. Could Greg be behind these antics? He had been a prankster at heart. His shop fridge had blown the day of the funeral, and now the lights were going out. What would be next?

My son came bounding up the stairs the next evening sporting a Cheshire grin, wanting to talk. It was odd and uncharacteristic behavior for a self-defined introvert. "Guess what happened!"

I offered a few possibilities to no avail, and then asked, "What happened?"

"I was doing homework in my room, and the lights went out."

"Anywhere else or just your room?"

With the biggest of grins on his face, he replied, "Only my room."

"Are you okay?"

"Yep," he announced with pride.

My daughter's turn came a week later. She was home alone, so when her name popped up on my phone, I immediately became concerned.

My hello was met by, "Mom, you won't believe what just happened!"

Her words evoked further panic. "Are you okay?" I asked.

"Yep," she replied.

I shook off my worry and then continued the conversation. "Good to hear. So, what happened?"

"The lights went out in my room. I'm sitting in the dark."

"Are you scared?" I asked.

"No, I think Dad's watching out for me," she said confidently.

"I know he is," I replied.

As the weeks and months passed, we continued to have what we lovingly came to call "Random Check-ins from Dad." We never knew when they might happen, and we were continually caught off-guard when they did. The constant was that the power outages only occurred in rooms we occupied.

The most memorable episode for me came on a Sunday evening in September. The kids headed downstairs to shower and organize schoolwork while I packed lunchboxes and filled water bottles. Afterward,

I headed to the bathroom to wash my face and prepare for bed. We all have nightly rituals, and washing my face every evening is important to me. In addition to good skincare, it functioned as a cleansing of the day.

I pulled my hair back and gazed at the mirror image before me, visually tracing the edges of my face. *Who is this person in front of me?* I asked the reflection. And with that, my mind began to spiral through nonresolvable questions. *How did she get here? How do I go on without you?*

At that moment, the bathroom lights went out.

I was dumbfounded for a time and then turned my gaze toward the bottom of the bathroom door. A tiny sliver of light shone beneath it. Light was coming from areas that were tied to the same breaker as the bathroom. *That's not how breakers work. I'm not alone.* And with that thought, I stepped back, leaned against the wall, and slid to the floor.

"It must be you," I said.

What once were thoughts became words. I talked. I cried. I hoped he was listening.

People are typically in one camp or another about these types of encounters. My family responded as expected: undeniably supportive. If they questioned my sanity, they kept it to themselves. My brother, an avid ghost-hunter fan, hung on my every word. He frequently called to ask about our encounters and seemed let down when there was nothing to report.

During a call with my mother, she asked if anything odd had happened lately. Just as the words crossed her lips, the lights went out where I was standing. I paused and then answered, "Well, you're not going to believe this. I was about to say no, but the lights just went out. So, in fact, yes."

My parents would get in on the action in the months to come. During their fall and winter visits, the den lights went off on their own three times, my son was awakened several nights by his PlayStation turning on and off of its own accord, and my daughter and I had two experiences where bedside lamps turned themselves on or off without human intervention.

When my parents returned in the spring, I picked them up from the shuttle station on my way home from work. Our conversations were mainly catch-up in nature. My mother gave me a blow-by-blow inventory of who, what, when and how the people around her had been affected by the changing nature of life. Dad, essentially silenced, threw an occasional word in edgewise. Once settled, Mom joined me in the den and began our exchange with an odd yet, for us, routine question. "Have you had any more signs from heaven?"

I paused, inventoried the past months, and replied, "No, it's been a while." Almost instantly, the lights went out, and we were left staring at each other in the darkness. "Guess that must be hello," I offered.

Later that month, I ran into our electrician at the local home-improvement store and seized the opportunity to ask his opinion about our peculiar power phenomenon. He offered to stop by the following week to inspect the house.

"Today's electrical codes call for more sensitive breakers. I can put an older model in your main areas, which may help." I gave him a thumbs-up, and he went to work.

"So, what do you think the problem is?" I asked.

"Power surges," he replied.

"Coming from where?"

He shrugged his shoulders, shook his head, and said, "I have no earthly idea."

— Beth Bullard —

Last Embrace

Those we love don't go away; they walk beside us every day.
Unseen, unheard, but always near; still loved,
still missed and very dear.
~Author Unknown

I felt the moment my mother died. It happened while I was at work on a beautiful, sunny day in the middle of summer. The shop I worked at in Vancouver's Gastown district had floor-to-ceiling windows offering one of the city's best views of Burrard Inlet and the cedar-covered North Shore Mountains.

My mother was living out her final days at the base of those mountains in the hospital's palliative-care unit. Though she'd fought valiantly, extending her six-month life expectancy to three years, her body had been ravaged by cancer, and there was nothing to do but wait.

The last time I saw her was her fifty-second birthday. She sat in her hospital bed with her face waxy and pale, her lipstick and mascara smudged. She'd still managed to style her hair in its usual bun, albeit a slightly messier version. For someone who never left the house without wearing lipstick or being impeccably dressed, this spoke volumes about her state. My aunts Elaine and Maureen sat on the chairs beside her hospital bed. The three of them were playing cards when I walked in.

I sat at the foot of Mom's bed, careful not to move the mattress, or it might jar her. At twenty-one, I wasn't ready to lose my mother. Knowing this birthday would be her last, I had no idea of what kind of present to get her, so I brought the most beautiful bouquet of flowers

I could find.

Mom didn't seem to notice me until Elaine announced my arrival. Though it didn't make sense at the time, in hindsight, I realized Mom had been so heavily medicated that the card game took all her focus. I greeted her with a kiss, told her I loved her, and wished her a happy birthday.

When she thanked me and looked away, my throat tightened with unshed tears. I knew she loved me, too. She was my mom. But were these going to be our last words?

The next day, the doctors put Mom into a morphine-induced coma. My grandmother visited her daily but advised me not to come, saying there was no point because "she wasn't there anymore." I guess she was trying to protect me. At the time, we didn't know as much about comas. We believed Mom wouldn't know I was there.

Every day, I went to work and came home to our empty house. Every day, I'd check in with Grandmother and my aunts to see how Mom was doing. Every day, they told me it would be "anytime now."

The magazine store was one of my first jobs. At the time, I knew nothing about bereavement leave or how compassionate care worked. Until Mom was hospitalized, working all day and looking after her at night exhausted me. As an only child of divorced parents, I needed help, so Grandmother came often. It was a difficult time for all of us.

Now that Mom was in a coma, there was nothing I could do. I didn't know how the news would hit me when it came. I didn't want to cause a scene or be forced to work the rest of my shift in tears until someone came to relieve me. So, I asked my grandmother to not notify me of Mom's death in the middle of my workday but to wait until the end of my shift instead.

That sunny day in early August. The lunch rush had just ended. Sunlight filtered through the large windows as I paced the empty store. Despite the air conditioning, a hot pressure came over me. The air shimmered with a sparkling, golden hue. I felt a hand on my shoulder. I turned, but nobody was there. Then, a pressure came over me, like I was being squeezed, enveloped in a tight bear hug. With it came a feeling of love combined with such grief. Tears filled my eyes. My heart pounded like a gong in my ears.

Then, the sensation lifted. I gulped in air as the feelings and the shimmery, golden light subsided.

Later that afternoon, at the end of my shift, my grandmother called right at 6:00 to let me know that my mother had passed. I asked her what time it had happened. She told me it was just after 1:00 P.M.

In hindsight, I realized what had happened.

My mother had come to say goodbye, and this was her last embrace.

— Lisa Voisin —

Butterfly Effect

A grandmother is like an angel, who takes you
under her wing. She prays and watches over you,
and she'll gift you anything.
~Author Unknown

It was November 11, 2003, and my mother had given me a ride to Dillard University, where I was a freshman. "Do you know what today is?" my mom asked as I grabbed my backpack from the car.

"Yes, Mom, I do. Today marks one year since Grandma passed away," I answered.

My maternal grandmother had passed away the previous year after enduring a third stroke that left her bedbound.

"So, how are you feeling?" asked my mom.

I nonchalantly replied, "I am feeling good. I know that she is always here with us. I just don't want you to be sad, okay?" I urged.

I gave my mom a hug, waved goodbye, and started to walk toward the chapel.

My nonchalant response was a façade. Truthfully, I often thought about the events that surrounded my grandmother's passing. I acted lowkey about it because I did not want to fall apart and make my mother more upset.

"God, please send me a sign if my grandmother's spirit is still around me," I silently pleaded.

Suddenly, a butterfly gently landed on my left shoulder.

Absentmindedly, and being that I am not a lover of insects, I swatted away the butterfly.

Then, I thought, *What if that was the sign I had asked for?*

"God, if that was indeed the sign, please send it back," I pleaded.

As if on cue, the same butterfly landed on the same spot. It stayed on my left shoulder and accompanied me until I reached doors to the chapel where my class was meeting. I watched it fly away and felt reassured that it was a definitive sign from above.

However, I was not expecting a second sign of reassurance on the same day.

That afternoon, I was assigned a work-study position in the university's computer lab. It was near closing time, and I was eager to lock up in order to board the city bus at a specific time.

"Please make your final copies. The computer lab closes in ten minutes," I announced.

Almost everyone cleared out in a timely manner with the exception of one young woman. Initially, I was quite patient, but as each minute passed, the slower she moved. I did not want to be rude, so I did not rush her. Instead, I decided to take a later bus.

As she made her way to the exit, she turned around, stared at me and calmly said, "I love you, Jennell, and God loves you, too." I stood frozen in shock. My mind flooded with many questions. How did she know my name? I was new to the campus, I was not outgoing, it was only my third shift in the computer lab, and I was not wearing a name badge. Why did she tell me — a stranger — that she loved me? Most importantly, why did she feel compelled to tell me that God loved me?

I snapped out of my trance and ran to find the young woman, but she was gone.

I decided to look up her name in the computer lab's sign-in log. There was a unique number associated with each computer, and users would sign the log in the space assigned to the computer they chose to use.

I found the space associated with the computer that she used and, after seeing her name, was in absolute shock. Her name was Naomi Smothers. Naomi was my grandmother's first name, and Smothers was her last name during her first marriage.

November 11, 2003, will always be a special day to me because I received two separate messages of confirmation and love from above.

P.S.: As I was reading the rough draft of this story to my mom in the car, a butterfly landed on the windshield.

—Jennell Melancon—

Smoke Signals

Because I feel that, in the Heavens above,
the angels, whispering to one another,
can find, among their burning terms of love,
none so devotional as that of "Mother."
~Edgar Allen Poe

My husband and I were the perfect example of when opposites attract. I was opinionated and outspoken; he was quiet and chose his words carefully. I liked going out and trying new things. He liked staying in or going on solo adventures like riding his bike and fishing. And when it came to sharing a bed, there was no negotiating. Even when we traveled, the left side of the bed was always his.

When my exasperation with newly married life mounted, I would call my mother.

As soon as I blurted out my frustrations, I could hear the click of the cigarette lighter. After a pause (which I knew to be the first exhale of smoke), I would imagine her setting down the cigarette in one of her colorful ashtrays.

In an era when most of her peers had been smoking since they were teens, my mother was in her mid-thirties when she started. After years of secondhand smoke in her home and social circles, she began her own love affair with cigarettes. A year later, the Surgeon General's warning appeared on the packaging, and the next year my dad and many of her friends were quitting. But not Mom. Long after everyone else stopped, she held out. She took her smoke breaks with dignity and determination, cherishing her time in isolation.

Her routine had a dance-like choreography. She walked outside with her beaded cigarette pouch and found a comfortable place to sit. She surveyed her surroundings, and then removed a cigarette and held it to her mouth with two beautifully manicured fingers, using the other hand to strike the monogrammed lighter she gave my dad when he still smoked. The ritual displayed both my mother's elegance and her will.

"Karen," she would begin after I finished ranting, "have you tried seeing this situation for what it really is?" Or "Is this really important?"

No matter what I fretted over, her advice always de-escalated the situation or forced me to own up to my part. Her favorite adage was, "Well, sometimes the tide is in. Sometimes, it's out."

As my life and hers changed, we lived in different places and at different stages of life. When my dad retired, they traveled and did things on their own. They began their second shift of being grandparents when my brother's kids were born. Mom divided her time between all of us and was never farther away than the phone if I needed her.

I looked forward to the times she came to stay with us. We shopped and had lunches out. We cooked together, and she spent time with the kids and our friends.

My favorite, though, was time alone with her on our porch swing where she took smoke breaks.

There, in my garden, where no one kept track of time, we talked for hours.

Despite the decades I had to prepare for it, I was not ready for my mother's death. The phone silence was the worst.

My need for her counsel on being a wife and mother was just beginning, and I had so many questions. How did she and Dad fill their days after my brothers and I left home? When would I stop worrying about my kids, and when would they start listening to me?

I missed not being able to pick up the phone and call her anytime I thought of her or had a problem only she could solve.

Our connection was so deep that sometimes, as soon as I started worrying, the phone would ring. For weeks, I prayed for a sign that I hadn't been disconnected from her forever.

And then I started smelling smoke—in my garden, in my car, and in random places in the house. When I shared the phenomenon with Mike, he agreed that it would be just like Mom to make her presence known this way. Once or twice, even he commented on a cigarette-like presence when we talked about her.

Almost as suddenly as they started, the smoke signals stopped, though.

Years later, when our daughter was just days away from delivering her baby, she developed preeclampsia. She had been so diligent her entire pregnancy that I couldn't imagine how or why this happened. I was concerned for them both and felt helpless there was nothing I could do. Every night, I prayed for them and fell asleep wishing that I could call my mother.

A few days later, Mike and I were having our morning coffee when he put down the newspaper and smiled at me.

"I've been meaning to tell you that I've had some strange dreams about your mother lately," he said.

"What kind of dreams?" I asked.

"All kinds of dreams," he said. "But the funny thing is she's somewhere in every one of them. Standing. Sitting. Walking with her hands on her hips. Always with a cigarette in one hand."

We both laughed. "But in the dream last night, she came up to me and told me to tell you she heard you. And that everything will be fine." I laughed, and then I hugged him and shed a few tears. My prayers had been answered. I wasn't disconnected from her after all.

— Karen Ross Samford —

Eternal Love Takes Wing

Those we love never truly leave us.
There are things that death cannot touch.
~Jack Thorne

M y late husband wasn't even sure he believed in heaven. "But if there is one," he used to say, "I'm going to hover up there and play tricks on you, angel-style."

When Roxanne told me that John was sending her messages from beyond, I scoffed. After four years of watching him painfully succumb to cancer, I missed my husband every day. No doubt about it, my faith was shaken. I couldn't seem to heave myself up out of my pit of sadness.

John had never met Roxanne, a fact that also tested my belief. I made her acquaintance after his death when I adopted my kitty Posey from her. I sensed that John's cat Sam, who had been his constant companion and source of joy, needed a playmate. I understood Sam's sorrow when he crept around the house, meowing softly and searching for his buddy. So, I brought little Posey into my newly restructured family.

Besides fostering kitties, Roxanne works as a registered nurse. She told me that nurses and others in the helping professions tend to be more intuitive about souls who are no longer on this Earth. These caregivers, who are special kinds of angels themselves, often witness people transitioning to heaven. Thus, they are naturally more open to messages from beyond.

"He told me to send you a butterfly card," Roxanne said after she received her first message from John. "I'm making something for you right now. I need to know, what was John's favorite saying?"

Why butterflies? I thought to myself. We hadn't had any particular connection to the little creatures. Cats? Yes. Butterflies? No. It didn't make any sense to me.

I finally said, "Well, he used to be so good at soothing me when I was worried. He'd say, 'Don't borrow trouble.'"

A few days later, Roxanne brought me a beautiful card strewn with touches of glitter and gold, showcasing butterflies aloft. In dainty calligraphy, she had penned John's words. I clipped the card to my display shelf, nestling it in amongst the sympathy messages. During the ensuing weeks, my gaze was often drawn to the card. Each time I focused on the butterflies, my spirits seemed to flutter a bit higher.

A couple of weeks crawled by. I still wrestled with the concept that my husband could really be out there somewhere, watching over and caring for me, although I hoped beyond hope that he was.

Then, something happened that truly gave me goose bumps. One morning, I was lugging my groceries to the car when I noticed a small object tucked under my windshield wiper. Sliding it out, I saw that it was a library card from San Francisco, which is three hours away from my home.

I peered at the card, wondering how in the world it had landed on my windshield, in this parking lot. Several butterflies adorned the margins. Flipping it over, I saw the name on the card, and butterflies seemed to take up residence in my stomach. The name was "J. Kim" — J for John, followed by my name, Kim. One of John's best qualities was a great sense of humor. Could this be one of the tricks he promised to play on me to make me smile? When I arrived home, I stuck the card on my refrigerator with a butterfly magnet.

Soon, my birthday came around — one more landmark day to get through without John. Roxanne treated me to lunch at my favorite restaurant overlooking the ocean. On my way home, several monarch butterflies swirled around my car, creating an orange-and-yellow entourage. As I waited at a stoplight, one swooped so low that I could see the small white dots decorating the black edges of his wings.

"Hello, John," I whispered with a smile. I could no longer label all these happenings as coincidental. My angelic soul mate was reaching out to reassure me of his eternal love. "Bravo for you for getting out and celebrating your special day," he seemed to be saying.

I Googled butterflies and learned that they are a symbol used by many grief counselors and support groups. A butterfly symbolizes life after death because of its transition from a caterpillar that crawls on the ground to a beautiful, ethereal creature that flies through the air. This image called to mind my own metamorphosis from a sleepwalker wrapped in the inertia of grief to a free spirit moving toward happiness and light.

I accepted the fact that I might be flying solo. John had tried to have a heart-to-heart talk with me about this topic shortly before he passed. He told me sternly that he didn't want me to remain alone. "You've got to be with someone who has a sense of humor since I won't be here to cheer you up," he said. "But the most important quality I would wish for you is kindness." He realized that his innate kindness had been in short supply due to chronic pain.

I remembered pressing my lips together, refusing to talk about life without my husband. If I couldn't be with John, I wanted to be alone. But time can soften the edges of the most stubborn stances. As I neared the one-year mark since John's passing, I realized that perhaps he had a point. Doing whatever I wanted, when I wanted, without worrying about anyone else's opinion, was a bit overrated. A friend urged me to go on a date. I was hesitant and, frankly, terrified, but I went.

My date and I were sitting out on the restaurant's patio when a monarch butterfly fluttered around our table. Keith said, "That's weird, I've never seen a butterfly here before."

I just smiled to myself and whispered, "Thanks for the endorsement, John." And, yes, Keith turned out to be not only funny but one of the kindest men I've ever met.

A few weeks later, my parents and I scattered John's ashes off the coast. I had been putting off this task for a long time, not sure I wanted to face the finality of it. Though sunny, it was a blustery day and sprinkling lightly. The ocean roared with giant, wind-driven waves. The scents of rain and sea mingled, creating an intoxicating freshness. As I opened a small, engraved box and prepared for the ritual, a heavenly rainbow burst onto the horizon. "Would you look at that?" Dad exclaimed.

Afterward, we sat quietly together on a log, reminiscing about John and watching the rainbow slowly fade into the horizon. Just then, a butterfly landed on the end of the log and fanned its wings.

"Great trick, John," I said, and smiled through my tears.

— Kim Johnson McGuire —

51

Jackie's Angel

The bond between friends cannot be broken by chance;
no interval of time or space can destroy it.
Not even death itself can part true friends.
~Saint John Cassian

Jackie was tall, thin, lovely, and extremely quiet. To say that we were exact opposites is an understatement. Despite our obvious differences, we were both believers in the Lord and became the best of friends.

We met while working at a water district in the foothills of San Diego County. There were no restrictions at that time regarding smoking within the workplace, and unfortunately Jackie shared an office with an employee who was a chain smoker. Although Jackie never smoked a day in her life, it became apparent that she was not well. She had become short of breath and had a nagging cough. We didn't think much about it until she developed what we thought to be pneumonia.

Jackie made an appointment to see her personal physician, who sent her to see a pulmonologist. Several tests were scheduled, and the results were not what any of us had expected: Jackie had lung cancer.

The doctors advised her that they could possibly remove the infected lung, but after further testing, they realized that it had already spread to her other lung. She was sent home with medication that would keep her relatively comfortable while awaiting the inevitable.

Jackie worked for a few more months until her breathing became extremely labored and exhausting. She had taken a turn for the worse, and her doctor decided to admit her to our local hospital for observation. I went to visit her and asked if there was anything special she wanted. She said, "I've always loved angels!" I told her that I had seen one at our local Christian bookstore and headed off to purchase it for her. I returned within the hour, but she had fallen asleep. I placed the porcelain angel on a shelf next to her bed and left her to rest for the evening.

I checked on Jackie the next day, and the nurses said that she had experienced a difficult night. They almost lost her. She said, "Thank you so much for my angel, but how in the world did you get him into your car?"

I told her that I had just set it on the seat next to me. "It's really not all that big, so I set it on the shelf by your bed."

She said, "Oh, not that angel! I'm talking about the one that stood at the end of my bed and kept watch over me all night! He was at least seven feet tall and had huge wings! He never said a word, but I felt such peace with his presence. He stayed until daybreak, and then he was gone."

Jackie knew that her time was short, so the doctors released her from the hospital to spend her final days at home.

At 5:30 on a Sunday morning, my husband sat straight up in bed. He was noticeably shaken and said, "Did you hear that?"

Coming out of a sound sleep and totally confused, I replied, "No, what did you hear?"

He said, "It was Jackie's voice! She said, 'Goodbye, see you later!'"

Five minutes later, the phone on our bedside table rang. It was Jackie's husband, Morrie. He said, "Jackie passed away a few minutes ago. You were her best friend, and I wanted you to know first."

I turned to my husband, and we just looked at each other in amazement. Jackie had bid us one last farewell.

Her angel had come to take her home....

— Sharon E. Albritton —

Chapter
6

Miracles Happen

52

No More Doubt

Death ends a life, not a relationship.
~Jack Lemmon

O n a Thursday evening in late July 2019, I was sitting in a room on an unfamiliar church campus. Around me, men and women of all ages had come together to share their stories, pain, and tears. But, most importantly, they were there to provide comfort to one another. This was a grief support group for bereaved parents.

First-timers were asked to introduce themselves and state their child's name and when they passed. I drew a deep breath. "My name is Mark Mason, and my daughter's name is Makenna. She died last month." I paused for a moment. "She was twenty-five years old." A few people seated near me offered kind words of welcome with knowing smiles. I felt a profound sense of belonging sitting there among these strangers, this community of shattered hearts. These were my people.

I continued attending meetings in the months that followed and became familiar with many in the group. Their stories of loss were as varied as the people sharing them. But many of the stories had one thing in common: an event that was interpreted to be a sign from their loved one who had passed. Some believed that they had received a visitation in the form of a dream. Others were convinced that the strange behavior of a family pet was the departed's attempt to communicate with them. Still others felt that the sudden appearance of butterflies or hummingbirds at odd times was their child signaling to them that they were happy and at peace.

I did my best to keep an open mind as I listened to these accounts, but I always felt there had to be a logical explanation for these "supernatural" occurrences. I certainly understand a person's need for hope in the face of indescribable loss, and I sincerely believe that I will see my daughter again one day. But signs? Whenever someone in the group encouraged me to be aware of the myriad ways that my daughter would contact me in the months and years to come, I would smile and thank them while secretly dismissing the idea.

Summer ended, and with it came a growing feeling of dread. The ever-shortening days of fall would lead me to the beginning of the holiday season and then, ultimately, inexorably, to my first Christmas Day in twenty-five years without my daughter. I swallowed hard every time I thought of it.

C.S. Lewis, in writing about his grief over the loss of his wife, observed, "Her absence is like the sky, spread over everything." This certainly applied to how I now experienced every day of my life. With the approach of Christmas, I made no attempt to distract myself from the reality of my loss but decided to acknowledge it. Immediately after Thanksgiving, I ordered a custom-made ornament online in memory of my daughter. It was a white, plastic disc that would have a photo of her smiling face printed on one side. Beneath it were the words, "Always in our hearts," along with the dates of her birth and death.

When it arrived, I removed it from the package and held it for a time. It was perfect. A thin strand of green ribbon was threaded through a small hole at the top, tied together to form a loop.

I chose a branch on our artificial tree near the top and bent the tip of it upward at a ninety-degree angle for an extra measure of security. (It was unnecessary given that the ornament was unbreakable, but I did it anyway.) Hanging it on the branch was a bittersweet moment, but I was glad I had purchased it. It felt healing somehow.

A few weeks later, it was Christmas Eve. My wife Judy and I were exhausted from all the last-minute preparations for the following day. It was very late by the time we finally went to bed. As I lay in the darkness, my mind filled with images from years past when Makenna would spend Christmas Eve at our house. It was our tradition. I wiped away the tears and tried to relax.

Suddenly, we heard the sound of an object dropping onto the hardwood floor in the front room. It was a familiar sound. Our cat liked to bat the low-hanging ornaments on the tree and would knock one off on occasion. That would have been the logical explanation if we still owned a cat.

"Should we go look?" Judy asked.

"Give it a moment," I replied. Once we were satisfied it wasn't an intruder, we fell fast asleep.

The next morning, Judy was the first one up. I was just beginning to stir when I heard her call out from the front room. "Mark! You need to come out here!" She didn't sound alarmed, but the tone of her voice had an urgency to it.

I walked over to where she was standing near the tree. There at her feet was Makenna's ornament, lying face-up on the floor.

"This is what we heard last night," she said.

I stood for a moment in stunned disbelief before picking it up. The ribbon had not come undone. Then I examined the branch where it had been hanging. The tip was still bent up at a right angle. There was no physical way that ornament could have come off on its own.

Was this the sign that others had told me to look for?

With tearful eyes, I turned to look at Judy, who gave me a loving smile as if knowing what I was thinking. As I returned the ornament to its place on the tree, I whispered, "Merry Christmas, sweetheart. Thanks for stopping by."

— Mark Mason —

53

Heaven's Hummingbirds

You may be gone from my sight,
but you will never be gone from my heart.
~Henry van Dyke, Jr.

I had hit the snooze button and dozed off again when my cell-phone started ringing. It was my dad, trying to explain through sobs that my mother had suddenly passed away.

While most of the day was a blur, I can remember the drive home after making her arrangements. I sat in the passenger's seat, gripping a small, sealed envelope handed over to me by the funeral director.

"Give it to her," my dad had said to him, barely able to speak.

I held the envelope tightly. Silent tears streamed down my face as I thought about what was inside. It was my mother's necklace, the one that she never took off — a thin, gold box chain with a hummingbird pendant.

Both my children were always mesmerized by the shiny hummingbird, their small, dimpled hands reaching for it when Grandma was reading them a story or just cradling them on her lap.

Mom wore the necklace whether she was in sweats doing housework or all decked out for a formal occasion. It felt wrong to have it now, but my dad had insisted.

My mother was an avid bird lover, and hummingbirds were her favorites. Starting in early spring, she hung nectar feeders throughout her garden, which was overflowing with flowers that would attract hummingbirds. The yard was filled with hummingbirds well into September.

My mother tried desperately to share her love of hummingbirds with my children and me. She purchased feeders, planted flowers, and even made her own "special recipe" nectar to attract them, but to no avail. The hummingbirds would never visit our yard, although she kept trying — for seven years.

On the morning of my mom's memorial service, I picked up the small envelope that hadn't moved since I laid it on my dresser three days before. I cried as the gold chain containing the little hummingbird pendant fell into the center of my hand.

It was time to wear it, to honor my mother, although I did tuck the pendant under my collar so as not to upset my father more. I was hoping, praying, that wearing it would give me the inner strength I needed to get through the day.

After the service, I was the first to leave. I made up some excuse for why I needed to stop at home before meeting for a family meal. Truthfully, I wanted time by myself to think, cry, and process the past few days.

After a very tearful drive home, I pulled into the driveway feeling a little better. I was gathering up my purse and the photos and albums from the service when I heard a vibrating sound. I was sure it was a bee, and in my hurry to get away I dropped my purse in the flowerbed. When I went back to get it, I heard the buzzing again. As I was about to make a mad dash for the door I found myself eye-to-eye with my attacker, which wasn't actually a bee at all.

Hovering in front of me was the most stunning, emerald-green hummingbird I had ever seen! I instinctively reached into my purse for my phone to call my mom.

Even as I moved, the little bird lingered for a moment, just inches from my face, before it circled me and flew up into a nearby tree. That's when I saw a second hummingbird, at the nearest feeder.

More than seven years without a single hummingbird visit, and now on the day of my mother's funeral, they arrived.

It's been fifteen years since my mama's been gone, and those little, buzzing beauties have visited every year since, bringing with them long-awaited blessings of comfort I so look forward to.

Although I was unable to call and tell Mom on that day when they first arrived, something tells me she was well aware of it.

—Valerie Archual—

54

Let There Be Light

*Miracles are instantaneous, they cannot be
summoned, but come of themselves, usually
at unlikely moments and to those
who least expect them.*
~Katherine Porter

The phone call from the emergency-room physician informing my husband and me of our adult son's sudden passing hit us like a wrecking ball. Marc, we were told, had just died of an aortic dissection — a rupture or tear in the aorta wall that comes on suddenly and almost always results in death.

It's tough enough to bury a close friend or parent, but the grief that accompanies burying one's child is indescribable.

Questions plagued me, as if a macabre script kept playing over and over in my mind. How could such a tragedy have happened? How could God allow my son to die? As a thick shroud of helplessness and sorrow engulfed me, part of me knew God was near, but another part, the shattered part, felt as if God were a million miles away. I needed to feel God's comforting presence more than at any other time in my life, but I struggled.

Heavy storms were predicted for the day of the burial, with warnings to stay indoors. I stared out of my bedroom window, refusing to believe that, along with my grief, I'd have to bury my son on such a day. I'd been praying for clear skies and sunshine, knowing that inside my broken heart, dark skies, rain, and howling wind would only exacerbate the heaviness of this monumental loss.

I prayed for the sun to shine. But as I drove to pick up a wreath of Marc's favorite flowers for the grave, dark, threatening clouds seemed to mock me through the windshield.

We gathered at the gravesite, umbrellas at the ready, and waited for the minister to begin. The beautifully wrought copper urn that held Marc's ashes sat atop a marble pedestal beside the open grave. I clasped my husband's hand as the minister spoke words of comfort that I could barely comprehend. My mind was filled with questions. How would I be able to go on without my son? He'd no longer laugh with me over my grandchildren's antics or have those newsy telephone conversations with me. How could I bear his absence at family gatherings where he always brought laughter and joy?

As the pastor continued the service, I couldn't imagine how anything this side of Heaven could remove the enormous grief and emptiness I felt. Did God truly know how helpless I was feeling? Did He understand the immensity of my loss? Would I be able to sense His loving presence in the difficult days and weeks ahead? Did He hear my whispered pleas?

Just then, the minister, who was about to settle the urn in its resting place, paused. In that brief moment of time, something dramatically changed. The atmosphere became electrified. We all looked up from the ground to the sky. The immense, black ceiling of clouds overhead suddenly began to shift, separate, and split in two. Sunrays streamed through the breach toward the earth, filling the atmosphere with glorious light and warmth. As sunrays struck it, the copper urn that held Marc's ashes glowed in the minister's hands.

"Oh, wow. A small miracle," the minister announced to the mourners.

For the first time in days I felt a measure of peace.

Now, when I'm having a particularly difficult day, I remember that radiant, sunlit urn and what I consider to be the small miracle God performed that day, those magical moments of sunlight that lasted until the service ended. I may not have all the answers as to why tragedies happen, but I do know this: God's light can penetrate the darkest hour, even when we least expect it.

— Paula L. Silici —

55

Miracle or Coincidence?

*Believe in miracles. I have seen so many of them come
when every other indication would say that
hope was lost. Hope is never lost.*
~Jeffrey R. Holland

Years ago, my wife Linda and I owned a hardware store in Hysham, Montana. The property encompassed about three-quarters of the block. There was a large area outside where the previous owner had farm and ranch items and lumber. But when we bought it, those items had been depleted, leaving a lot of unused space.

One day, a man whom we didn't know came into the store. We later learned he worked for an oil-drilling company that had just completed drilling a dry hole north of Hysham. After looking around the store for a few minutes, this man asked me if I knew of anywhere around town he could store his travel trailer for a few weeks between jobs. I told him I didn't, but then I realized we had plenty of room in that empty lumber yard.

"On second thought, I have a lot of space out in the yard, and you could park it out there while you're gone," I said.

He smiled. "That's just what I hoped you would say."

I directed him to the gate in the yard and asked him to park it out of the way. Then, I returned to my work. He headed out and parked his trailer far away from everything I had out there.

About a half-hour later, this man returned to the store with a large box of groceries in his arms. "These will go bad before I get back. Could you use them?"

This was in March, and things were slow throughout the winter. I took the box from him and thanked him for his generosity, and he left.

When I closed the store for the day, I returned home with the box of groceries in my arms. When I showed the box to Linda, she got a strange look on her face. Tears streamed down her face as she stared at this box.

A few minutes later, she explained her tears of joy to me. Since it was a hard time of the year for our family, our budget was extremely tight. She walked me over to the cupboards and showed me they were empty. We didn't have anything left in the house to eat. This box contained meat, flour, sugar, canned vegetables, and a lot of other things.

She told me she had been praying about this situation at about the same time this man entered our store. With shouts of joy, she said, "God did it! God did it!" She had an answer to her prayer.

I can't say that this man was an angel, but I know that sometimes we entertain angels and are not aware of it. I also know that God uses ordinary people to accomplish His will and answer prayers.

I will never forget this incident as long as I live.

Was it a miracle or was it a coincidence? You decide.

— Lee E. Pollock —

56

My Miracle at Seventeen

Faith is not only daring to believe;
it is also daring to act.
~Wilfred Peterson

It was August 1976, a few days away from my seventeenth birthday. I had just had a sleepover at a friend's place. Holding a plastic bag with my overnight belongings, I walked the few blocks home to the Parkside housing project in the Bronx. I felt relieved that I had packed my halter top and shorts the day before in preparation for this latest heat wave.

I entered the elevator of my building, followed by a man I did not recognize. I noticed that he was wearing a cap pulled down so low that I could barely see his face. He appeared well-built, even under his jacket. I thought it was odd he was wearing a jacket in that heat. I pressed the button for the 14th floor and he then pressed the button for 12. And then, as the elevator rose, the man removed a knife from his jacket and held it to my belly. I saw the sharp blade resting against the bare skin below my halter top. "I am taking you to the roof to check your bag for money," my assailant said. "Don't scream or resist."

As a child who grew up witnessing domestic violence, I understood how crucial it was to stay calm in certain dangerous situations. My mother's partner back then was extremely violent, and I learned as a young child to be hyper-vigilant and controlled in his presence so as not to incite his rage. Unfortunately, my mother never learned that lesson, which meant many beatings, especially in the middle of the night. He would break down the locked apartment door and go after her with his fists. The banging would jolt me awake, and I'd jump out of bed and run to the kitchen phone to call the police, knowing that the door would soon be hanging from its hinges. The cops were a constant presence in my household, but he always managed to escape before they arrived.

I looked at that knife, and every fiber of my being went on high alert. I immediately became very, very still. From a deep place within, I knew that there was no way I would allow this man to hurt me. Watching helplessly as my mother was beaten for so many years strengthened my resolve; I would never let myself be a victim like my mother.

"Put the knife away and I will do whatever you say," I lied. I continued to repeat the words calmly as the elevator approached the twelfth floor.

The elevator doors opened across from the entrance to the staircase. The man grabbed my arm to lead me there. I knew I could not let him take me behind that door. Once inside, I would be helpless against him, and no one would hear my screams. As my mind raced with thoughts of ways to escape, I suddenly remembered that my friend Matty lived in the apartment at the end of the hallway. I looked toward Matty's apartment door, and I said to myself, "Matty, I need you NOW." It was more than a mere plea or a burning hope. My words felt more like a command. I knew that I had run out of options and that my safety depended on Matty showing up.

At that moment, I entered the space of miracles. As soon as the words were uttered in my mind, Matty walked out of his apartment into the hallway. I quickly glanced at the man's free hand but did not see the knife. I screamed, "Matty!" The man dashed across the hall, through the staircase door, and down the stairs. Matty ran to me, and I burst into tears as he held me. He ran into his apartment to get his machete and dashed down the stairs after my assailant.

I spent the next few days at the police station poring through hundreds of photos to identify my attacker. The police believed he was the same man who had raped two young women in the Gun Hill projects a few miles from where I lived. He had also cornered them with a knife in the elevator, leading them up to the roof, where they were violently assaulted.

I struggled with survivor's guilt after that. I kept imagining what those girls had experienced and wondered why they became his victims while I managed to escape. The police told me my decision to remain calm was crucial and that I was lucky Matty showed up when he did. But I knew luck could not entirely explain what happened. I felt I had experienced divine intervention — a miracle I had somehow called forth.

I found a confirmation of this many years later on another hot summer day around my thirtieth birthday while scanning the shelves at Barnes & Noble. While passing the Bible section, I suddenly wanted to pull one off the shelf. I never had any interest in religion or in reading the Bible. But at that moment, I was overwhelmed with curiosity, and I picked out a maroon-colored Bible with gold lettering on the cover. It was the King James version. I sat comfortably on the floor and flipped through the thin pages until I came across some words in Matthew 7:7- "Ask, and you shall receive, seek and you shall find, knock and the door shall be opened unto you."

I suddenly burst out loud laughing with absolute delight! I was delighted because I realized that on that day when I was threatened at seventeen, I had a deep abiding faith in a higher power that I could not name but somehow knew I could tap into. That faith fueled my conviction that I could bend the Universe to my will. Declaring "Matty, I need you NOW!" worked because I expressed it without a seed of doubt that my request would be fulfilled. I didn't know it back then, but it was my faith that saved me.

— Susanne Saltzman, MD —

57

Small Miracles

Don't believe in miracles — depend on them.
~Laurence J. Peter

One fall, during the heart of the Covid pandemic, I pulled into the crowded parking lot of my local grocery store and slid into an available slot. It was one of those breezy New England days when the leaves on the trees are bright orange and red, the autumn air crisp and alive with a hint of lingering summer. It was 2021, a year of distance, isolation and uncertainty. It was also the year I published my first book, a memoir called *The Angle of Flickering Light*.

Like all memoirists, in order to write my own story, I had included the stories of others. I had written about my father's infidelity, his and my stepmother's verbal and emotional abuse, and falling in love with a man who was addicted to heroin and making a home with him when I was in my twenties. I had detailed my own struggles with drugs and alcohol, my disordered eating, and my weekend drives to visit a close friend who was in jail for drug charges. And, like so many writers who have come before me, a part of me thought, *What have I done?* I not only worried about revealing intimate moments from my own life, but I worried even more so about what others' reactions might be to parts of their stories being included. What would my estranged father, former stepmother, or ex-boyfriend say or feel if they read the book and saw themselves within its pages?

In the months leading up to publication, when I remembered what

I had written, I experienced moments of profound fear and panic. I envisioned worst-case scenarios — being hated, sued or ostracized by someone I cared about. Ironically, the fear I experienced was similar to the fear I'd felt in my early twenties, which I'd detailed in the memoir. I wrote about how I'd become prone to anxiety and phobias, debilitated by intrusive thoughts and a sense of impending doom. I'd become frightened of going to sleep each night, of dying before waking up. These moments of dread, both back in my twenties and now in my forties, often approached me without warning — like sudden gusts of turbulent wind threatening to blow me away.

That fall day in 2021, inside the store with my grocery list in hand, I perused the aisles, weaved between carts and people, and inspected avocados and heads of cauliflower. My thoughts were far from the memoir I'd written, and even farther from the Acknowledgments page I'd included, which detailed a list of people who had been essential to my writing process. One of the people I'd mentioned was my former therapist — the woman who began working with me in my early twenties, and continued working with me for years, even as I was diagnosed with post-traumatic stress disorder, obsessive compulsive disorder, and anxiety disorder; even when I refused to go on medication for my symptoms; even when I blew off our appointments; even when I lost my health insurance and could barely afford to pay her for her time.

She worked with me until I arrived at her office one day, and she told me that it would be our last visit. She had to close her practice abruptly due to unforeseen, unavoidable circumstances. While I stood frozen in shock, she said, "After working together all this time, if there's one thing I can leave you with, it's this." She handed me a Post-it Note with the words "Use Your Voice" printed in black ink. In the Acknowledgments, I'd expressed gratitude for this note and the three crucial words that eventually morphed into an entire book.

Seventeen years later, at age forty-two, I stood in line to pay for my groceries. As the cashier scanned a natural cleaning spray I was purchasing, she asked, "Does this work well?" I told her that I didn't know yet because it was my first time buying it. She nodded and went on to tell me about how she used vinegar to clean the windows, floors, and toilets. "Everything," she said. She stopped working to talk as a line of people behind me waited while she explained that vinegar is non-toxic. She even went on to tell me about a book she owned that contained dozens of uses for vinegar.

Finally outside, I pulled my face covering down around my chin, unloaded my groceries, and steered my empty cart toward the corral. A woman motioned toward it. "Can I use your cart?"

She was masked, but I recognized the shape of her glasses and the color of her hair. I paused, wondering if this woman was who I thought she was. I almost didn't ask. But suddenly, I found myself saying, "Are you Deb?"

"Yes," she said, her expression still concealed.

"I'm Gina. I was your client a really long time ago. I wrote a book. And you're in the Acknowledgments. I've been wanting to give you a copy."

Her eyes searched mine. "Gina T," she said, remembering.

"This was totally meant to be, meant to happen." I spoke as if someone had pulled strings from above, dictating my words. "I didn't know how to find you." I jogged to the passenger door of my truck, grabbed one of my books from the seat, and handed it to her. She studied the cover as I told her how I thought I saw her a few times throughout the years, but was too shy to approach her. I told her how grateful I was for the time she spent trying to help me, for her kindness, and for charging me only ten dollars a session. I spoke as if this was the last time I'd ever see her again.

"Thank you," she said. "I love to read."

I didn't tell her I'd been thinking of her on and off for months since I had written the Acknowledgments. How I searched for her online but found nothing. How I'd even thought that one day I might ask my friend, who is a private investigator, to find her address so I could mail her a copy. And, without consciously deciding to, I began to lean toward her to embrace her. At the same time, with our eyes watering, she asked, "Can I give you a hug?"

That day, as I drove away elated, I thought about this strange collision of events: the odd experience of the cashier prolonging the one-way conversation about vinegar in the checkout line and the lone woman in the jam-packed parking lot pointing to my cart out of all the others. I knew these circumstances had been aligned, timed, and orchestrated perfectly by something far beyond my comprehension. I thought about the urgent need I'd felt to give this woman a copy of my book and the uninhibited way I'd spoken to her. Finding her was a miracle of sorts. But perhaps this miracle was not for me but to remind this woman of her own gift. She'd made a distinct, unforgettable imprint on one person's life. On so many lives.

— Gina Troisi —

58

No Vacancies

*Faith is unseen but felt, faith is strength when we feel
we have none, faith is hope when all seems lost.*
~Catherine Pulsifer

I turned off the light, crawled into bed, and glanced at the clock on my nightstand. It was almost 10:00 P.M., and I desperately needed to sleep. For the past few nights, I had felt so worried about finding an apartment to rent that I had tossed and turned until morning.

After my mother and brother died, I moved in with my older sister temporarily. But a year and a half later, it was time for me to find my own place. Unfortunately, the monthly rent for all the apartments that I had looked at was too expensive for me. Finally, after finding a place that was affordable, I learned that smoking was allowed in the building. Since I have asthma, being around secondhand smoke or possibly moving into a unit where a smoker had lived prompted me to cross that apartment off my list, too.

"God," I whispered as I lay in bed. "Please, help me!"

Before I could finish my short, desperate prayer, a bright light suddenly appeared and illuminated an entire wall of my bedroom. I immediately sat up in bed and looked around, feeling bewildered. A large beam of light was streaming through the ceiling into my room, but I couldn't figure out where it was coming from. I had never experienced anything like this before. As I continued looking at the light, it seemed to be shining directly from heaven into my bedroom.

Instead of feeling afraid, I was filled with an overwhelming sense of peace. For the first time in more than a week, I finally was able to relax and stop worrying about finding an apartment. All my stress and fear had gone away as soon as the heavenly light appeared.

Suddenly I heard a man's voice speaking to me. No one, of course, had entered my bedroom. The door was still closed, the windows were shut, and the blinds were drawn. I couldn't see anyone, yet I sensed that there was someone standing inside the beam of light that was still streaming into my bedroom.

And then I heard a compassionate voice. "Carolyn! Everything is going to be all right. You will find an apartment."

I let out a loud sigh of surprise and relief, and then I silently thanked God for this unexpected celestial reassurance. My body was so relaxed now and my eyes were so heavy with sleep that I had to force myself to keep them open. Although I felt bone-weary, I wanted to stay awake and continue to look in amazement at the beam of light that had brought me such peace. But, within minutes, I was sound asleep.

When I woke the next morning, it was already 7:00. Thanks to my angelic vision, I had slept soundly through the night. I was still so awestruck from that encounter that, when I looked at my cellphone to check my emails, I almost missed seeing a message from someone named Victoria.

"Are you interested in an upstairs apartment?" the subject line read.

The name of the building I had looked at, which allowed smoking, was The Victoria Springs Apartments, so I assumed this email was from the manager. *That's strange,* I thought, since I had already told her I couldn't move there.

As I looked closer, though, I realized that the email wasn't from The Victoria after all. A few days earlier, I had phoned the manager of another apartment building. The woman, Victoria, told me that there were no available units, and there was a long waiting list for the building. Undeterred, I had given her my contact information anyway.

"Yes, yes, yes!" I immediately typed back to Victoria. "I'm very interested in an upstairs apartment."

Two weeks later, I sat across from Victoria in the manager's office and signed my lease. I could barely believe that not only had I found a place to live, but it seemed perfect.

"Do you have any questions?" Victoria asked as I handed her the signed lease.

"Yes," I replied. "When I phoned a couple of weeks ago, you told me that there wouldn't be any vacancies for a long time and that many people were on the waiting list."

"I remember that," Victoria responded, nodding.

"So, how did I end up with this apartment?" I asked.

My new manager paused a moment and leaned back in her chair. "It was the most unusual thing," she began to explain. "First, one of our residents had to move suddenly and break his lease. Then, none of the people on the waiting list responded to my e-mails about the vacancy."

Victoria looked at me and smiled. "There's only one word that I can use to describe how you ended up with this apartment," she added. "It was a miracle."

— Carolyn Bolz —

My Truly Spectacular Christmas

Don't give up before the miracle happens.
~Fannie Flagg

I grew up a stone's throw from New York City. Over the years, my family explored many of the notable landmarks, including the Statue of Liberty, the top of the Empire State Building, Times Square, and the Christmas windows at Macy's.

The one thing we never attended was the Christmas Spectacular at Radio City. My father worked as a baker, so purchasing tickets for six of us was deemed an extravagant expense. I was always intrigued by the long line of Rockettes that would dance across our television screen, and I vowed that one day I would see the iconic show in person.

Thus it was with great excitement that I finally found myself at the age of thirty-eight heading into the Big Apple to score tickets to the show. My husband Jay was at the helm of our Jeep. His sister, her boyfriend John, and our eight-year-old son were nestled in the back seat. The traffic was minimal because we had strategically planned our visit for a Sunday morning.

Our plan was to park the car and head directly to the box office. But the city was bustling, and it took us fifteen minutes to find a spot. We weren't in a hurry though, so we enjoyed the walk to the theater. By the time we got to Radio City there were long lines and people everywhere.

I went to wait in one of those long lines. I saw people walking away disappointed in front of me, but I told myself that it was probably too expensive or the show was at the wrong time to fit in their itinerary.

It'd been a bad year for me. My grandma and great-aunt had passed away. The deaths of these matriarchs had left me doubting my faith, particularly in regard to my aunt. She was the most devout person I knew. She attended church every Sunday, belonged to the rosary club, and prayed for all of us. She had become so debilitated from cancer that she was barely recognizable at the end.

Finally, I reached the cashier. "Good morning," I greeted her cheerfully. "I'd like to buy five tickets for the next show."

"I don't even need to look. The last seven people asked me the same thing. We are sold out," she responded.

"Okay, so how about tonight's show?" I said.

She looked at me like I was the village idiot. "Um, girl, we are sold out for this day, this week, and this month. I might be able to get you in the middle of January."

I was shocked. It was worse than I could have imagined. "Are you serious?"

"Totally. I'm sorry."

"Not your fault. Thanks anyway," I said as I turned away disappointedly.

John came back and reported that even the scalpers didn't have tickets. He and Jay went off to find my sister and my son, and I stood alone in the magnificent building coming to terms with our defeat.

A man approached me. "Are you looking for tickets?" he inquired while extending a slip of paper to me. "Here, take this. We can no longer use it."

"Yes!" I answered enthusiastically. Then, I added, "But I need it for five people. And how much are they?" I reluctantly reached for the paper while also watching to make sure I was not the victim of a scam.

"This will work. No charge. It's meant for you," he assured me. There was an aura about the stranger that I could not explain. A radiance of warmth exuded from him. His eyes glistened. As soon as I grasped the paper, he disappeared into the crowd.

"Wait!" I whispered. I looked down at the paper. It said SRO for the show at any time. I was perplexed. My crew returned. I relayed what had occurred.

"What?" Jay exclaimed. "Some guy just came up and gave you this? Why didn't he use it?"

"I have no idea," I answered truthfully.

"It can't be real. That's worth hundreds of dollars." Sheri was skeptical.

"But what would he gain? He didn't ask for money," I said, perplexed.

"Well, let's try," John encouraged.

"Eh, okay, but don't get too excited. I doubt we will get in," my sister-in-law advised.

We saw the show that day. We all got in for free, and we didn't have to stand. They brought chairs for us right beside the stage.

I sat there in awe. I couldn't quite process what had occurred. But that year, 1998, the play had a particular slant. The story was based on the true biblical interpretation of Christmas. In the last scene, when the nativity was presented on stage, the hair on my arms rose.

I felt as if I had received a message to continue believing in the magic and miracles of Christmas. I was reminded of a verse my aunt would often quote: "We walk by faith and not by sight."

I'd received an emotional manna that day. It was truly a godsend. I was restored that Christmas, and it truly was spectacular.

— Patricia Senkiw-Rudowsky —

The Miracle Ride

Every day holds the possibility of a miracle.
~Author Unknown

I was determined to be one of the first cars at our city's recycling center. The center opened at 8:00 A.M. and allowed city residents to bring leaves and yard waste there to be recycled into mulch. I quickly loaded several leaf bags in my car, grabbed my billfold, and drove the short distance to the recycling center to wait in line until the center opened.

Being the fourth car in line, I accomplished my task and drove back home. Upon arriving, I exited my car and laid my billfold and car keys on the rear bumper of my husband's pickup truck parked in the garage next to my car. I cleaned out the back of my car where some leaves had escaped the bag and put away the used leaf bags. Then, without a glance, I walked right by my aquamarine billfold and car keys sitting on the rear truck bumper and entered the house.

My husband Richard was heading out the door as I came in. He said he needed to fill his truck with gas and stop at Target. That sounded fine with me.

About ten minutes later, while sitting at my desk, I reached into my purse for a pen, and suddenly it felt like a lightning bolt went through my hand. I'd left my billfold and car keys on the rear bumper of Richard's truck! Immediately I thought to myself, *Maybe if I use the spare set of car keys and drive the route he might have taken,*

I will see my billfold on the street or along the road. Maybe it bounced off the bumper just down the street from our house.

I grabbed the spare car keys and slowly drove down our street, scanning the roadway and neighboring lawns. I saw nothing. I decided to keep going and drive to Target. The store is located off a busy, four-lane state highway with a large, grass median strip between the roads. That section of road has a 45-mile-per-hour speed limit, though most people drive 50–55 miles per hour. It seemed impossible that anything would remain on a rear bumper given the speed limit and roughness of the road. I looked for Richard's truck in the parking lot but did not see it. Many cars filled the lot because it was Christmas shopping season. I started feeling physically ill as my angst grew.

I returned home, totally defeated. During my frantic drive to Target, I had tried calling Rick several times, but he didn't pick up. Feeling stupid and embarrassed, I almost felt relieved that he didn't.

After all these fruitless attempts to help myself, I finally turned to God, which is where I should have started. I said a simple prayer asking God to somehow protect my billfold and keys. Admittedly, my faith was weak, but praying did lower my stress level. I decided to do something useful and started listing the credit cards and corresponding telephone numbers necessary to report the credit cards as lost. A total of seven card companies and five banks would need to be called. It seemed like a daunting task.

I tried one more time to call Richard, and he answered. I told him what I had done. He didn't know what to say. He could clearly hear in my voice how upset I felt. He was in the check-out line and said he would call as soon as he got to the truck in the parking lot to tell me what he discovered.

The call came a few minutes later. My hands were shaking as I answered. Amazingly, both items were still sitting on the rear bumper of his truck! We could not believe it. He had traveled at least 45 miles per hour on a busy bumpy four-lane road. Even while parked at Target, no one had taken the billfold. Whenever I think God doesn't answer prayers or care about the details of my life, I remember the miracle ride of my aquamarine billfold and car keys.

—Jane Williams—

61

Star Sapphire

Perhaps, they are not stars in the sky
but rather openings where our loved ones
shine down to let us know we are loved.
~Based on an Inuit Proverb

One afternoon in August, five years after Mom passed away, I was unpacking my groceries on my kitchen counter. When I lifted my left hand out of a grocery bag, I suddenly couldn't swallow. Looking at the ring on my finger, I saw four silver sprockets eerily sticking up from an empty setting like winter tree branches. The star sapphire was gone.

Mom had given me the ring on my twenty-first birthday with a card that read: "May the Angels and God watch over you always, as I know they will." I had worn it every day for twenty-nine years. It was a connection to Mom, a symbol of our love, and a touchstone of healing and hope.

"No! No! No!" I yelled, grabbing my phone and car keys and running out the door. On the way, I called my best friend, Marie. "I need you to meet me at ALDI. The star sapphire in my mom's ring fell out. I need help looking."

"I'm on my way."

"Please, don't panic. Bring positive energy only."

Keeping faith and hope in seemingly impossible situations was a gift I'd been given by Mom. As a young child, I had witnessed her courage and strength when my two brothers passed away less than two years apart. And, seven years later, I had sat on her lap when the police officer told her that my dad, her husband of thirty-five years, was tragically killed in a plane crash.

For forty-five years, Mom and I shared an unshakable and loving bond forged by life's wondrous joys and sorrows. We sat for hours on each other's beds, at our backyard picnic table, and at Burger King, washing down Whopper Jr. burgers and fries with vanilla shakes. We talked about my brothers and dad, how my parents fell in love, God, faith, fear, sadness, and, most of all, that we are never alone, no matter how lonely we feel.

One night, while sitting on the picnic bench underneath the summer sky, Mom told me to look up. "When I see stars, I feel at peace. I know everyone I love is okay and right here with me," she said, her Southern voice soothing me again. "When your dad was away on extended flights, no matter where he was in the world, we'd talk on the phone, walk outside and see if we could find the same stars. Whenever I see stars, I feel like he's right here."

I glanced down at my star-sapphire ring and smiled.

When Mom passed away, I felt devastated and lost. She had been my best friend, confidante, and travel companion. She knew me better than anyone and taught me how to grieve and live, cry and laugh, hurt and get up, and be heartbroken and love again. For five years, I had grasped for something to rekindle my zest for life and fill the hole in my heart. The star-sapphire ring, her tattered and worn Living Bible, a lifetime of beautiful memories, and photos of us laughing together were priceless anchors in times of extreme grief. Prayer, faith, therapy, nature, yoga, meditation, writing, sports, and the love of friends and family helped me along my journey, but I couldn't shake the feeling that I was not only lonely but alone.

Back at the grocery store, I pulled into the same parking spot and looked everywhere for my star sapphire. My bare hands and knees felt the hot pavement as I searched frantically around and under my SUV.

Marie pulled up a few minutes later and immediately started looking, too. I was grateful for her help. She was the friend who always found my keys or sunglasses when they went missing.

I rushed inside the store searching for a familiar face. I spotted Amanda, whom I had met on previous shopping trips, and urgently tapped her shoulder. "I was just here twenty minutes ago and lost the stone to this ring. It's very special to me. Can you help me?"

Her eyes softened and then focused. She understood. She grabbed a large mop and strategically started sweeping it back and forth down the first aisle.

I called after her, "It's light blue and small." My voice sounded so small, and I realized how enormous this store was. Grocery aisles I'd shopped earlier turned into cavernous hallways. Boxes where I'd picked bananas became deep, dark traps. And the line of freezers chilled more than the food inside.

The stone was so small. What if it had bounced and landed under a pallet? How would I find it? Was it even in the store? It could have been anywhere.

I snapped out of my paralysis and sprung into action, searching the floors, looking under shelves, and flailing my hands in produce boxes. Nothing.

God, I can't lose this. Please help me. It means so much to me. It's part of Mom and me.

I rushed outside to see how Marie was doing in the parking lot.

"Did you find it?" Marie asked hopefully.

I shook my head.

"Di, I've looked everywhere: in the car, under it, around the parking lot. Multiple times. I can't find it. It has to be inside."

My next words came from somewhere other than my rational brain. "I'm gonna find it. I have a feeling I know where it is," I said, getting down on my hands and knees. I rested my right cheek and ear on the pavement and stared under the belly of my SUV, scanning from tire to tire, searching for any irregularity in the pavement.

Then, I spotted a small bump resembling a pebble on the pavement silhouetted against the setting sun. Lightness came over me. I stretched my arm and plucked up the stone. I rubbed my thumb over its smoothness. I stood up and cupped the sapphire in the palm of my hand like a fragile robin's egg, shifting it around until the light hit it just right. Its luminous, white star shone.

"Oh, thank God," I said.

Marie came closer to look at my hand. "No way."

I hugged Marie and dashed into the store to tell Amanda the amazing news. Back in my car, I removed the empty ring setting from my finger and placed it in my wallet's coin section. But I kept the star sapphire tightly clenched in my left hand.

Thank you, God. Thank you, Mom.

I started the car. The ten-minute drive was surreal. I don't remember any sounds, the route, the passing buildings or the landscape. I don't remember driving. All I recall is a deep feeling of peace and knowing that I'd witnessed a miracle, a sign from heaven, and a love nod from my dear mom.

I was not alone.

— Dianne E. Beard —

62

Gifts from Grandma

*I would maintain that thanks are the highest form
of thought; and that gratitude is
happiness doubled by wonder.*
~G.K. Chesterton

It was December, and instead of enjoying the Advent season and preparing for Christmas, I was praying for my grandmother, who was losing her battle with cancer. For months, my siblings and I took turns caring for her until she had to be admitted to hospice care. For me, it meant a costly 180-mile roundtrip every day.

Grandma passed on December 21, 1989. It was common practice in our Polish neighborhood to have a three-day wake with the funeral on the fourth day. To alter this tradition was considered disrespectful, but the family made the difficult decision to hold the funeral on December 23rd as the fourth day would have fallen on Christmas. Postponing Grandma's funeral would have been more difficult for everyone, especially for those of us from out of town. We all prayed that we had her blessing and she would have understood.

I was inconsolable. The loss of my beloved grandmother was particularly hard for me since I had lost my mother when I was only nineteen years old. To make things worse, we'd recently discovered that my husband was in danger of losing his job. Money was tight even with him working, and if he was without work, I wondered how we'd survive.

As I huddled at my grandmother's gravesite with my husband and two young daughters on that frigid December day, I prayed for the repose of her soul. I also prayed that my beloved grandmother would watch over us and pray for us.

The next day was Christmas Eve, and for my young children's sake, we left Buffalo to return to our home in Rochester. I had to put on a happy face for our two daughters.

Arriving home, we unloaded the car and rushed to prepare for Christmas. My husband went to the basement to retrieve Christmas decorations, only to find the floors flooded. The hot-water tank had ruptured and spilled water everywhere.

Fortunately, my husband knew how to install one, but purchasing a tank on Christmas Eve was another matter. The Buffalo trips had drained the savings earmarked to cover the mortgage, and I had no idea where the money would come from to pay these mounting bills. We'd have to go a few days without hot water until we could figure out how to get the money.

I felt overwhelmed. All I could do was pray and talk to my grandmother. "Grandma, I miss you. Please pray to God for us. We need a little help right now."

When Christmas morning arrived, I knew that going to church would bring everyone some comfort. So, I bundled up the girls and got ready myself. My husband grabbed a pair of boots that he hadn't worn in months. As he tried to pull on his left boot, something blocked his foot from slipping inside. He sat down and turned over the boot. To our surprise, a wad of money tied by ribbon only used by Grandma fell out. We untied our unexpected find and counted twenty-five crisp twenty-dollar bills! $500. It was the exact amount we needed to purchase a new hot-water tank.

We looked at each other in astonishment. My husband asked, "Did you put this in here?"

I shook my head as I swiped at the tears on my cheeks. "It's Grandma! I asked her to pray for us and to send us help. There's no other explanation."

Just then, the phone rang. My husband answered and heard his boss say, "Sorry to bother you on the holiday, but I wanted to let you know your job is safe. Merry Christmas!"

—Terry Hans—

Chapter 7

Guardian Angels

63

Need a Hand with That?

I think that someone is watching out for me. God,
my guardian angel, I'm not sure who that is,
but they really work hard.
~Mattie Stepanek

In 2009, I had recently started working with my boyfriend Chris at a warehouse in Oklahoma City. He purchased large lots of government surplus from the local FAA and resold them on eBay. The majority of items were desktop computers, but sometimes we got other stuff, everything from a lifetime supply of chalk to a centrifuge to vintage servers that used giant floppy disks.

One day, we had a large cabinet with a stack of computerized components. We had not been able to identify exactly what it was or what it did, but somebody bought it and seemed happy to get it.

It stood nearly four feet tall and was about two feet square. And it was heavy, weighing at least four hundred pounds! It had the oddest wheels. I could not imagine their intended purpose. Two of them faced one direction, and the other two faced another direction. They only swiveled a little, so when we tried to push it in a straight line, it zigzagged.

The buyer sent a truck to pick it up. Chris had specified that the truck must have a Tommy lift because our forklift had died. But when the driver was lowering the lift, I couldn't help but notice how it jerked and tilted.

We zigzagged the monster out of the warehouse and across the parking lot. We wrestled it onto the lift. The driver went to push the lever while Chris steadied the machine. I watched from the other side.

When the lift was about two feet off the ground, it jerked and tilted again. The machine started to move! Chris tried to hold on, but it tore out of his grasp and continued to roll—and it was headed straight for me!

As the machine reached the other side of the lift, I instinctively stepped forward to catch it so it wouldn't break—as if a 140-pound woman could stop a 400-pound behemoth with gravity on its side!

One of the wheels slid off the lift, and the machine pitched forward, smashing into my face. My sunglasses went flying, and I had just enough time to realize that my last thought was going to be, *Well, that was pretty dumb!*

And then it stopped. That giant machine froze in mid-air, resting against my face and body with no weight or pressure at all. There was total silence, and I felt a gentle yet powerful presence on either side of me. And then I could see them!

The moment seemed to stretch for several minutes before it was abruptly broken as Chris and the driver arrived to grab the machine and push it back onto the lift.

As they resumed the process of getting the monster into the truck, I picked up my shattered sunglasses and wandered into the warehouse. I was in a daze, filled with wonder, and lucky to be alive. I went to the bathroom and looked in the mirror. I had a cut above one eye, but I seemed otherwise unscathed.

When the truck was on its way with its cargo, Chris came in to check on me. He said, "That was crazy! When that thing started to roll and I couldn't stop it, I thought I was going to lose you. There was no way I could get there in time! Then, it was like everything was in slow motion, and the machine was just hanging there. How did you stop it?"

I told him, "I didn't. It wasn't me at all. Two angels saved me."

He wasn't surprised. Chris had several angel stories of his own. This was my first, though, and I was still very surprised. He gently asked me, "What did they look like?"

I described what I had seen: two young men with muscular arms and curly, light hair, with a golden aura around them. They had tan skin and light brown eyes, and they were wearing dark vests and lighter colored pants that I would best describe as breeches. They looked like twins, or at least brothers. They had stood on either side of me, smiling, holding the machine back until Chris and the driver could get there.

Chris sneered, "That's not what angels look like." I was taken aback for a moment, shocked at his reaction. Granted, he could be a jerk at times, but this seemed like an odd hill to want to die on. Finally, I just smiled and shook my head, saying serenely, "Maybe that isn't what your angels looked like. Maybe that is what I needed my angels to look like. Maybe they appear the way we think they should. I don't know! I only know they were there, and the only reason we are having this conversation is because they were."

He stalked off, apparently more offended by my choice of angels than grateful that I was alive. We never talked about it again, not even when I was picking bone fragments out of the cut above my eye.

Chris has been gone from my life for many years, but the scar from that cut remains, a small, tangible souvenir of an unforgettable experience.

I've always wondered if those two young men are my assigned guardian angels (it figures I would need two!) or if they just happened to be passing by that day. Even more, I have always wondered why they chose to show themselves.

Someone once asked me, "Have you ever been touched by an angel?"

I softly replied, "I've been touched by two."

I've never seen them again and I've never had a similar experience. However, there have been several additional times when I should have been seriously injured but wasn't, so I know someone is looking out for me.

— Linda Sabourin —

64

Three Angels and a Road Trip

A dream which is not interpreted
is like a letter which is not read.
~The Talmud

"Honey, your grandma has passed away." My mom's voice sounded strained and hoarse through the phone. I knew she had been crying.

"What?" I asked. I didn't really believe her. My wise and wonderful grandmother had seemed so healthy the last time I was home. She was still living by herself in the little house where she had raised fifteen kids. I could close my eyes and see it surrounded by gardens, flowers, and dogs.

She couldn't be gone.

"It was sudden," Mom explained. "She was getting ready to come over to our place for a fish fry, and she just fell to the floor and was gone." My aunt and uncle had been visiting from Florida, so she was not alone.

The visitation and funeral were planned for a couple of days from then.

I couldn't seem to focus on what she was saying. Grandma was gone. It seemed so unreal.

"Honey, I need you to come home," Mom said.

Usually, my mom accepted that I lived halfway across the country with two of her grandchildren. My Army husband was stationed in North Carolina, while I had grown up in the middle of Missouri. I visited home several times a year, called Mom a lot, and sent endless letters. And Mom and Dad came out to visit me once a year and took a little vacation from their responsibilities on the farm. We all understood this was just how things were.

"I need you here," she repeated, her voice cracking and close to tears.

Mom never asked me for anything — until now. She had just lost her mother. The least I could do was go home.

My husband, Jason, walked into the room. With one look at my face, he pulled me into a bone-crushing hug.

I explained everything the best I could through a lot of tears.

"I have to get home," I said.

"I can't go with you," Jason said, shaking his head. "There is no way that the Army is going to let me take time off right now." Jason was in the middle of training to become a Green Beret.

I made my way slowly back to the kitchen to finish up dinner. Six-year-old Nicholas ran to me immediately when he saw my face. He gave me a big hug and asked what was wrong. I pushed off answering the questions and sent him to wash up for supper. I lifted ten-month-old Gabriel into his highchair.

The next morning, I was on the phone with several travel agents and airlines. Ticket prices to fly home were impossibly high and did not fit into our budget. Besides, the airport was two hours from my mom and dad's farm. Someone would have to pick me up, or I would have to rent a car, another expense that I couldn't afford.

By the time Jason got home, I had exhausted all the transportation sources I could think of to get home. Jason had more bad news. He had confirmed that he would not be able to take time off from work. If I wanted to get home, I would have to drive the 1,000 miles by myself with the two boys. The thought was overwhelming and terrifying. This was long before the days of cellphones and GPS. I couldn't stop thinking about all the things that could go wrong.

Then, Jason dropped another bombshell. He would not have time to watch our Golden Retriever, Daisy, while we were gone.

I was going to have a six-year-old, a ten-month-old, and a rescue dog to deal with on an eighteen-hour road trip. I stayed up all night. I was terrified by the whole idea of the long road trip by myself. I did not think I could do it, no matter how much Mom needed me or how much I wanted to be home.

About 3:00 A.M., I fell asleep on the couch. I had the most wonderful dream — or maybe it was a vision or a message. I could see my now deceased grandma as clear as day. She was with Grandpa, who had died when I was in grade school, and my Aunt Therese, who had died of leukemia. I could see them so clearly. They didn't say anything. They were just smiling, happy and peaceful. The image seemed to last the whole night.

The next morning, I woke up a different person. I felt eerily calm and had a clear plan on how to get through this road trip. I made a quick inventory of things I would need for the trip, and the boys and I ran to the store to purchase snacks and a road atlas. Back home, I packed coolers, bottles, snacks, and clothes. While the boys played, I sat at the kitchen table with the map and marked all the pages for the states we would need to drive through. Then, I wrote the directions back home with colorful markers on index cards. By the evening I was ready to go.

There was no explanation as to why I suddenly had so much confidence in my ability to make the trip home by myself. I just knew everything would be okay.

It took eighteen hours and a lot of caffeine, but we made it back to Missouri safe and in time for Grandma's visitation. It meant everything to Mom that we were there. After the funeral, the boys, Daisy and I stayed a couple of weeks to help at the farm.

One afternoon, as Mom and I were folding laundry, she said how glad she was that we made the long drive safely.

"I just knew that it would be okay," I said. "Grandma was watching over me. Grandpa and Aunt Therese, too."

I explained what I had seen in my dream, a little embarrassed that Mom might think it was silly. Mom grabbed me in a tight hug. A devout Catholic, she explained that it must have been the Holy Spirit watching over me.

The night before I was ready to head back to North Carolina, I had the exact same dream. The next morning, I had the same calm, confident feeling and the sense that someone was watching over us on our drive back home. I made it back to North Carolina safely and never had the dream again. Over the years, Mom maintained her belief that it was a vision from the Holy Spirit.

Other people I've told the story to have tried to give me a more practical explanation — that I needed something to help me get through the drive so my subconscious made up the vision to help myself.

But I know that three angels came to me in my dream, and they watched over me on that road trip.

— Theresa Brandt —

A Heavenly Hand

The guardian angels of life fly so high as to be beyond
our sight, but they are always looking down upon us.
~Jean Paul Richter

Peter entered our world weighing a whopping eleven pounds, eleven ounces. The name Peter means "rock," and after our first two delicate, little girls, this robust boy seemed to fit that description perfectly.

We prayed over this new addition to our family, asking God to give him a strong guardian angel — one who would follow him through his life to keep him safe, especially when that job was out of our control. But, at that time, we had no idea how important the answer would turn out to be.

Pete seemed fearless, with a love for the rugged outdoors, hiking, biking, climbing, wielding tools to build his forts, and, of course, any kind of athletic endeavor. Seldom would a day go by that didn't require a bandage or a sling, but it didn't stop his love of adventure... and the occurrence of incidents. But there was one specific day when we most appreciated the significance of that early prayer.

I was busy with baby number six when Pete came to ask if he could take a bus across the great city of Montreal to spend a day or two with his friend Bill. He was only twelve years old, but it was summer holidays, and he was restless, ready to explore and venture out on his own. I called Bill's mom to make sure she was okay with it. She assured me all was good, so off he went.

After spending their allowances on junk food at the closest convenience store, the two boys stopped to stare in the window of the neighbourhood arcade. The boys had been told that under no circumstances could they ever go in there. They were just too young, and often the crowd collecting there could be rough, so it was not a safe place for them. Still, they were tempted. But after watching and wondering if they should break the rules, they decided to return later.

The day was passing quickly, and the sun was low in the sky as they strolled by the local high school. Walking around the deserted building, they threw stones and peeked through the windows into the vacated classrooms. They were about to leave when the farthest corner of the school caught their eyes where a grouping of pipes leaned against the wall. The pipes wound their way from the ground all the way up to the roof of the building.

"Hey, look. I think we could climb up those." Pete was already excited.

"Think there would be tennis balls up there?" Bill asked.

"Probably," Pete answered.

Their eyes met as both shouted, "Let's do it!"

Pete went first, scampering up the pipes like a master climber, and Bill was not far behind. As the pipes ended, the two boys clawed their way onto the roof.

"You can see the world from here!" Bill shouted.

Pete looked around in awe. "I can see your house, man! And there is the arcade! Wow, this is awesome." They ran around picking up balls and stuffing them into their pockets.

Pete stood up, slowly turning in circles, but suddenly stopped. "Hey, what's that?"

At the far end of the roof was a series of five domed skylights. The two boys strolled over to have a look. As they leaned over one of the windows, they could see a basketball court on the gymnasium floor three stories down. It was dark in the room, but the remaining streams of daylight filtering through the glass enticed them to look closer. They got on their knees.

"That's so cool. It would be fun if we could get in there, but it's so far down." Pete stared longingly at the bin of basketballs.

Bill stretched his back as he stood up. "I wonder if this will hold me up." He gave a little kick and then placed one foot on the skylight, slowly transferring his full weight with both feet planted.

Suddenly, the terrifying sound of shattering glass filled the air. The dried-out, forty-year-old window gave way, and Bill fell through the hole.

Later, as my son relived this story, he did not remember exactly what or how it all happened. But somehow he managed to reach out as Bill was falling and grab hold of his friend's one visible hand. Pete grasped it tightly and, with his other hand, grabbed the edge of the broken window to stabilize himself. And for a few seconds, the two young boys remained suspended in time.

Peter's twelve-year old body had been preparing for this day for years, but it was not enough. He could feel Bill's hand slowly slipping through his.

"Help me!" came Bill's anguished cry.

"I'm not going to let you die, man," Pete groaned, struggling to hold on. "I'm not going to let you die!"

Bill's body hung in the hole. His sweating hand was difficult to grasp. Terror held them, and death loomed as Pete felt himself being pulled into the gaping hole that was swallowing his friend.

At the point of hopelessness, something incredible happened. Pete started to pull his friend's dangling body up through the space. Between the jagged shards came Bill's head, shoulders, waist and then legs. He was soon lying flat on the roof of the school... right beside Pete's exhausted body. "I told you I wouldn't let you die," Pete gasped.

"Thanks, man. I thought I was dead already. How did you do that?"

"I don't know. Do you have any cuts from the glass?"

"Yeah. The broken glass cut my leg." Blood oozed from an open gash.

"We are in so much trouble," Pete moaned. "Let's get out of here."

Bill rolled over. "I have to look once more at where I almost died."

The boys slowly crept to the open space and looked in. Thirty feet down, shards of glass lay scattered across the floor. Pete punched

Bill in the arm. "Why did you do that? We both almost died, man."

"I know. Sorry." Those three simple words were all that was needed.

They made their way back to the pipes and, with trembling muscles, slithered back to the ground.

Years later, blinking back tears, Pete recounted, "I still don't know what happened that day. Bill's hand was slipping, and I was sure we were both going to fall. Yet, I pulled him up!"

I knew there could be only one answer.

This was not the only time that guardian angel showed up to rescue my son. In fact, there have been many times when nothing other than miraculous intervention could explain Pete's escapes from disaster.

So, each night before I close my eyes, I thank God for the answer to that prayer so long ago and hug my boy every chance I get.

— Heather Rodin —

Angel in the Storm

Angels represent God's personal care
for each one of us.
~Andrew Greeley

As an eighteen-year-old, I was fortunate to have a full-time job as a stenographer, which helped me afford night-school classes at the University of Missouri–St. Louis. But sometimes I felt overworked and unappreciated.

After one particularly busy day at work and an extra-long commute, I arrived home in St. Ann, exhausted.

Mom had fixed one of my favorite suppers, but I pushed the food around on my plate. Since a spat with my boyfriend the week before, I'd lost my appetite. We'd dated for six months and were on the verge of calling it quits.

After supper, I helped Mom wash dishes and clean the kitchen. I needed to study for an upcoming quiz on conjugating French verbs but couldn't concentrate. All I wanted to do was sleep.

Worn out physically and emotionally, I announced to my parents, "I'm going to bed."

On my way through the living room, a TV weather forecaster warned of approaching thunderstorms and a possible tornado later that night. A tornado in January? That would never happen.

In my room, I turned off the lights and crawled under the quilt. The sound of rain pattering on the window next to my bed lulled me into a sweet slumber. I was dreaming about taking a train ride to Paris on a breezy day.

Then, the clickety-clack of the train rolling down the tracks grew louder until it became a deep rumble, which finally switched into a terrifying shriek that shook the entire house. I opened my eyes and trembled in fear, unable to move.

No lights were on, yet the room glowed. A beautiful lady with long, silver hair in a flowing, white gown stood next to me. She looked similar to what I had imagined my own guardian angel looked like. Still a bit groggy, I thought I was dreaming.

The angel touched my shoulder and urged, "Get up and run."

With a sudden burst of energy, I tossed off my cover and bounded for the door, just as the bedroom window shattered into a thousand shards of glass and tore into my bed.

My mom, out of breath and her eyes wide with fear, met me in the hallway. "The sirens just went off. It's a tornado!"

With no basement, we joined Dad, my two brothers, and little sister in the bathroom — the safest place to ride out a twister. There we huddled, all the while praying until the chilling sounds of wind and hail pounding against our house died down.

After the all-clear signal, I told my parents about the broken window. Even before Dad checked for damage, he hugged me. "Are you okay, sweetie?"

Fighting back tears, I admitted, "Just a little scared."

As soon as Mom entered my room, she wept and said, "It's a miracle you weren't killed, honey."

I wasn't sure they'd believe me, so I didn't mention the lady in white. I had a hard time understanding what had happened myself, although in my heart I knew she was real.

In the morning, we learned that the January 24, 1967, F4 tornado was one of the worst in Missouri's history. Several homes in our neighborhood lost roofs, and a few were lifted from their foundations. Others miraculously remained untouched. Tragically, two girls who lived just a few miles away lost their lives.

Thankfully, the only damage to our home was the bedroom window that shattered and collapsed moments after I ran.

I shivered at the sight of the pieces of glass scattered across my bed and floor, and I lifted a quick prayer of thanks. My guardian angel had appeared just in time to save me from being hurt — or worse — when she warned me, "Get up and run."

That winter day, the beautiful lady, bathed in shimmering, white light, did more than rescue me during the storm. She proved to me that angels really do exist.

— Donna Duly Volkenannt —

The Unseen Bodyguard

Prayer is man's greatest power.
~W. Clement Stone

t was already dark, and I should have been heading home after running errands in town. "Just one last stop," I told myself.

I wanted to clean the car, even though my husband had cautioned against going to the car wash in the bad part of town. We had barely been married a year, and I suppose I hadn't yet learned to value his advice. I drove into the secluded lot, intent on fulfilling my mission. Pulling up to the meter, I got out of my car to pay for my selection. That's when I noticed him. Stepping out from the bushes not ten yards from me, he approached unhesitatingly. Immediately, my blood ran cold. There was something about him, a look in his eyes, that told me I was in trouble.

I retreated back to my car. He was already calling out to me, just a few steps away. I managed to get myself in the car, but my window was down, and he was at the door. I had nothing to defend myself with. No one was around to assist me. He was asking me something. I started to pray quietly but fervently to myself. All the while, I hoped to placate him with my words.

Suddenly, his eyes shifted to the passenger seat of my car, and his sickly smile faded. He looked confused and a little scared. He took a step back, bid me goodnight, and retreated back through the hedge. Shaking, I rolled up the window, locked myself in, and got out of there as fast as I could. It was only on the drive home that I realized what must have happened. He saw Something or Someone in that empty seat. Something he didn't want to tangle with.

I imagine there are many times when we are saved from perils we know not of as we go through life. But, that night, I knew.

—KC Polon—

68

Slapped by an Angel

*You don't find love; it finds you. It's got a little bit to do
with destiny, fate and what's written in the stars.*
~Anaïs Nin

The slap came while I was talking to some friends. My husband Chris and I weren't dating at the time, but we had gone to this particular party together. Chris had asked me out several months prior, but I was hyper-focused on my next adventure: going into the Peace Corps. I had already received my assignment, and I would be leaving for a two-year stint in Africa in a few months.

I could have dated before leaving, but I knew that I would have to either try to end it when I left or attempt a long-distance relationship. Neither of these options appealed to me, so I decided to enjoy the single life for a few months.

The party was like many college parties. It was held in an apartment, so there were only about thirty guests. It was warm outside, so several of us congregated on the back deck. We were standing in a small circle, and Chris was beside me. One of our friends in this group looked at Chris and me having so much fun together and asked if we were dating. I remember hearing Chris respond, "No," but I lost a bit of time after that.

An all-encompassing feeling came over me, and I became paralyzed while watching a premonition play out as if on a movie screen. Chris was wearing a black tux, and I was wearing a white dress. We were walking hand in hand, and we had just gotten married.

The visual was short enough that I didn't think anyone had noticed that I had zoned out, but I couldn't recover. I felt weak and sick to my stomach. I felt as if my guardian angel had just slapped me and said, "This is THE ONE."

I couldn't stay at the party any longer. This new feeling I had was too overwhelming, and I asked Chris to take me home. I needed some time to process what I had seen and felt. Chris and I weren't even dating, and I had just envisioned us walking down the aisle!

It was the next day before I could vocalize my feelings to Chris. Of course, I couldn't tell him that I saw marriage in our future. That's how you get rid of a guy, not how you start dating one. Instead, I explained that even though we might only have a few months, I thought we should give dating a try.

It didn't take long before Chris and I were dating exclusively, and I withdrew my Peace Corps application. The Peace Corps would have been a unique opportunity, but I couldn't ignore the divine intervention I had just experienced.

Twenty-seven years have passed now, and Chris and I are happily married with two grown children. I am so thankful that I had an angel taking control of my best interests at that time of my life because I was clueless. Had it not been for that jolt from an unseen force, I would have some great stories to tell about Africa, but I would not have married the man of my dreams.

— Tammy Brown —

69

An Angel in the Classroom

There are no miracles for those that have no faith in them.
~French Proverb

I was lecturing in my classroom when one of the students inadvertently stretched out his leg as he sat, tripping me as I walked backward while talking. There was nothing to stop me from falling and landing on the rock-hard floor.

But, in mid-fall, two hands suddenly connected with my back, pushing me up and forward until I regained my balance. I turned around to stunned faces. The first thought I had was that the boy who had accidentally tripped me had somehow reacted fast enough to catch me, preventing my fall. But their faces said differently.

"Ms. B., are you okay?" they blurted out. Everyone was talking at once.

I looked at the boy in my class. "Did you stop me from falling?" All he could do was shake his head. "Did all of you see what happened?" They all nodded.

Finally, someone said, "Ms. B., you fell, but before you could get hurt, something caught you in midair and pushed you back up on your feet. We all saw that."

I processed their eyewitness account, realizing it was exactly what they had described because I had felt the hands upon my back.

"What was that?" another student asked.

"I don't know what I think about that right now, but it's all okay, so let's get ready for dismissal."

After my students left, I tried to figure it out. As I realized the full extent of what had happened, a feeling of peace and comfort came over me. Being a teacher was difficult for me and this was like a pat on the back. Why was it difficult? Because right after I got my master's degree in instructional technology and became a teacher, I began to lose my voice.

It began as a slight tremor to my neck, followed by a progressive paralysis of vocal cords. It didn't improve for a very long time. Sure, I pursued a diagnosis and treatments followed, but the spasmodic dysphonia, the medical term for it, is largely incurable. Teaching involves lots of talking, but when I'm having a bad day I rely on other resources, mostly technical ones, to help me.

I've been teaching for thirty years despite my disability. I've learned to live with it. To be honest, if angels were going to help me, I would have thought a different kind of intervention would have occurred, like fully restoring my voice. But what matters is that I was saved from that fall to teach another day.

— Tamra Anne Bolles —

70

Never Judge a Book...

Things do not pass for what they are, but for what they seem.
Most things are judged by their jackets.
~Baltasar Bracián

Had you asked me eighteen months ago what an angel looks like, I would have given you the stock answer: a beautiful, shimmering being with long, blond tresses, dressed in a golden caftan. I would also have added the caveat that that's what they would look like if they existed... which they don't. Of course, that was then, and this is now. If you ask me today what an angel looks like, I will give you an entirely different answer, and I can emphatically confirm that they are out there.

Before I share my encounter with you, I should probably explain where I live and what I was doing on that dark, damp November evening. I am fortunate to live in the county of Norfolk, England. It's a rural area made up of sleepy hamlets and isolated villages. Buses don't run in some areas more than once a day, so a late-night visit to my parents' house was always going to end in a long walk home.

On this particular occasion, I had said my goodbyes and was making my way back with my walking stick and trusty torch. A storm had been forecast for that evening, and I wanted to get home before the worst of it. Sadly, I had misjudged my timing, and the wind had already started to rattle the branches of the trees as I passed the church with its weathervane spinning frantically. The rain quickly followed, pelting me with cold, heavy water droplets. By the time I reached the outskirts of the village, a vicious thunderstorm had arrived, momentarily lighting up the sky before plunging me back into the darkness.

As the beam of my torch bounced from tree to tree in front of me, it lit up something in the middle of the road. I steadied my hand and swept back and forth until it rested upon a truly terrifying sight. An enormous, snarling dog stood blocking my path with its hackles raised and teeth bared. I had never seen such a monstrous creature and, had you told me it was a wolf, I would have believed you despite the fact that such beasts haven't existed in East Anglia for centuries.

I must confess that I was frozen to the spot as his iridescent eyes bored into mine. But as he stretched his neck towards me, growling menacingly, it broke the spell, and I took a step back. I made a jump to the left in a futile attempt to escape, but the creature lunged towards me, forcing me to sprint across the road onto the other side. At that moment a car came careering down the lane, skidding on the wet leaves, and ploughing into the trees where I had been standing only moments before.

The driver fell out of the car, unharmed but clearly intoxicated. In his statement to the police some hours later, he claimed that a huge dog had followed him as he left the local pub and had galloped past him on the road. The police put his ramblings down to the alcohol. After all, how could a dog sprint past such a fast-moving car? Of course, the answer is that it couldn't.

The police said that I had been incredibly lucky. Had I been on the other side of the road, I would almost certainly be going home in a body bag. They also asked me if I had seen the supersonic hound, and I replied truthfully that I hadn't seen anything of the sort.

That snarling creature with its glowering eyes and sharp, glinting fangs was no dog, and I now realise that it offered me no harm despite its terrifying appearance. It wasn't a beautiful, shimmering being with long, blond tresses, and it certainly wasn't wearing a caftan, but it was most definitely an angel. It was my guardian angel who had saved me from a truly ghastly end on that cold, dark November evening.

So, if you ask me today what an angel looks like, I would have to shrug my shoulders and shake my head. I suppose it can appear in any form it chooses. But one thing is certain: You should never judge a book by its cover… just in case.

—Joanna Elphick—

71

A Force Unknown

The human being is very resourceful. When you fight
for survival, you don't think much; you just do.
~Frank Lowy

Throughout my childhood, I always felt someone watching me, but I didn't connect that presence to protection. As a young girl, I'd stand on the bathroom toilet to crane my neck out the small window above, expecting someone to be looking back at me to confirm I wasn't crazy.

Fast forward to my senior year of high school. My work shift started at 11:00 A.M. I parked my first car, a 1987 Plymouth Reliant, in the grocery store's staff parking area, just a short distance to the entrance. I was troubled, though. I couldn't shake the feeling that something didn't feel right.

Punching out at 7:00 P.M. sharp, I exited through the automatic doors and met the dark, crisp winter air. As I scurried toward the edge of the lot where I'd parked during the daylight, I swung my head back toward the grocery store. A man dressed in dark clothes leaned against the building.

Unlocking the driver's side door, I plopped into the front seat, remembering I needed to empty my mini garbage bin. I backed out of my spot and turned toward the store entrance. The trash bin by the door was my target. I parked in the fire lane, left the car running, and ran to dump my rubbish. The looming man still leaned against the wall.

I jumped back into the driver's seat and leaned across to place the bin on the floor. The instant I sat up, my eyes pulled to the rearview mirror. A shadowy figure appeared behind my car. It was the man! He was putting on black gloves. Instinctively, I yanked the driver's side door handle shut.

But I was too late! He grabbed the inside of the door, ripped it open, and slammed himself next to me in the driver's seat. With all the strength of my ninety-five-pound body, I slapped, scratched, and shoved, screaming, "Help! Someone! Please help me!"

No one came.

Sensing my resolve, he body-bashed my light frame and slammed the car door, jamming us together in the driver's seat of the running car. "Noooo!" I screamed. Once his hand moved the automatic-transmission shifter to Drive, I grabbed his arm as he pressed the gas pedal. In an instant, my hand was on the shifter, forcing the car into Park.

The car jolted and banged onto the curb with an awkward stop, suspending the front half of my car over the barrier. My wide eyes met the stunned face of a man in the parked car to our left. "Help me!" I begged. A lifetime passed. He did nothing.

"Shut up and move over," my kidnapper yelled, seizing the shifter for Reverse, "or I'm going to kill you!"

I turned my head to the passenger-side door and heard a voice calmly say, "Unlock the door, and you will be free." In one fluid motion, I slid over to the passenger seat, reaching the lock and handle. I pulled at both, opened the passenger-side door, and escaped.

Suddenly, I was screeching inside the store lobby, frantically banging on the locked manager's door, terrified the man was close behind. "Let me in!" I begged. With a click, the door unlocked. I burst through the door, past the area where cashiers wait to count their drawers, and met the cinderblock wall of the dark back room filled with bins of recyclables.

The manager brought me back to the cashier waiting area and sat me down at a metal desk. She handed me a cordless phone and said, "You're safe now. The police have been called. Can you call your parents?"

I shakily punched the number for my grandparents. It was Sunday night; dinner with extended family was standard. That's where my parents would be.

"This is Elissa! Are my parents there?" I blurted out when my aunt answered. "Someone tried to kidnap me!" I couldn't hear her response.

My parents were out the door in seconds to make the seven-minute drive to the store. I trembled like I had been plucked from an ice bath.

"If we knew it was you," a couple, who were store regulars, said near customer service, "we would have helped."

What? I barely made it out of the car.

Their words dissipated as my parents entered the secure area. I hugged them and burst into tears. They wrapped their arms around me. I took my first deep breath since the ordeal started.

A police officer arrived. Tall and muscular, he made me feel safe. I relived each moment of terror as the officer gently listened to my story, taking notes on his pad. After I finished, he informed us that a chase was in process. The man was driving my car wildly through our rural town, speeding through stoplights and hitting cars and mailboxes.

"Stay close," the officer said. "I'm confident we'll catch him soon." Without a cellphone, my parents told the officer we would wait at the local diner for him. My parents held me up like a ragdoll as we walked out of the store and made the short drive to the diner. Completely detached from reality, I silently waited.

An hour later, the officer came into the diner. "The perpetrator crashed your car. He's been apprehended." Quickly, we followed the officer out of the diner and into the darkness. With emergency lights on, the officer led, and my dad followed. Two miles later, we turned down the last road in town — a one-lane road under the train tracks.

My dad parked. More flashing lights. Stunned in the dark loneliness of the cold back seat, the spinning lights from the ambulance ahead shined through the front window. My mangled car sat on the hillside of the train tracks overpass.

The officer approached us and asked me to identify my assailant. I got out and shuffled toward the ambulance, my protective parents on both sides of me. There were people all around — even the couple from the store who hadn't helped me.

I stumbled up the steps to the back of the emergency vehicle. Bloody and bruised, the man in dark clothes lay on the gurney. I didn't have a doubt. "It's the attacker," I told the officer. As we moved away, the couple's voices followed us in the cold air. "That doesn't look like the man from the store." Their words stuck in my head like a wall blocking the truth. I had seen his face inches from mine. It was him.

Before we started the fifteen-minute car ride home, the officer said, "He'll receive treatment before going to jail."

By then, I was numb.

The following day, my parents took me to the impound lot. There, the sun illuminated the total damage. The passenger's side of the car was completely destroyed, with the dashboard nearly touching the seat. Only then did reality hit me.

I would have died if I hadn't escaped.

But that wasn't my fate. The commanding, calm voice made sure of that. Still, the near-death experience has been a pit I've been crawling out of for twenty-three long years. Now I realize something though. An unknown force has always been watching me, ready to protect me. I have nothing to fear, and I am not crazy. I am blessed.

— Elissa Rowley —

72

Angel on the Highway

Alone is impossible in a world inhabited by angels.
~Author Unknown

How do you know if a miracle has occurred in your life, and it wasn't just luck favoring the fortunate? What happened to me one snowy February convinced me that miracles and divine intervention happen, often in "the blink of an eye."

As a Texan, I am not experienced in or comfortable with driving in snowy, icy road conditions. So I was reluctant, even afraid, that snowy February morning to embark on my twenty-five-mile commute. I dressed for work anyway, listening to weather reports and watching the radar, hoping to receive a text message from my school district telling me that schools would be closed for the day.

The text message never came. So I warmed up my car, melting the fresh layer of ice on the windshield, and then left for campus, slowly inching my car along city streets and keeping my eyes peeled for patches of black ice.

I approached the freeway entrance ramp relieved that road crews had treated it with sand and salt, making it less hazardous. I tensed my shoulders and leaned forward like a race-car driver, gripping the steering wheel so hard that my knuckles turned white. I made my way onto the freeway, slowly accelerating and decelerating to maintain traction, passing several abandoned vehicles along the side of the road with their flashers blinking. I drove cautiously, staying well within the lanes the snowplows had cleared, keeping a safe distance between me and the cars in front of me. Despite my vigilance, I swerved a couple of times and all but spun out once or twice, terrified that I'd collide with another vehicle or the concrete median.

In the distance, I could barely make out the treacherous, unavoidable High Five — a twelve-story-high, massive, five-level freeway interchange that I'd soon have to navigate to reach my destination. I forged ahead, looking for my familiar exit ramp, only to discover that it had been closed, forcing me to take the next higher-level ramp. My heart raced as my fear of heights kicked in. "Relax," I told myself. "You'll be fine." But in a flash, the clouds burst open, releasing blinding snow.

My heart raced, beating even faster, keeping time with the windshield wipers' frantic *schwump, schwump, schwump*. Within minutes, the blowing snow blended together with the existing snow cover. Visibility was instantly reduced to next to zero. Directional signs quickly vanished. The road itself disappeared as did all the cars around me. I had no sense of direction, no idea how high I was or where my exit ramp was. I knew that I was experiencing what's called a whiteout.

Suddenly, I hit a large patch of ice and began sliding, horrified at the sound of dozens of merciless tires screeching toward me. I spun out of control, heading straight for a badly damaged metal guardrail — the only thing that could possibly stop me from plunging off the High Five. A sense of utter helplessness and fear enveloped me. I gripped the steering wheel harder, staring at my sweaty, trembling hands, unsure what to do because I didn't have the skills or experience to maneuver myself out of the slide, let alone avoid crashing into other cars. I was about to drive off the edge of the High Five and plummet to my death!

My mind raced with the acute awareness that comes when facing imminent death. I would never again see my husband. How would he cope without me? What about my family, friends, and colleagues? I would never see them again or share a holiday or birthday with them. I would never again teach a class, assist a student, grade a paper, or attend a staff meeting. All my tomorrows would be gone.

I spun even closer to the edge, convinced that my death was inevitable, and wondered what heaven would be like. And then I called out, "God! Help me! I don't want to die, not today."

Then, in the blink of an eye, something unexplainable happened. My car effortlessly veered back to the left, dodging one car after another, skirting past the damaged guardrail. Time crawled to a standstill, and my car slowed on its own, positioning me in a clear lane of traffic. I looked at my hands. They were loose on the steering wheel, having done virtually nothing to take me out of the death spin. "What just happened?" I blinked in disbelief. Had I blacked out, or had some divine force moved me out of harm's way?

At that moment, I felt like the hands of an angel were on my steering wheel, directing my car safely onto the lower ramp and keeping it from nose-diving off the bridge. Although I didn't actually see an angel, I definitely felt its loving, protective presence guiding me to safety. Thirty minutes later, I arrived at school, humbled, grateful, and transformed.

That experience gave me a new perspective on a lot of things, including angelic protection. The highway can be a dangerous, sometimes deadly place, with cars speeding and careening like big, heavy missiles of metal, glass, and gasoline. People don't always pay close enough attention to where these rolling projectiles are headed, all made even worse by inclement weather, poor road conditions, and reduced visibility. It can be a harrowing thought to realize that we are at the mercy of fate out there on the road, racing along in a thin shell of metal that will likely not do much good to protect us if danger comes calling.

But what if we're not alone out there on that stretch of road? What if we're not alone on the highway of life? What if there are benevolent, angelic forces watching over us, looking out for us, protecting and guiding us safely to our destination much like the protective angel who led me to safety that snowy winter morning? My freeway incident convinced me that angels, seen or unseen, are patrolling the roads and highways just as surely as is the specter of death. They come to us in times of need, distress, or danger like the one I faced on the freeway that wintry February morning.

In hindsight, I can vividly recall other times in my life when I've unknowingly encountered an angel who, without saying a word, protected me from harmful conflict and the fray; who cushioned me from a physical, emotional, or spiritual fall; who inwardly strengthened and comforted me in times of sorrow and pain; who guided me away from potentially harmful choices; and who provided me with guidance and encouragement during difficult times in my life.

I take comfort in knowing there are angels behind the scenes looking out for me, angels watching and waiting to help me, angels guiding me, and angels snatching me from danger when I venture onto any of life's highways.

—Sara Etgen-Baker—

Chapter
8

Divine Messengers

73

The Bond Between Sisters

Do you think the universe fights for souls to be together?
Some things are too strange and strong to be coincidences.
~Emery Allen

There was a lot of love in my mother's family — and a lot of bickering. Each Sunday, when I was young, the families would gather at my grandparents' home in Astoria, New York. Mother had one brother and two sisters; they would be there with their spouses and children.

These visits would begin with fun, laughter and plenty to eat. The aroma of Grandma's deep-fried donuts lured us in as we walked in the door.

Maybe because there were so many of us, or maybe because we all spoke so enthusiastically, somehow an innocent conversation would soon turn from an opposing point of view into an angry shouting match. Sooner or later, one person or another would walk out yelling, "I never want to speak to you again!" The loud and rowdy slamming of the doors told us all it was time to go home.

The following Sunday, all the families would show up at our grandparents' house again, as if nothing unpleasant had ever happened.

The arguments were more likely to occur between my mother and her sister, Mary. They were close in age, and there was a rivalry between them. I never knew why they didn't get along, but I do know that they loved each other very much.

When Mother immigrated to America with my brother and me, Aunt Mary took her under her wing to help her get adjusted to life in another country. She got Mother her first job working as a seamstress in the same factory where Aunt Mary worked. Mary was always there for my mom, and my mom was always there for her.

After my grandparents passed away, Mother and Aunt Mary met only once more. It was at my grandfather's funeral. It was a somber occasion, and the sisters hugged, grieved and clung to each other throughout the day. But as the service ended, some words were exchanged, and a short but bitter feud erupted between the two sisters — something about the will.

Mother and Aunt Mary did not speak again.

Eventually, news came that Aunt Mary had passed away. By this time, no one knew where the rest of the family lived, so no condolences or words of sympathy were conveyed.

I knew it bothered Mother very much because she had sincerely loved her sister. I was too young to advise her. Thinking back, I should have tried.

Eight years later, Mom and I went to visit Slovakia, where my family had originated. One day, we happened to be at a restaurant and had to use the restroom. In separate stalls, we heard two women by the sink speaking in perfect English.

"Have you heard that Mary's sister Florence is coming to visit Slovakia?"

Our ears perked up. My mother's name was Florence.

"Really?" answered the other woman. "It's a shame she and Mary are so estranged."

"I know," said the other. "It bothers Mary tremendously."

Mom and I burst out of our stalls.

"Who are you? And who are you talking about?" Mom and I questioned the women.

They looked at us, puzzled. "Čo to hovoríte?" they replied in Slovak. Suddenly, mysteriously, they didn't speak English.

We spoke to them in Slovak, and they explained that, indeed, they knew Mary. She had been to Slovakia to visit a few months earlier.

Mother and I were not certain what to believe. Could it be that Mary was still alive? The hope that radiated in my mother's eyes was a remarkable sight.

We exchanged names and addresses with the two ladies and asked them to join us at our table for some coffee and conversation. The ladies promised to be there in a minute.

Back at our table, Mother was overjoyed. "Can you imagine? She's alive! My dear sister Mary is alive!"

Eight years of sorrow and grieving had suddenly been erased from my mother's face. I knew in her heart that she had always loved her dear sister, and their breakup had hurt her immensely. Not that she had ever admitted it — until now.

"I should have reached out to her. I should have reunited with your aunt." She looked so forlorn.

From our table, I had a view of the ladies' room door. I watched for the two women to emerge. We waited and waited. When a few minutes had passed, I went back into the restroom to check. It was empty. They had disappeared. How did I miss them?

We tried to contact these women using the phone numbers they had given us. The numbers didn't work.

We never saw the women again. The two women who seemed to know things about our family that we didn't, who spoke perfect English and then didn't, suddenly didn't exist.

After our European trip, as soon as we landed in the United States, Mom couldn't wait to get back to check on the whereabouts of her sister. From a New York airport, she called directory assistance and got a number for Mary's husband in New Jersey.

I'll never forget the hopeful expression on my mother's face. I heard her almost whisper, incredulously, "Mary? Is it you? Is it really you?"

On the other line, I clearly heard what sounded like an overjoyed roar, "FLORENCKA!"

The sisters reconnected. Their love prevailed. Both stubborn women came to their senses. Eight years had been wasted.

The two women in the ladies' room in another part of the world had accomplished their miraculous intervention. Aunt Mary said she had never heard of them, and Mother never met them again. Yet these two mysterious angels reunited the two sisters.

Although eight years had passed, Mom and Aunt Mary picked up where they had left off. Living in different states by then, they still managed to get together one way or another. They called, visited, laughed and cried. And, yes, they fought and made up, just like in the old days.

—Eva Carter—

74

Your Heart's Desire

*Important encounters are planned by the souls long
before the bodies see each other.*
~Paulo Coelho

The daughter whom I dearly loved, the little girl I had coached
in soccer, nursed through endless ear infections, and helped to
write research papers the day before they were due, was getting
married.

And I was a mindless, doddering basket case of nerves.

"Why can't they just elope like we did?" I asked my wife.

"You mean have their nuptials performed in the break room of
the courthouse by a justice of the peace?"

"They could buy a house with the money they'd save."

My wife flashed me one of those looks. If you've ever been married, you know what I mean.

"I'll be in the front yard doing a little gardening," I mumbled,
retreating to the relative safety of the outdoors.

The garden had become my place of refuge. My mother had
started it when she came to live with my wife and me. And up until
the day she passed away, it was her domain and source of inspiration.
After she was gone, I tried my best to keep things up. But the soft,
understanding touch of my mother for all things growing had obviously
been left out of my DNA package.

I started with the roses, which were seriously overdue for a prun-
ing. I tried to remember what my mother had taught me: Cut each

branch back to an outward-facing bud.

"Good afternoon."

I turned quickly, startled. He was standing on the other side of the waist-high picket fence that bordered the front yard. I had not heard anyone approach, no footsteps. Stranger still, my Lab had not barked to alert me and, even now lay on her side dozing.

He was tall, thin, gray-haired, and dressed smartly in a dark suit jacket and pants, a gentleman who looked as if he had just stepped out of a movie from the 1940s.

"I apologize for surprising you like that," he offered in a deep, comforting voice.

"Oh, no need to apologize. I didn't see you coming up the walk, that's all. I'm a bit preoccupied with the garden."

The stranger surveyed my front lawn, which featured an array of flowering plants, shrubs, grasses and vines.

"Impressive," he observed. "You are quite the gardener."

"No," I insisted, "this is my mother's doing. She was the gardener."

"Well, in that case, your mother must be quite the gardener."

I paused, hesitating, unsure of how much I should share with this man I had never before seen in our neighborhood. But his smile seemed genuine and engaging.

"My mom passed away a few months ago. I've been trying to keep up the garden since then. Most of this," and I swept my arm in a wide arc, "she planted when she came to live with my wife and me."

"It's a beautiful memorial to your mother," the stranger quietly observed.

"I find great peace when I'm out here. Getting dirt under my nails reminds me of what is important in life. Especially right now."

"Go on," he quietly encouraged.

And, for some reason, I did.

"Well, my daughter's getting married next month, and it's all a little overwhelming—the bridal shower, the bachelor and bachelorette party, rehearsal dinner, and, of course, the wedding itself."

"Sounds like you've got your hands full."

"That's why I come here. To the garden. Mom's garden. I feel close to her here. She and my daughter, the one getting married, were very close as well. I had so hoped that Mom could hold on until the wedding but…." My voice faltered, and I realized I had said much more than I intended.

And then, the man did something I did not expect — and, for some reason, I did not mind. He reached over the fence and gently touched my shoulder.

And, with his touch, I began silently weeping.

"I'm sorry," I apologized, struggling to regain my composure. "I don't know why I'm acting like this. I mean, I don't even know you."

The man smiled warmly. "It's perfectly natural considering everything you're going through. Say, have you ever heard of Heart's Desire?"

"Pardon?

"It's a perennial. Dianthus Heart's Desire. Pink flowers with a ruby-red center and a clove fragrance. I was thinking it's the one thing your garden — I mean, your mother's garden — needs. Right over there," he said, pointing.

"Oh, that's where Mom planted tulips. They're dormant right now. I couldn't plant anything there."

"Yes, yes, I suppose you're right," the man conceded. "Still, that looks like the perfect spot for your Heart's Desire, William."

And, at that precise moment, Scout, my fifteen-year-old Lab, stirred and began barking.

I bent over to quiet her, an act that took just a few seconds. But when I turned back, the stranger was gone.

A quick survey of the street in both directions revealed nothing. He had simply vanished.

Puzzled, confused, and maybe a little frightened, I stumbled into the house and recounted everything to my wife.

She listened patiently, expressionless. And when I had finished, she simply asked, "Do you believe in angels?"

"I don't know."

"Well, let me ask you this then. Did you tell him your name?"

"No."

"Then how did he know yours? William. Your middle name. The

only person who called you that was…"

"My mom," I interjected.

"I think we need to go to the nursery."

An hour later, we were back with trowels, garden soil and three containers of Heart's Desire in hand.

And we began planting. Right where the stranger had pointed.

The soil was rich and easy to work. In short order, we had one of the Heart's Desire planted and were working on the second.

That's when my trowel struck something. At first, I thought it was a rock and was about to dispose of it. And then, I brushed it off and looked closer. "Oh, my God."

"It's your mother's diamond ring," my wife gasped, "the one we've been looking for."

We had been searching for Mom's ring ever since she had passed. Our daughter's fiancé had asked for one of the diamonds from her ring, wanting to have it set in the wedding ring he was presenting to our daughter, knowing how close she had been to her grandmother. We had searched everywhere — the hospital, hospice, her personal belongings — without any luck.

Now, that had all changed.

It would be the connection between the old and the new, between two generations, between a grandmother and her granddaughter.

And it would lead to something else as well: my belief in angels.

Obviously, I had just met one.

— Dave Bachmann —

75

My Storm Guide

While we are sleeping, angels have
conversations with our souls.
~Author Unknown

"Are you sure you want to watch a scary movie?" my husband asked. When I told him I was sure, he looked at me with narrowed eyes and raised eyebrows. "Are you feeling okay?" he said jokingly. My husband Harold knew me well. I usually gravitate toward romance and comedy movies. Harold told me I'd be watching solo that night. He had to get up early for a meeting at work, so he was going to finish up some paperwork and head to bed. So, it was just me, the TV and a bowl of popcorn. I lowered the lights to get in the full effects of a spine-chilling experience.

About halfway through the movie, fear got the better of me. Every noise in the house made me jump. My horror-movie fest was cut short. I turned on the lights and changed the TV channel to a cooking show instead. After a few minutes of watching cake decorating, I couldn't shake the creepy feeling of the horror movie, so I decided to turn in for the night.

Walking into the bedroom, I had an eerie feeling as if someone was behind me. "This is why I shouldn't watch scary movies," I said aloud to myself. It was nice to finally get into bed. Hearing Harold gently snore made me feel safe, and I fell asleep quickly.

My dream that night was vivid and realistic. I was walking in a park, enjoying the brilliant sunshine, when an elderly woman approached me. The lines and creases on her face showed her age and perhaps a hard life. But her sweet smile said otherwise.

"Hello, dear. Such a lovely day," she said as she motioned toward the sky. I agreed with her by smiling back. As I was walking away, she said something unsettling. "We don't always have nice days, you know. You should be aware and take shelter." I turned to her to ask what she meant by that, but she had vanished. I started to weep and kept asking her to come back to tell me what she meant. Instead, I woke up from the dream.

In the morning, I told my husband about my dream and asked him what he thought it meant. "It means that you shouldn't watch scary movies, especially before you go to sleep." He laughed. He made me feel better about the dream. If he could joke about it and make light of it, surely I was overthinking.

Thankfully, my day was filled with work, chores and errands. I didn't give my dream a second thought.

Coming home after a long day, my two dogs looked at me with anticipation and tails wagging. "Okay, girls, let's go for a walk before it starts to rain," I cooed, as I put on their leashes. The day's forecast said it would rain most of the day, but the sun had other ideas. There wasn't a cloud in the sky all day. It wasn't until the early evening that it started to look like it was going to rain.

I put my dogs in the back seat of the car for the short drive to a local park. We were enjoying a quiet walk when I heard the first sounds of raindrops hitting the leaves of the trees. It was a gentle rain, so we continued to walk slowly toward the car that was parked on the other side of a field. The rain started to come down fast and hard, so we took shelter under a maple tree.

"It's okay, girls. We'll wait here until the rain tapers off," I said to soothe my frightened pups. I looked off to the side and saw a woman walking with a huge umbrella. I couldn't see her face, but she was coming toward us. As she approached, my dogs calmed down and sat beside my legs. I stood cautiously as the woman lowered her umbrella to reveal deep furrows in her aged face. She smiled warmly and simply said, "It isn't a nice day, dear. You should take shelter." She pointed toward a picnic pavilion in the distance. Shivers went down my spine. Her words and familiar face were so similar to the dream I had had the night before. It was pouring at that point, and I was hesitant to run in such torrential rain with my senior dogs. The woman instructed me sternly, "Hurry up and take shelter!"

I picked up my two dogs and made a mad dash toward the pavilion, sliding on the wet grass as the woman surprisingly kept up with us. Just as we reached the pavilion, I heard a booming, thunderous sound. Looking out onto the field, where we had been moments before, the tree we had stood under was now smoldering. It was struck by lightning!

In disbelief, I tried to absorb what had just happened. I remained frozen for a few minutes, staring at the tree. When I calmed down, I turned to the woman to thank her for helping us. But, just like in my dream, the woman had vanished. I realized then that, though horror films are usually fictional, angels and miracles are most certainly not, and I am truly grateful for that.

— Dorann Weber —

76

My Surprise Genealogy Lesson

Angels are not merely forms of extraterrestrial intelligence.
They are forms of extra-cosmic intelligence.
~Mortimer J. Adler

I t was a very busy night. I was a twenty-one-year-old college student, working as a cocktail waitress at a trendy jazz club in downtown Austin. One of the more popular local bands was up on the stage entertaining the crowd, and the small, smoky room was packed to the gills, overflowing well beyond peak capacity.

I made my way through the throngs of thirsty patrons, taking drink orders, dropping off martinis and beers, and picking up credit cards. One of the other waitresses went on her break and asked me to cover for her. I noticed two older women sitting at one of her tables, watching me and whispering to one another.

I knew they must be eager to order some drinks, so I delivered a round of shots to a table of college kids in my section and then hurried over to greet the two women. "I'm so sorry for the delay," I said, smiling, as I grabbed my pen to jot down their order. "What can I get you?"

One woman whispered something to the older woman, who continued to study me intently. I noticed they were both quite beautiful, with long, black-and-gray hair and espresso-colored skin. The first woman said, "I would simply like a glass of water, and she will have an iced tea."

Oh, great, I thought to myself sarcastically. *These two are really going to leave me a big tip.*

"I'll be right back," I told the women, flashing a smile anyway and hurrying off to the bar to fetch their drinks. I was back at their table in just a few minutes, setting down napkins, along with their glasses and straws. "Enjoy the music," I said. "I'll be back to check on you in a bit."

The older woman leaned over and whispered something to her friend, who lightly touched my arm. "Before you go, we were just wondering what tribe you're from."

I frowned slightly, not sure if I had heard her correctly over the loud music. I put my hand to my ear. "I'm sorry," I giggled. "Did you say 'tribe'?"

The first woman nodded her head, not even breaking a smile. "Yes, I asked what tribe you are from."

Now, I was beginning to think these two might be slightly off their rockers. I giggled nervously again. "'Tribe' as in a Native American tribe?" The women both nodded their heads in unison.

"I'm not Native American, ma'am," I responded, slightly confused.

"Yes, actually, you are," she said, continuing to look very serious. "We can tell because of your medicine shield."

I looked down at my outfit, which consisted of rather nondescript blue jeans and a black T-shirt. "My medicine shield?" I really had no idea what they were talking about. "What is that?"

"It's your ancestor walking around behind you, protecting you from evil."

I looked behind me but only saw a packed room full of people drinking, laughing and enjoying the music. "I really don't know anything about that, but I have to admit that I'm intrigued. Is this something you can see?"

"Oh, no, not me," the first woman replied. She nodded at the older woman. "But she can. Only the medicine woman can see this. Her grandmother was the medicine woman of our tribe and taught her the ancient ways many moons ago."

At this time, I noticed there were several people at other tables looking around for a waitress, so I knew I needed to wrap this up and get back to work. "I'm so sorry," I said, motioning to the busy room. "I need to go check on a few other tables but would love to know more about this. I'll be back in a minute. Please, don't go anywhere."

I hurried off to make my rounds. By the time I made my way back over to their table, they were gone. I quickly scanned the room from side to side, but they were nowhere to be found. *How strange,* I thought, glancing down at the table. The two drinks were untouched, but a one-hundred-dollar bill had been folded up and nestled neatly between the two glasses. I was rather stunned and, I have to admit, slightly ashamed at my dismissive attitude.

The next day, I called my parents, eager to tell them about my strange run-in with the Native American ladies. I had expected my father to laugh but he surprised me and said, "Well, I've always had a strong suspicion that your grandfather was part Native American."

"Which one?" I asked. "Grandpa Steve?"

"Yes," he responded. "And you know how much you've always taken after him."

My maternal grandfather and I had always had a very strong connection. Different people over the years had commented that he and I shared similar facial traits, too, especially the long face, large eyes and high cheekbones. "But why would you think he's part Native American?"

"Well, we don't really know," my dad answered. "You know your grandpa was adopted, right? He was adopted from an orphanage when he was just a baby. He loved his adoptive parents very much but was always curious to find out about his actual roots. Many years later, as an adult, he went back to the orphanage to try and find his biological parents, but the orphanage and all their records had burned down. So, he was never able to find out anything about his actual heritage. The bottom line is, we still don't know where he came from."

Although I never saw the two ladies again, I still to this day often feel like my grandfather is in the room with me, even though he passed away a very long time ago. Whether he was Native American or not, I will probably never know. I do, however, believe that he's always there protecting me, and that single thought makes my invisible medicine shield shine just a little bit brighter.

—Susan Taylor—

77

The Bull

I believe that tomorrow is another day,
and I believe in miracles.
~Audrey Hepburn

About a year after my father passed, my mother decided she was ready to go through his clothes and sort them into keep, donate, and toss piles. I had volunteered to help. We were in their room with clothes spread out on every surface. She was quiet as we sorted and folded, likely deep in her thoughts about the last time he wore that sweater or those cowboy boots or his favorite Western shirt. In that moment, drowning in memories of Dad, I needed the comfort of hearing one of Mom's legendary stories about how divine intervention had saved someone's life.

"Mom, tell me the story about the black bull," I said.

She sighed as if she was too mired in grief to scratch out the details of that long-ago tale. "You know it better than I do."

"Yeah, but it's your story." When she didn't respond, I nudged gently. "I'll start it for you: It was late Friday afternoon, and you were rushing home from work because you, Dad, Shelby and I were going to Dad's parents' farm, and it was a four-hour drive."

Mom carried on from there.

"Once I got home," she began, "we loaded up and headed out. It took about a half-hour to get through the rush-hour traffic, but finally we reached the interstate and headed east. Because I was tired and eager to get to the farm and sleep, I drove as fast as the speed limit allowed—70 miles an hour."

I stifled an eye roll. Mom never drove the posted speed limit; she always went at least five miles over. But if I reminded her of that, story time would come to an abrupt halt.

"Time passed, and it got dark. You girls fell asleep in the back, and Dad nodded off next to me. Seat belts weren't mandatory at the time, so no one was buckled in. Hours later, I exited the interstate onto the little state road. The speed limit was 50, but I kept going 70. There was no traffic after all, and I knew your grandparents were waiting up for us."

I'd spent summers with my grandparents as a kid, and they did indeed go to bed early, as farmers do.

"At last, I reached the turn that would take us to the farm. The road was a narrow, less maintained farm-to-market road that locals used. It was pitch-dark, and the only light was from my headlights. I pressed the pedal harder and sped up."

This was the point in the story that always sent chills up my spine.

"Suddenly, a large, black shape appeared in my headlights, right in the middle of the road. I knew that, at the speed I was going, I wouldn't be able to stop in time to avoid hitting it. If I swerved to miss it, I'd hit the bar ditch and overturn the car."

"A voice inside you said, 'Hit the brake,'" I whispered, needing to be part of the story.

"I gripped that steering wheel and stomped that brake as hard as I could, knowing that any second we were going to plow into the object and be killed. The sudden action threw you girls onto the floorboard and pitched your dad into the dashboard. It felt like a lifetime before the car finally stopped.

"Then, to my complete astonishment, the object disappeared. In the chaos that followed—you and your sister crying and your dad asking what the hell happened—I tried to explain what I'd seen and why I had slammed on the brakes so violently. But I couldn't explain what the dark shape had been and why it had disappeared.

"For several long minutes, I sat there trying to stop shaking. Eventually, I resumed driving, but I was still so unnerved that I was incapable of driving more than 20 miles an hour.

"A mile or so down the road, my headlights lit up a large, black shape. This time, the shape didn't disappear. Standing in the middle of the road, just as the first shape had, was a huge, black bull. Because I was creeping along, I had plenty of time to stop the car and avoid hitting the beast. A few horn honks sent it lumbering off the road, and I drove on to the farm.

"If I'd hit that 2,000-pound bull driving 70 miles an hour…" She choked up as if the thought of what could have happened still shook her, even after all these years. "The only way I can explain it is that one of us had a guardian angel looking out for us that night."

Over the years, my mom has received many visions warning of danger, and each time those visions saved us. Whatever power is protecting us — guardian angel, divine being, or something else — I wholeheartedly appreciate and respect it… and my mom for being open to receiving and believing these visions.

— S.M. Green —

The Bird that Restored My Faith

Faith is the bird that feels the light
when the dawn is still dark.
~Rabindranath Tagore

After losing my mother, my faith was challenged in ways I never saw coming and in ways I'm often ashamed of. My grief made me question my belief in a higher power and everything else I'd been taught within my church walls. I was lost and hurting.

One day, as I sat alone on the couch, overwhelmed with grief, I sobbed. My body shook as I struggled to breathe. I cried. I yelled. I asked questions. I demanded answers for the pain I was facing. I asked my mom why she had left so soon and what I was supposed to do without her.

Suddenly there was a loud tapping on the window. And right there in front of me was the brightest, most vibrant red cardinal I had ever seen. I stared intently, and it seemed to do the same. As I sat, frozen in disbelief, it tapped one more time, gently, and then stood steadily on the wood divider of the window, looking in at me.

My crying paused, and my breathing slowed. We'd seen many cardinals at our house, but never standing there and staring in the window. I couldn't believe my eyes.

I was trying to decide if it was real or if my grief was playing tricks on me when my husband came in and asked what the noise was. I pointed to the window. He stood with me in disbelief and awe.

Cardinals are significant in our family. They have always been our family's sign from those who have passed.

We remained there, silent and still, watching this bird watching us. It didn't move. It just kept looking intently in my direction. And I knew without a doubt, and without any need for confirmation from the man I loved sitting beside me, that this was my mother coming to calm me down.

I knew as I watched that crimson bird that this was a moment I'd never forget, one when love transcended time and eternity. One when my mother showed up for me, even after death, just like she always promised she would. I knew that some people would view it as a coincidence, but to my husband and me it was an undeniable gift from my mother.

Right there in that living room, I had hit the deepest valley that grief had to offer, and I saw no way out. I let grief's pain and consequence paralyze and debilitate me. And those *tap, tap, taps...* Well, they set me free. They gave me hope and faith again. They reminded me whose daughter I was, and that there is nothing bigger or greater than the love of a mother.

That day, in that dark room, a bird restored my faith.

— Chelsea Ohlemiller —

79

It's Going to Be Okay

Butterflies are nature's angels. They remind us
what a gift it is to be alive.
~Robyn Nola

I didn't have a lot of hope. I sat on the hood of my outdated Oldsmobile, staring at the fields that went on for miles as tears ran down my face. That car reminded me of my life—rust where there had once been promise; something that had been handed down from one person to another. No one should feel that way at seventeen, but I did.

That day, it hit me all at once. My future was barreling down on me fast. I would graduate soon and be forced to leave the safety of my foster home for a world that I already knew was flawed. The pressure of moving forward had left me frozen and terrified.

Who would I talk to? Where would home be? Where would I go for the holidays?

The financial-aid paperwork had been the last straw. As the college staff tried to walk me through the complicated pile of pages, I asked for help once again when the questions started asking about family support. The answer was quick.

"Just mark 'orphan.' That is what all the foster kids mark."

Orphan?

But my biological parents were not gone. I knew where they lived and even talked to them. Why in the world would I mark "orphan"?

Suddenly, the gravity of my life hit, and loneliness took over.

I had wonderful friends and amazing foster parents. But this was a system, and my time as one of its members was almost over. Then who would my family be?

The tears poured down and fell upon the faded, pea-green paint of the car that now felt like the only thing in the world that might understand me. The beautiful plains before me that usually brought me solace could not soothe me.

I wiped away the tears at the sound of an approaching car followed by slow footsteps on the small, limestone cliff I was parked on.

"I should have known this is where you would be."

After those few words, my friend stood next to me in silence and let me cry until I didn't feel like I had any water left inside me. I finally looked up just as a pure white butterfly flew in front of my face and fluttered around me several times in a circle. It hovered in front of me for what felt like forever as I stared, amazed at the beauty of it. Before I could reach out my hand, it was gone, disappearing into the blue sky.

"Hmm," my friend said. "You must be pretty special."

"Why is that?" I said, wiping away the smeared mascara I was suddenly aware of before turning around.

"Because white butterflies have special meaning. They mean someone is trying to tell you that everything is going to be okay."

"You are just telling me that to make me feel better," I said.

"No, it is actually true. Look it up."

I didn't look it up that day. I didn't look it up several years later when I walked out of a courthouse after my divorce hearing, and a white butterfly followed me to my car. I didn't look it up when my one-year-old got a devastating, lifelong diagnosis, and a white butterfly was waiting on the porch when we came home from the hospital. I didn't look it up after watching a white butterfly flying outside my office window as I sat at my grandmother's desk only days after telling her goodbye.

I didn't have to look it up. I knew my friend was right. I knew it every time a sudden peace came over me that I could not explain. I knew it every time the anxiety faded. Throughout my life, in some of my hardest moments, that white butterfly has brought me comfort when

I thought there was no comfort to be found. It has brought me hope.

It also brought me a way to give that hope to someone else. In 2019, I was sitting on my porch swing on the phone with a friend, telling her about a dream I had for a nonprofit. It was a vision of how I could give back to foster children who were living in their worst moments — children who felt life was no longer promising and questioned their value as they were handed from one person to another. I told her I did not want those children to feel lonely anymore — right as a white butterfly flew by my front porch.

That day, I finally looked up the meaning of the white butterfly. Comfort. Someone watching over you. A sign of a fresh start. A symbol that someone is there with you. A message that it is all going to be okay.

Three years after that phone call, a nonprofit for children in crisis, for children who could not go back home, was born. The white butterfly is our symbol. I want to make sure that any child who feels like an orphan and feels alone gets the same message a friend gave me all those years ago: permission to hope and know it is going to be okay.

— Shannon Leach —

80

Hospital Visit

*I find hope in the darkest of days, and focus
in the brightest. I do not judge the universe.*
~Dalai Lama

The hospital felt colder than normal as I made my way to my mother's bedside. She had been in the ICU in a medically induced coma for the past week. They had her on a ventilator because her oxygen levels were too low, her carbon-dioxide levels were too high, and she was fighting pneumonia.

She had been diagnosed with severe COPD and bronchial asthma and placed on oxygen a few years ago. Honestly, this part didn't shock me as this seems to run in our family and she was a smoker.

Right now, that wasn't my concern. My concern was the ventilator that she was on because she was deathly afraid of it. A ventilator had blown a hole in her mother's lung, which killed her the day before my fourth birthday. I knew that technology had come a long way since 1999 but I couldn't help but worry. There hadn't been any positive movement in her condition, and I was starting to think the worst. What if this was how she died? In the ICU on the ventilator just like her mother?

She lay there, sleeping as peacefully as she could in the coma. The TV was set to Nick at Nite. One of my sisters must have visited before I got there. This was the channel she kept on at night because she couldn't go to sleep in silence. I walked over to the couch they had in the room for guests. It had been a long day at work, and all

I wanted to do was get off my feet. So, I sat down, leaned my head back, and closed my eyes.

Not even a minute later, I was startled awake by a female voice in the room. The voice was familiar, but I couldn't quite place it. I looked around before spotting the woman standing next to the bed. She had one hand over my mom's and the other smoothing my mom's hair back. Slowly, I got up and stretched to make it seem like I was just trying to get comfortable. In fact, I was trying to get a better look at her. This woman stood a little bit taller than me, and her face resembled my mom's, but she looked a bit thinner, softer, and older. I was trying to figure out who she was and how I knew her when she spoke again.

"There's nothing to be afraid of. They'll wake her up tomorrow and start the process of getting her off this machine." She was soft-spoken, but she also sounded confident, like she knew what was going on. She wasn't a nurse, though, based on what she was wearing: a purple shirt with Snoopy on it.

"Oh, that's great. I know she's not fond of the ventilator…," I started to say. The lady smiled at me before offering her hand to me.

"Heather, it's okay. I know she's afraid of it, but everything will be okay. She'll be taken off this in no time." She wiggled her fingers a bit, beckoning me to grab her hand. How did she even know my name? I reached forward and grabbed her hand gently. It felt cold but not in a bad way. She felt inviting and like everything was going to be okay. That's when I noticed she seemed to be a bit transparent — or maybe I was just tired. "I know she's going to be okay. You're going to be okay, too. So smart and brave for being here next to her this entire time."

"I appreciate you saying that," I said. I paused when I heard my name. It was coming from behind me and sounded like my sister. I turned around. My oldest sister was walking into the room. She was carrying a soda and some chips for herself.

"Who are you talking to?" She sounded confused. I looked forward. The lady who had stood in front of me was no longer there. I made a weird face and walked over to sit down on the loveseat. My sister walked over and sat next to me. Even though I knew it was going to make me sound crazy, I told her about my whole experience. I described the woman who had just been there. She sat and listened to me without judgment. After I finished telling her everything, she told me it was our grandmother — our mother's mom, who had died before I could start retaining memories. She even showed me a picture of her.

Maybe I was going crazy and had been thinking about it too much. Or maybe it was my grandmother appearing before me to give me hope and the positive attitude I had been missing these past few days. Those moments popped in my head the next morning when the doctors and nurses came in during their morning rounds. There had been a lot of improvement in my mom's health, and they were going to start the process of waking her up. Just like my grandmother had said.

— Heather Powers —

81

An Unexpected Call

The love between grandmother
and granddaughter is forever.
~Author Unknown

It was a normal Wednesday by any measure. I had just gotten home from work and was getting dinner ready when suddenly a painful ring sounded in my ear. I knew instantly that I needed to call my grandmother. Something was wrong.

Pushing aside any doubts, I dialed her number quickly and waited with a growing sense of dread as she did not answer. That was extremely unusual because she always answered, her cordless phone always by her side. I called again. "Pick up! Pick up!"

I knew rationally she could be out or was away from the phone but as I dialed again and again, only getting her answering machine each time for over two hours, I began to panic. She had no car, she lived alone, she only took short walks around the neighborhood.

I knew she needed help. I don't know how I knew; I just did. Casting all rationale to the wind, I called my sister and my father and told them I thought something was wrong and we needed to drive one state over to my grandmother's house to check on her. I was out the door before either of them could mount much of an argument via text.

I picked them up and we headed toward I-95. "She's probably at church," my father kept saying. "Maybe she's taking a nap," my sister chimed in, but I just stepped on the gas and a half hour later we pulled into my grandmother's driveway.

Her red brick duplex was completely closed off, the gate was shut, and the blinds were drawn. Not a speck of light could be seen inside. Now, sensing I was right, and something was clearly amiss, my father began pounding on the locked front door while I checked the back door. Locked. My sister leaned on the doorbell and although we could hear the chimes ringing there was no other noise inside. I raced around the side of the house to look inside one of her windows, but the heavy blinds were shut tight.

My sister rushed over to the neighbor's house to see if they had seen our grandmother, but they were out. The other house connected to our grandmother's duplex sat empty after a foreclosure. Not a soul was around.

I tried to pry open a window, feeling more desperate by the second. Then I realized one of the blinds was sitting crookedly and I might be able to see inside. I hoisted myself up onto the windowsill and pressed my eye against the windowpane. Straining to see inside the darkened room, I could just make out a pale hand on the floor. I pounded on the window and this time I could hear a faint cry for help.

I sprinted toward the back door, yelling for my father and sister to help me break into the house. My father smashed the window of the back door open with a rock and I was able to reach in and unlock the door. We were in.

My poor grandmother lay prone on the floor of her dining room, her shoulder clearly broken.

"You got my call?" she asked hoarsely. Then she began to weep. I held her hand and lay on the floor beside her while my sister called 911 and my father started to clean up the broken glass.

"It took you long enough," she said but I barely heard her before she burst into tears again. She was unable to tell me what had happened, but I could tell by the plate of food on the floor, an overturned chair, and the wetness of the carpet beneath her that she had been lying there since dinner last night. I thought I might be sick at the thought of her lying there for hours in such pain, but

I kept it together and held her hand until the paramedics arrived.

My grandmother became confused as she lay there, asking for relatives who had passed years before, and wondering why her dining room furniture was upside down. It wasn't. The paramedics were angels and calmed her and all of us down while they assessed her injuries. Before I knew it, I was sitting in the front seat of the ambulance, with my grandmother strapped to a gurney in back. Soon we were at the local hospital's emergency room.

Thankfully, she had not suffered any other injury besides her broken shoulder. I called my aunt and she and her two children arrived shortly thereafter with my father and sister bringing up the rear.

The smell of hospital antiseptic was nauseating as we waited to be allowed in to see her. Eventually, her doctor informed us that a UTI brought on by dehydration was the cause of a dizzy spell that made my grandmother fall to the floor and break her shoulder. I had no idea dehydration, so common in the elderly, could cause so much damage. I wasn't surprised to hear she was dehydrated. The closest my grandmother ever got to water was by way of coffee or iced tea.

As visiting hours were ending, we each took time to say goodbye. I lingered by my grandmother's bedside, knowing she was in good hands but feeling terrible over the whole situation. She looked lost in the big white bed and her confusion was not going away despite her fluid intake. I didn't want to leave her.

She took my hand and said, "I was calling and calling you to come over and help me. Thank God you picked up."

I stared at her blankly for a moment and discreetly took out my phone to check my call log. There were no incoming calls from her, only outgoing.

My grandmother smiled at me so sweetly and patted my hand in gratitude.

And then I knew. Even though she hadn't called me, somehow, I still received her message. How in the world was this possible? I could find no logical reason for any of it but instead of worrying over it I decided to trust my instincts once again. I set aside my shock, held on to my grandmother's hand and thanked God I "answered" her call that day.

— Melanie R. McBride —

Comfort from Beyond

82

A Father's Final Gift

We never lose our loved ones. They accompany us;
they don't disappear from our lives.
We are merely in different rooms.
~Paulo Coelho

The day my dad died, I asked him for a favor. It was mid-January, just nine days before his birthday, but I hadn't bought him a gift. I was too scared to have his present in my house all wrapped and ready to haunt me if he wasn't still around to receive it. Unfortunately, I was correct in thinking that way.

I had been by his bedside all through the night with my two sisters as he lay there, eyes closed and breathing heavily, in a state the staff members at his assisted-living facility referred to as "actively passing." Essentially, he was in the deepest kind of sleep… one he couldn't be awakened from. We were told that his hearing would be one of the last things to go, so we kept the conversation as light as we were able to, and we each took turns talking to him individually. It is impossibly difficult to say everything you want to say to someone you love when you know it's your last chance to say it. The longer Dad remained in the process of transitioning from one world to the next, the more I thought to share. Repeatedly, I whispered, "Thank you," "I love you," and "I'm going to miss you."

My mother and brother were out-of-state and drove through the night to be with us, arriving before the sun rose. It had been some time since the six of us were all together, and it was heartbreaking to realize that we never would be again. None of us was ready for this goodbye. I think the only one of us who may have been prepared to let go was Dad. After suffering from cancer and dementia for several years, I believe he had had enough. It was only two months prior when we had admitted him into this facility because his health had deteriorated to the point that we, his children, were no longer capable of taking care of him.

I gazed upon my father's face with all its familiar contours and lines and felt an overpowering surge of emotion. Anticipating this day's arrival had not softened its crushing blow. I was losing my Superman. I was unable, or perhaps more accurately, unwilling, to imagine all of my tomorrows without him. I looked away from his face and studied the steady, although increasingly labored, rise and fall of his chest. My throat constricted with the awareness that at any second that movement would come to a forever halt.

Please, God, I thought, *let him go peacefully and painlessly.* I had uttered this prayer to myself so many times by this point that I decided to make a mantra out of it: "peacefully and painlessly, peacefully and painlessly, peacefully and painlessly…" These three desperate words looped in my brain, and while their echo filled my soul, I put my hand over my father's heart and leaned in to speak. My father, like all adoring daddies who turn to jelly when their little girls peer up at them with doe eyes, always had trouble saying "no" to me. I dared to ask him for one more "yes."

"Dad," I began, "after you go, could you send us some snow to let us know you're alright?"

My siblings immediately voiced their objections. "Snow? Why'd you ask for snow? We don't want snow. Couldn't you have asked for a rainbow or something? How about the winning lottery numbers?"

"No, I want snow," I explained. "Snow is peaceful; it soothes me." I glanced at their dubious expressions and laughed. "Just a light snow. I'm not asking for a blizzard! Just to let us know he's still with us."

They accepted that qualification, and everyone quieted. None of us had gotten any sleep, and we were exhausted. There were fewer comfortable seating options in my father's small room than there were people. We also had no idea how long Dad might remain in this state. (One nurse had informed us that it could last for quite a while, even days.) As a result, a couple of us were urged to go home, get some shuteye, and come back later. I reluctantly agreed to leave with one of my sisters. I had just gotten over being ill and was feeling rather weak, so my family insisted. I trudged away with wet salt trails running down my cheeks.

Some hours later, shortly after noon, following a restless bit of sleep and a shower, I was about to step out the front door to make my way back to my father when my phone rang. It was my brother. "He's gone," I remember him saying.

The rest of the conversation is a blur, but I do know I choked back a sob and asked, "Did he go peacefully and painlessly?"

"Yes," my brother responded. "It was very peaceful."

I wept with grief and gratitude. My father was gone, but he had felt no pain.

My sister and I returned to our family. I noted on the drive there what beautiful weather we were having and felt torn over it. On the one hand, it was a lovely day for my father's spirit to ascend to Heaven on a golden sunbeam through a bluebird sky. On the other hand, however, it conflicted so drastically with what I was feeling that it almost made me angry. I wanted the skies to be dark and the clouds to be weeping with torrents of rain. I wanted the world to reflect my agony.

When I reentered my father's room, Dad was in his bed, just as before, but eerily, shatteringly still. I embraced my mother, sisters, and brother. We would wait there together, as one newly incomplete unit, until hospice came to examine Dad and transport him to the funeral home. It was 2:25 P.M. and we were still waiting, when my sister yelled, "Oh, my God, it's snowing!" I was standing with my back to the window and whipped around to see the gentle snowfall. We all burst into a fresh batch of tears as we watched the sparkling, crystalline flakes dance in the air outside. I checked the weather forecast on my phone. No precipitation of any kind was predicted. It was nearly forty-five degrees and sunny. I called my husband, who was working just a couple of miles away, and he said it wasn't snowing where he was.

My father had done it. He'd granted my last request. I knew he would; he never let me down. He was okay. He was with us... and always would be.

—Kerry Farraday—

83

The Perfect Dog

The gift which I am sending you is called a dog,
and is in fact the most precious and
valuable possession of mankind.
~Theodorus Gaza

Two weeks after my husband's passing, my sixteen-year-old daughter barged into my bedroom and ripped the covers off me. "You need to get up," she said. "We need to go to ARF." ARF was the Animal Rescue Foundation, a place to which we certainly did not need to go.

I pulled the covers back over my head and mumbled, "No, we don't. We have three dogs and three cats. There are only two of us. We're seriously outnumbered as it is."

"Mom, we used to have five dogs." She pulled the sheet back again. "Come on, you can't stay in bed all day."

On it went. Somehow, she leveraged my maternal guilt, and soon I was driving us to the shelter — but only to look, like a visit to the zoo.

We entered a sunlit atrium and walked past glass-walled enclosures that housed the animals available for adoption.

Ari bent down to look at a small dog named Mighty Mouse who looked like a Chihuahua on steroids. An adoption counselor walked by and asked if we'd like to meet her. Before I could say, "No, thank you," Ari said, "Oh, yes, we'd love to!" We were led into a large room with Mighty Mouse trailing behind us. Once the adoption counselor dropped the leash, Mighty Mouse began whirling about like a dust devil. She literally bounced off the walls.

"Don't worry, there are plenty of dogs for you to meet," the counselor said. I tried to give Ari a dirty look, but she was careful to avoid eye contact.

Out came an assortment of dogs, and I found fault with each and every one. A little frustrated, the representative finally asked us what we were looking for. Instead of telling her that we were not looking to adopt, and that we were, in fact, wasting her time, I described my late husband's dream dog.

Mark loved mutts. A mutual fondness for pets was one part of our bond as a family. An autumn earlier, before he was sick, we sat snuggled up together on a bench at the local dog park, where he regaled me with his thoughts on the perfect pup.

"First," he said, "she should be a thick — but not too thick-boned — dog with a delicate, feminine face. She shouldn't exceed 75 pounds but come close to it. Her ancestors would be Labrador Retrievers, German Shepherds, Rhodesian Ridgebacks, and Hungarian Vizslas, with a great-grandfather who's a Staffordshire Terrier — I love those guys."

I asked, "What color would she be?"

"A reddish-brown, but her face should have a darker sable mask. And she should have a heart-shaped, cowlicky stretch of white fur on her chest."

"What else would she have?" I asked.

"She'd have silky-to-the-touch, hound-like ears. Her eyes would be a warm brown. She'd have jet-black toenails, which would stand out against the few white hairs at the end of her toes."

"She'd be ridiculously sweet, right?"

"Of course, sweetheart. She'd have a perpetual smile and a wagging tail, but she'd never knock over our wineglasses."

I decided that I would only adopt a dog if she met all of Mark's criteria, which I described in detail. And that was impossible. Then, the counselor said, "Have you met Cherries Jubilee? She sounds like your perfect dog."

I pulled out my phone to check the time and saw the many texts reassuring me that life would get better. I tucked it back into my purse and then looked up.

Into the room, the adoption worker led the very dog that Mark had once envisioned. I got goose bumps. How could this be? How could a blend of breeds result in this precise appearance? The only difference between Mark's phantom dog and this very real flesh-and-bone dog was that she had some scarring on her left hind leg.

Cherries Jubilee slobbered us with kisses. She showed off her talents. She sat and lay down upon request and then gave us high-fives. After meeting this dog, I felt as if I'd stumbled through the wardrobe door into Narnia. We were told to come back with our other three dogs for a meet-and-greet.

On our ride home, I was hoping to talk to Ari about her dad, but instead she talked endlessly of the exciting new adventures she was going to have with our new dog.

We returned to ARF with Aggy, Apollo, and Isabelle. I was especially worried about Isabelle, the Chihuahua, but I didn't need to be. Cherries went up to each dog and flipped onto her back as her way of greeting them. They then romped and played, jumped and rolled, with lots of licking in between. The ARF representative said, "It looks like a match made in heaven. This doesn't happen every day."

Ari smiled quietly in their midst, looking to me for agreement.

"What about cats?" I asked. "We have three of them."

"Cherries treats cats like dogs; she's very affectionate and tries to play with them. But one slap on the nose or a bit of hissing, and she gives them a wide berth."

There was no way we weren't taking her home; she was our family. I had to wonder if this development was a manifestation of Mark. I could think of no plausible explanation. Since Mark's death, I had looked for signs of his presence, and this glaring example was certainly one. He used to joke occasionally about returning as a dog, so I pondered that possibility. If this dog wasn't the reincarnation of Mark, she was at least the dog he wanted us to have.

While it would have felt like a sacrilege to name her after Mark (although he probably would have liked it), we called her Dylan, after

Bob Dylan, Mark's favorite singer and songwriter.

Our Dylan was a reminder that Mark was still a presence in our life. I wasn't looking for another dog in my throes of bereavement, but how could I say no to this one?

In the process of welcoming her, I could see hope for our future and felt more whole again. The dogs piled onto the back seat of our SUV. Ari watched as they arranged and rearranged themselves before settling in. She then turned to me, smiled, and said, "You know that Dad orchestrated this whole thing." I simply nodded. It was the first time she had mentioned her father since his death.

— Victoria Lorrekovich-Miller —

84

In Good Hands

Mothers hold their children's hands for
a short while, but their hearts forever.
~Author Unknown

The monotone hum of the flatline drowned out the other noises in the room — not that I was paying attention to anything else. "I'm so sorry," the nurse, an old friend of mine, whispered before leaving the room.

I hardly acknowledged her. My mind was too focused on that hum and the body lying in the bed: my mother's.

I should have been happy for her. After years of physical pain, I knew her freed soul was lifting to a better place, but she was still my mom. My rock. The one who encouraged me whenever I was too nervous to leap. The one who supported me even if my ideas seemed crazy. The one who was always there with open arms when life's problems became too much to bear alone.

No more.

A week slowly passed. The wake and funeral were a blur. I pretended to be okay as friends and strangers shared their condolences, but nothing could ease my worry. Was my mom in a better place?

I knew she should have been, but how could I be sure? What if my mom's soul was stuck on this Earth?

No matter how many times I told myself that I was being silly, that those thoughts were ridiculous, that I should know my mother's soul was in a better place... How could I be sure?

Four years later, I was at the doctor's office with my shirt pulled up and a lot of slick goo swirled on my swelling abdomen. The ultrasound technician looked over with a smile and said, "It's a boy."

My son's due date was so close to my mother's birthday that the entire family placed bets as to whether he would be born that day. I was on the fence about whether I wanted him to be born on her birthday, knowing that she would never get to hold him.

One month before my due date, though, something went wrong.

"We have to go to the hospital," I said, waking my husband early one morning, trying to keep myself as calm as possible.

"What's wrong?"

"I'm bleeding."

Even though we hurried, and the hospital was only a fifteen-minute drive away, the bleeding had gotten much, much worse by the time we got there. Even though my husband had tried to say that everything was going to be okay as we drove to the hospital, one look in his eyes and I knew that he was thinking the same thing as me: It was not going to be okay — not with that amount of bleeding.

I never told him that I hadn't felt the baby move since the bleeding started. I didn't have to.

A day of pain and emotional torture later, I was lying in a hospital bed, using the time alone to say goodbye to my son. My cheeks burned after hours of wiping away the never-ending rush of tears, and still more tears flooded forward. I don't remember when I fell asleep; nor do I remember being asleep. When I woke up, it was dark and my husband was snoring on the couch.

The ray of pure, golden light first shone in the corner of my eye. Its blinding beauty intensified when I turned my head. The rocking chair in the corner that had been empty when I woke now held my radiant mother. Her body was no longer hunched, and youthfulness was shining in her features. In her hands was the tiniest of bundles. A miniature hand reached out and clasped her finger.

In that split second, before the light disappeared within a blink of the eye, my mother looked up and met my gaze with the happiest of smiles on her face.

To have called the light surrounding my mother and child golden did little justice to its true, majestic beauty, but it was the best I could do. With the room dark once again, two undeniable facts comforted me. My mother was in a better, happier place, and she was watching over my baby.

— Katrin Babb —

85

Give Me One Reason

There's no other love like the love for a brother.
There's no other love like the love from a brother.
~Author Unknown

"Give me one reason to stay here, and I'll turn right back around," sang Tracy Chapman from my car radio as I drove home from work one afternoon. Memories of being a teenager and "jamming out" to that song on repeat, while I made food or did my chores, came flooding back to me. I would play that song so often that my younger brother would become annoyed and stomp into my room, singing it with an exaggerated voice.

I missed my little brother. He had been dead for almost a year, and I still could not wrap my mind around the fact that I would never see him again. Things like particular foods and certain smells would stimulate fond memories of our time together, but music seemed to have the most profound effect. My brother and I shared similar tastes in music, but I had a tendency to obsess when I really liked a song. Even our mom would express frustration when I played the same song over and over throughout the day.

Tracy Chapman's song, "Give Me One Reason," was one of many songs that made it into my "Repeats Hall of Fame," and my brother never attempted to disguise his frustration as the song's lyrics constantly piped throughout our house.

Hearing that song on the radio as I drove home that afternoon, however, reminded me of his absence, and I began missing my little brother. I remember thinking that I would love to see him just one more time. I would have settled for at least a sign, something that would assure me he was okay.

I had heard other people explain how paranormal experiences had helped them believe their recently passed loved ones were reaching out to them and letting them know they were fine. But there had been no inexplicable or paranormal signs assuring me of my brother's wellbeing. Instead, I just felt empty and alone.

Once inside my house, not wanting the fresh memories of my brother to fade just yet, I decided to pull up YouTube and listen to the song once more. As I sat in my living room, belting out the lyrics, my brother's cat that I had adopted after his death jumped on the couch beside me and lay down. I was singing my heart out with the song when I suddenly noticed the cat looking up in that strange way animals often do, as if something invisible had entered the room. Staring in the direction of the cat's gaze, I noticed that the ceiling fan had started to spin on its own, circulating at least seven times before falling completely still. Chills on top of chills began to travel up my arms, and I felt myself smile for the first time in a very long while.

In that moment, I realized I had been given one reason to believe my little brother was not far away. He was okay, and I knew he was watching over me.

— Lindsey Burpee —

86

Aracely's Angel Visits

All the world is a laboratory to the inquiring mind.
~Martin H. Fischer

As a hospice physician, I have heard many reports from adult patients who have experienced visions of family members who had died years earlier. I admit, I was skeptical about these visions — wondering if they reflected the effects of drugs or low oxygen levels or delirium — until I met Aracely early in my years of pediatric hospice practice.

Aracely was a twelve-year-old girl with a lethal brain tumor. She underwent extensive treatment before her physicians ran out of chemotherapy options for her. She was a tough kid, but her most recent chemotherapy had resulted in significant damage to her heart muscle, even as it had failed to halt the progression of her tumor. This was not Aracely's first experience with severe illness. Prior to this cancer, she had been successfully treated for a tumor of her adrenal gland when she was a toddler.

I met Aracely for the first time at home at the initial hospice visit and found her lying listlessly on the couch in the living room. She barely spoke at that visit, offering only one-word answers to my questions. She did brighten briefly to point at specific pictures on the walls of herself with her parents and older brother. I noticed that there were distinctly more photos of the family's middle child, Alex, now dead for eleven years. Aracely pointed him out but said she didn't remember him.

Aracely's family members were the unlucky carriers of a gene called P53, which increased their risk of developing cancer. Alex had died of a brain tumor similar to his sister's when she was less than a year old. After his death, his mother Adele had descended into drugs and alcohol until her family staged an intervention and got her into treatment. Adele did well with her recovery, and the family had subsequently thrived, having found their footing once again. Luckily, DNA testing on Aracely's older brother revealed that he was not a carrier of the gene that had so devastated his family. He lived close by with his wife and baby.

Several weeks after I first met the family, as Aracely became weaker and more debilitated, her mother requested transfer into our inpatient unit, feeling that she could not bear for Aracely to die in the family's home. One day, Adele was napping and was awakened by the sound of Aracely talking to someone. Adele opened her eyes and looked around, but the two of them were alone in the room. She listened a little more and then asked Aracely, "Who are you talking to?"

Aracely responded, "Alex."

Adele asked, "Is he here visiting you?"

"He was, but he's gone now."

"What did he say?"

"He said he was glad to see me… that it wasn't time yet for me to come… that he'd be back later."

Adele responded, "Well, the next time you see him, tell him I love him."

"Okay."

A couple of days later, Aracely was once again speaking to individuals not visible in her room. After she quieted down, Adele asked, "Was that Alex again?"

"Yes, and he had Grandma with him today."

"My mother?"

"Yes, Grammy."

"What did she say?"

"We just visited. She told me it wasn't time for me still, but she'd be back. Then, she said, '%#$@&%$.'"

"Say that once more for me, Aracely."

"%#$@&%$."

That afternoon, Adele told me what had happened and said, "%#$@&%$ was a special phrase my mother and I always used to say to one another." [Adele did not share the actual phrase with me.] "Aracely has never heard that phrase before in her life because I never once said it to my children. It was just a little saying between me and my mom. My mother died before Aracely and Alex were born. Aracely never even met my mother."

"How does this make you feel?" I asked.

"For me, it's proof that my mother is watching out for Aracely. And as horrible as it is to imagine losing my daughter, it really helps to know for sure that my own angels, her brother and grandmother, will be there to usher her into heaven. I feel like the angels' presence bolsters my faith, and I feel more relaxed now. I'm less anxious and can focus on Aracely's comfort."

I encouraged Adele to be open and accepting of anything Aracely wanted to share with her but not to prod her into telling more than she felt comfortable revealing. Over the next few days, Aracely had visitations on an almost daily basis. Each day at my visit, I asked Aracely if she'd seen Alex as part of my routine assessment, just as I might inquire about whether her daddy had been able to spend the night. She would look right at me and either say yes or no, and I would ask how Alex was doing. Some days, she would say "not today" in response to my inquiry. Other days, she would say that he had come to check on her. To my knowledge, she never saw her grandmother again.

Aracely died peacefully and comfortably ten days later.

In my more than forty years of practicing medicine, Aracely's story is the most convincing one I have heard about "angels visiting" from the other side. For me, an innocent child's report held special weight as I don't think she could have made it up. Physicians are quick to label such visions as hallucinations, drugs effects, or delirium. None of those hypotheses applied to Aracely, and she certainly had no contextual framework upon which to anticipate visitations as she approached the end of her life. She was not requiring pain medication, and she was not depressed but tired of feeling bad. Aracely seemed matter of fact about her guests from the afterlife, accepting her fate with an eerie maturity.

A little more than two years later, Aracely's mother Adele was admitted to our inpatient unit. Having already battled breast cancer and another tumor even before Aracely became ill, she had developed leukemia and every possible complication of her treatment. Had she seen her angel children and her mother in similar visitations? I couldn't ask her because Adele was barely conscious upon arrival to the unit, and she died within a day or so. It was my hope that she experienced similarly comforting visits from her precious children and her mother before she died. Adele's death ended the curse of the P53 gene in this family.

I've thought a great deal about this experience with Aracely, grateful to hear her tell me about seeing her brother and grandmother, and grateful for the comfort it provided to Aracely and her mother. Now convinced that angels come to prepare us for our transition, this experience remains the most convincing evidence for me that we may see our loved ones again.

— Nancy L. Glass —

Morning Meeting

*Stop and smile. For you know when
you see me, it's our special hello.*
~Author Unknown

A screeching, sharp twitter like no other wakes me at 5:00 A.M. After twenty minutes of listening to the relentless sound, I get out of bed. Slowly, I shuffle down the hall to my office.

I love my office with its built-in daybed and bookcases, the many pillows, and the long desk with a view of the back yard and canyon below. Even at this hour, I don't bother to close the curtains. Having the opportunity to see a new day take shape is something I don't want to miss.

But at 5:00 in the morning, total darkness still rules. And if it wasn't for that one bird, all would be quiet. I open my laptop and begin to go through that night's e-mails.

Suddenly, I am startled by a thump. It sounded like a snowball hit the window. In Southern California, that's highly unlikely. How about a masked man with a chainsaw? Since I'd caught a glimpse of *Friday the 13th* the night before, I decide to go with that image.

I take a breath, brace myself, and reluctantly raise my head to see what's out there. That's when I see it: a black-and-white bird sitting on the window ledge. And it's looking right at me.

The bird doesn't move. I don't either. A minute goes by with the two of us sitting perfectly still, staring at each other. Then, it flies away.

That was weird. Could it be? No, that's silly. The bird simply needed some time to recover from its less-than-graceful landing.

I go on with my day — until the next morning when the same noise wakes me. The bird is on my office windowsill again.

This is when that conversation I had with my mother six months prior, the one I pushed aside the day before, can no longer be ignored.

Mom and I were talking about life, death, and life after death. It was a frequently discussed topic. Near the end of her journey, Mom was preparing for her grand exit. Her last wishes and funeral plans were written down, with copies made for each of her four children. Her self-penned obituary was in a clearly marked folder.

The practical details were taken care of as only Mom could. But the emotional stuff — the fears, regrets, and wishes for those left behind — were still unprocessed. I asked if she was afraid of dying. A pragmatist, she had a hard time envisioning a sequel to what had been her life. I, on the other hand, wasn't ready to let her go. I wanted her to at least consider the possibility of staying in touch.

"If there is a Life Part Two, please give me a sign. Why not come back as a bird?" I begged. She must have heard the desperation in my voice. She promised she'd try. With that, we changed topics.

Three months after my mother's passing, I'm at my desk with a bird staring down at me through the thin glass.

By the third day, the bird manages to wake not only me but also my husband. I tell him about our early morning staring contests and my mother's promise to me before she died. I figure he'd smile and urge me to go back to sleep. He doesn't.

"What if it's her?" he says.

Is this my husband speaking? The usually clear-headed, analytical person I thought I knew so well?

I remind him that Mom didn't believe in an afterlife. And, besides, if she did have the ability to come back, she'd never wake us up at 5:00 in the morning.

"Maybe it's the only time she can get your attention," my husband suggests.

He has a point. At that hour, everything is quiet. Things would be different if she tried to get my attention at noon when our yard is swarming with birds diving into the fountain, drinking from the birdbath, and conducting meetings in the many trees surrounding our property.

"Why don't you go outside and talk to her?" he urges.

What has gotten into him? Why would I venture out into the misty darkness, in my cheap, hot-flash-friendly cotton nightgown, pull up a chair and speak to a bird?

"I wouldn't even know what to say" I explain.

My husband looks at me in disbelief. Me not knowing what to say sounded more improbable to him than his dead mother-in-law sitting on a windowsill in the body of a bird. With that, he pulls the cover over his shoulder and closes his eyes.

And I? I grab my robe and head down the hall.

And so, it continues. Morning after early morning, the bird wakes us with that persistent, demanding song. I get up, walk over to my desk, and sit down. The bird lands on my windowsill. It stares at me, and I stare back until it flies away.

Then, one day, the chirping stops, and the bird is nowhere to be found. I finally get some sleep.

I feel at ease — until I don't. What if that bird was indeed Mom, and now I've offended her? I could at least have offered her a few breadcrumbs and a drink of water. Mother would never forgive me. Her grudges lasted for decades — and now maybe even from one lifetime to another. Mother-daughter relationships are complicated no matter what form they take.

A few weeks go by. Then, one early morning, there's that familiar early wakeup call again. I get up, hurry over to my desk, and sit down. And, once again, the bird lands on my window ledge.

I told myself that if the bird ever returned, I would at least acknowledge its presence. But how? Should I whistle, sing, say something nice or give it the thumbs-up sign? I decide to blow it a kiss.

And so starts a morning ritual. It's Mom and me and nothing else.

And, after a while, I learn to spot Mom among all the other birds in my yard. She's the only bird out there with a sound reminiscent of a car in need of new brakes.

Soon, she becomes part of my life. She watches my hill-climbing morning routine. In the afternoons, she bathes in the hot tub as we read nearby. And the second we remove our old living-room window — before we have a chance to install the new one — she leaves her spot in the olive tree and lands on top of the living-room chandelier inside.

When spring arrives, I crave more light, so I move my office across the hall to the room with the bay window and the large tree right outside. Less than an hour after settling down, there's my bird in the tree, chirping and staring straight at me.

A year and a half has passed, and she's still around. Now, we have a solid bond. Nowadays, I wave to her. I talk to her and thank her for coming, but I make sure to maintain my distance. Oh, I would like nothing more than to venture close enough for the bird to land on my shoulder, but I'm afraid. Better a mom in a tree than getting close and discovering the bird is nothing more than a desperate wish to keep Mom close.

But one thing I do know: If I had a chance to turn back time, that one request for my mother right before her death would be different. If I ever woke up and saw a giraffe in my yard, then I'd know for sure.

— Anna I. Smith —

88

Chicken Soup for the Soul

He Was Here

Love is something eternal; the aspect may change,
but not the essence.
~Vincent van Gogh

I could smell his cologne. I could feel his hands on my hands. I knew he had been there, but it made no sense to me. When I woke up in the morning, I immediately sensed his presence.

I proceeded to tell my husband of six years that my ex-husband had come to visit me during the night. My current husband looked very confused, concerned about me, and perplexed about what I was telling him.

I told my husband that my ex-husband, Kenny, had been to our house, and he had sat down on the side of our bed where I sleep at night. I said, "I could smell Kenny's cologne. I could feel the leather jacket that he wore when he was eighteen years old when we started dating. He was even wearing his corduroy pants." Without ever moving his lips, Kenny made it very clear to me that he still loved me and was watching over me and our daughter. His visit felt long; his presence was still with me.

I had never experienced this sense of presence before, and it made no sense to me. My husband told me to try to shake it off, get ready for work, and try and regroup. I felt shaken and couldn't stop crying, overwhelmed with a feeling of sadness and loss.

I got ready for work. I did not discuss what had happened the night before with my daughter. We headed for school and work like any other day.

That Friday, her first junior-high-school dance at a new school was taking place. There was an excitement in the air for my daughter.

It was difficult for me to focus at work that day. I had a pit in my stomach as a result of that dream. Then, the phone rang. It was Kenny's aunt. She said, "Kenny died today."

And then I knew. I said, "No, he didn't. He died last night."

I rushed back to school to pick up my daughter a bit early because she had to get home to a sleepover guest she had for the dance. I told her that we only had a few moments, but we needed to talk. I explained to her that her father had just passed away. Due to his life choices, he was not an active part of her life, but she still loved him. I said we could cancel her night if she wanted. She said she still wanted to go to the dance.

We had a four-year-old Beagle, Sara. Sara was my shadow and never left my side, but I started noticing that Sara was not next to me.

My daughter came in my room and said that Sara would not leave her room. She kept walking and sniffing every baseboard in the room. Then my daughter informed me, quite reluctantly, that her dad was sitting at the end of her bed watching her.

I had not told my daughter of her father's visit to me. I explained to her that his visit was a gift, and if she was afraid, she could ask him to leave or embrace it. She chose to allow him to stay. Night after night, for approximately a week, he sat at the end of her bed. I never got to witness this. My daughter said her father was peaceful. He didn't say anything, just sat in her presence. She finally told him it was okay to leave, and he did.

To this day, twenty-eight years later, I realize what a gift this was for both of us.

—L.M. Seidel—

89

Dimes from Devin

A true friend is for ever a friend.
~George MacDonald

evin had been dead for two months before I realized the dimes came from him.

He was twenty-one years old when, in the wee hours of the morning in April 2001, he walked out onto the ski slopes at Copper Mountain, Colorado, and climbed up a pole to a chairlift. Nobody knows if he made it to the chair because Devin fell and died there in the snow.

Devin was my daughter's best friend and soul mate. They met when they were in pre-school. Through many years and many moves, they never lost their friendship or their love for each other.

When Devin died, so did my daughter's heart. She was a month away from graduating from college.

After Devin's memorial service in Tennessee, I drove my daughter back to college in New York, and I came home to Massachusetts. We tried to get on with our lives. One day, I came home from work and my husband said, "The strangest thing happened today. There was a dime on the floor of every room I went into." I wondered whose pocket had a hole in it.

I went into my home office to put down my books and computer. There, on the floor, was a dime.

Over the next few weeks, dimes appeared everywhere in our house. It became a common occurrence. Open the drawer to get a fork, and there was a dime. Sit down at the table to eat, and there was a dime by the plate. Clean out boxes in the far recesses of the garage and, under the last box, against the wall, in the dirtiest, darkest corner, sat a dime. Go into the bathroom, and there's a dime in the toilet. Get ready for bed, and there's a dime next to the pillow. At first, I simply pocketed them. Eventually, I put them all in a small, wooden box. There are one hundred and ten dimes in that box.

How often do you find dimes on the ground? Pennies maybe. If you're lucky, a dollar bill in the wind. But every day, everywhere. Dimes?

In June, my daughter and I returned to Tennessee to be with Devin's mother to celebrate her fiftieth birthday. While swimming at a local park, I noticed something shiny on the bottom of the pool. I dove down to see what it was — a dime, of course.

I swam to the edge of the pool, dime in hand, and told my friends about all the dimes I had been finding. Someone said, without pause, "They must be dimes from Devin."

We went back to the car after swimming, and there was a dime on the front seat. We made a stop at the auto-parts store, and as I stood there with Devin's mom, something fell in front of us, rolled around two or three times, and then dropped — a dime.

The dime dam opened for Devin's friends. My daughter was thinking about Devin, wondering if he was scared when he died. There, on the floor in front of her, she found a dime. She then began to find dimes throughout her house. A friend visiting Paris heard something drop behind her. It was an American dime. Another friend dreamed about Devin and woke up with a dime in her hand. A friend bought a new comforter. When she pulled it out of the plastic bag it was in, on the bottom was a dime. My son, who was just learning to drive, almost crashed into an upcoming car. He stopped and opened his car door. There, on the ground by the car, was a dime. The stories go on and on.

There were the skeptics. One of Devin's old girlfriends didn't believe in the dimes until the day she attended an art class at the University of Tennessee. The professor was showing slides of art and architecture throughout Knoxville inspired by Greek artists and sculptors. One slide was of a fountain in Knoxville that Devin and this young woman frequently visited. The picture had been taken the year before, and, to her surprise, Devin was in the picture. After class, the woman went to the fountain to think about Devin and remember her time with him. She looked down and there, at her feet, she found a dime.

It's been more than twenty years since Devin died. He hasn't left us. Every now and then, he cycles around when we need him most. My daughter will call and say, "Devin's back." Sure enough, that's when I begin to find dimes — on the side of the path during a hike, under a tent after a camping trip, in the corner of a hotel room, on the floor in the gym.

I still have that box full of dimes from when Devin first visited us. Now, when I find dimes in the house, I place them on the nearest windowsill or baseboard. There are nineteen dimes on a ledge in the kitchen, twenty-four dimes by the front door, and eight dimes scattered elsewhere around the house.

When I find a dime in a hotel room, an airport, a restaurant, or outside, I say, "Thank you, Devin." I pick it up and put it high up on a picture frame, a windowsill, a ledge, or a branch of a tree. I leave it so that Devin can fill the space.

There is a thin veil between this world and the next, a mystery at the center of the universe. Somehow, dimes come to us. It is beyond my understanding.

When Devin died, I realized, as all parents eventually do, that there is no way I can ever protect my children from pain. My daughter's pain at losing her best friend was deep. I couldn't do anything about it, but Devin could and did.

From the dimes, I have learned that if you keep your eyes open, if you live your life fully awake, you will see those moments, those miracles, those angels who pass by every day. You will find your dimes. They will support you through the pain and fill you with delightful surprises and gentle memories that allow you to go on one more day. When you see a dime, say "thank you" and pick it up.

— Trudy Knowles —

The Bathroom Mirror

Love recognizes no barriers. It jumps hurdles,
leaps fences, penetrates walls to arrive at its
destination full of hope.
~Maya Angelou

I received a "nose kiss" from Heaven. On my bathroom mirror! In a prominent place so it would not go unnoticed. It was from my son. He knew I would be distraught that day, so he carefully chose its position.

Zachary Christopher is my forever thirty-four-year-old son. His burly build easily disguised the fact that he had the heart, soul and mind of a little boy. He had been diagnosed at the tender age of two with autism. Through the years, he encountered many challenges, one of which was the inability to speak. However, his sweet smile was so charismatic! Everyone who met him fell in love with him. No words were necessary.

When the pandemic hit, Zack and I spent most of our days together. Like the rest of the planet, our activities were somewhat limited, but we always had fun. *Sesame Street* and Disney films had been his perpetual favorites when he was younger. We dug into their vaults and revisited many of the movies that we had shared long ago. His memory fascinated me. It was just as though we were sitting side by side viewing the VCR tapes in the 1990s. He even laughed at the identical scenes that had been the most humorous to him in the good old days. Hearing the elephants chant "Hup, two, three, four. Keep it up, two, three, four" from *The Jungle Book* instantly brought that delightful smile to his face.

Fast forward to October 1, 2021. It was one of the first days of fall, a season I loved. There was a slight chill in the air. I had just covered Zack with his special *Minions* blanket, making sure to completely tuck in his feet. That was a requirement! Leaning over to give him a kiss on the forehead, I chuckled as I heard Cookie Monster's voice coming from the television. We both adored him. He was an old friend.

Lunchtime was approaching, so I went to prepare something for Zack. Suddenly, I noticed my son rounding the corner into the kitchen. He was looking for me. I thought this was unusual behavior because he rarely left an episode of *Sesame Street* unattended. As he bent over, my mother's instincts kicked in. His past history of seizures told me that one was coming, and we both knew it.

As he fell to the floor, I slid next to him. I called my daughter, and we both spoke to him as we always did during a seizure. But something was different this time. His breathing had suddenly stopped. Emergency assistance was contacted, and I administered CPR until they arrived. But I knew he was gone. A crushing feeling enveloped me. In a heartbeat, my universe exploded.

To describe the remainder of that horrendous day would be far too painful. Thankfully, positive memories started popping in and out of my head: his contagious smile, the way he held my hand, the "look" I received when he disagreed with me, and his magnificent "nose kisses."

Struggling to find balance between grief and gratitude was an enormous undertaking. Waves of anguish came out of nowhere. Tears attacked like raging currents. I was drowning.

Revisiting the amazing memories I had of Zack allowed me to breathe again. Finding ways to ride the waves was necessary to keep my sanity. There was so much solace in the visions that appeared in my mind's eye. Zachary came to my rescue every time.

The world was a different place. Nothing made much sense. I was searching for answers when there weren't any. To say that my emotions were in roller-coaster mode would be an understatement. There were times when I somehow found the strength to feel optimistic about the healing process. Moments later, I was spiraling into sadness and a pain so intense it was suffocating.

There was a choice to be made: allow the darkness to entirely engulf me or let Zachary's light shine within me. So, I took baby steps and focused on the thirty-four magnificent years that God allowed our family to spend with this young man — a little boy in a grownup body who taught so many lessons along the way.

Zack's passing has given me a new path to follow where the healing is slow and often excruciating. But I am confident that I will eventually discover a recipe that will change the pain as well as reveal ways of celebrating my incredible son.

Amazingly, there was a ray of sunshine on October 1st. I do believe that Zachary somehow knew he was going to join the angels because he left behind an indescribable gift: a life raft for me.

As I stood sobbing, my attention was drawn to the bathroom mirror. An imprint stared at me, one that definitely had not been there earlier. My heart was pounding as recognition set in. It was a perfect impression of Zack's nose and lips. His renowned sign of affection, the "nose kiss," was gazing at me, reaching out...

When did he put it there? How did he know that I would never erase it? Was he aware of the fact that it was going to save my life? I just don't know.

But my angel's kiss from Heaven greets me each day. It allows me to see his mesmerizing smile, hear his childlike laughter, and feel the true power of a son's love.

— Gail Gabrielle —

Together

*Angels encourage us by guiding us onto a path
that will lead to happiness and hope.*
~Andy Lakey

Something was seriously wrong with our dog. "This can't be happening now, "I said to my husband Dave, "Not just three weeks after losing Adam!"

Our eighteen-year-old son Adam died unexpectedly of an accidental drug overdose on July 14, 2016. We were overwhelmed with grief and barely able to get through the day. We were sleep deprived, eating only out of necessity and totally oblivious to the needs of the outside world. And yet, it was obvious to us that our dog was not himself. He wasn't eating, seemed to have less energy, and struggled to find a comfortable position.

When Adam was five, we brought home an eight-week-old golden doodle puppy. We each came up with ideas for a name, however it was Adam's suggestion of "Luigi" that we all agreed was perfect. Adam, along with our older son Al and I typically called the puppy "Louie." Dave usually referred to him as "Louis."

Typical of most dog owners, we adored our pet. Luigi was truly a member of the family and seemed to know when we needed a distraction of play or when we needed a quiet cuddle. He slept on the bed each night with Dave and me and took up more than his share of space. When Adam died, Louie instinctively knew something was wrong. He was especially attentive, and when I returned to work he kept me company in my office.

At first, we thought Luigi's change in behavior, which started a short time after Adam died, meant he somehow understood our pain and was lethargic in response to our actions and demeanor. When he stopped eating, though, it was apparent that something was wrong with him, something beyond grieving. We took him to the vet, and after an exam and x-ray, she relayed the sad news that Luigi's body was filled with cancer.

The vet said she might be able to lessen the dog's pain; however, the cancer was terminal. She sent us home to consider what we wanted to do. There was really nothing to debate. The three of us knew we had to honor the trust Luigi placed in us to care for him; we made an appointment to have him euthanized the next day. We did a lot of crying together that night, and made Luigi promise to deliver messages to Adam for us.

The next day the three of us took our beloved pet to the vet's office. Al sat on the floor gently stroking Louie and through tears, asked him to let us know when he found Adam. "Show us a sign that you're together," he said, kissing Luigi's big head goodbye.

Twenty-four hours later, Al called me sobbing. He was at work in Waconia, Minnesota delivering pizzas for Domino's.

"Louie and Adam are together!" Al was literally screaming into the phone. "Mom, they sent me a sign, a real sign…. Wait till you see this…"

He texted a photo to me.

There, right at the corner, was a street sign. The top sign said "Adams Ave." and right below, hanging perpendicular, was the name of the crossing road, "Louis St."

The message was indisputable. Adam and Louie were together.

— Rhoda Michaelynn —

How Did That Happen?

92

The Budgerigar and the Bald Spot

Miracles come in moments. Be ready and willing.
~Dr. Wayne Dyer

hen our daughter was eight years old, we lived in a small, rather dilapidated trailer next to the house that we were building. It was noisy and drafty, and its windows and doors didn't shut right, but it was our home for a time. We shared that home with three pets: a lively Spaniel, a lazy gray cat, and a parakeet, aka budgerigar. For some reason, our daughter took a liking to that unusual word better than the more ordinary "parakeet," so we called him Henry Budgerigar.

Henry Budgerigar had a cage but was rarely in it if we were at home. He liked to fly around the place, alighting on the curtains, the lampshades, and the heads of cat, dog and people alike. We have a picture of him sitting on the cat, with the cat looking askance over her shoulder at him. Because my husband paid a lot of attention to Henry, the bird was fond of him and often perched on his bald spot.

It was Easter morning, and the three of us were getting ready to set off for my in-laws' home for an Easter egg hunt and family dinner. While we were getting dressed, I asked our daughter to put Henry back in his cage. As she tried to catch him, the dog suddenly jumped on the door. The door flew open, and the bird flew out.

We watched horrified as Henry swooped up to the treetops, and then flew from tree to tree. He buzzed a group of starlings who scattered. We stood outside, heads strained upward, trying to follow his flight as he exultantly dipped, soared and circled.

"Henry Budgerigar, come back!" my daughter cried. My husband brought Henry's cage outside and hung it from a tree. He had filled the seed containers with fresh birdseed.

"Henry, come get some nice food," we called to him.

"Here's your cage!"

"This is your home!"

"Come back!"

We said all sorts of desperate and foolish things, trying to make this free and airborne creature head back to a tiny cage and the people who thought he belonged to them. All to no avail. We gave up after an hour. The bird was long gone. We got into the car and headed to dinner, full of remorse for having let our pet get away. We blamed each other, blamed the dog, and blamed the trailer door that didn't close right.

Our daughter was in tears. "Do you think he'll come back?" she pleaded.

My husband and I looked at each other.

"I don't think so, honey," I said gently, "but you can never tell."

When we arrived at our in-laws' house, our daughter's sad story overshadowed any excitement she might have had about playing with her cousins or finding the colored eggs PopPop had hidden on the lawn. Everyone tried to comfort her.

Then, the phone rang. Don's mother answered and then handed the phone to Don.

"It's for you," she said. "It's your brother, Bob."

Don's identical twin brother and his family were expected for dinner, too. Since they only lived a mile away, they should have been here already. Why was he calling now?

"What's up?" Don asked. "Is everything alright?"

Then, Don's face lit up, and he began to laugh. His brother had said the last thing my husband expected to hear.

"I have your bird," he'd said.

We heard the whole story when Bob and his family arrived for dinner.

"I was standing outside ready to get in the car to come for dinner when this bird came out of nowhere, swooped down on me, and landed on my head," he told us. "At first, I was startled and went to shoo it away, but then I recognized that it was Henry. I slowly walked into my house with the bird sitting on my head."

"I guess he found a familiar bald spot," Don chuckled.

Evidently, Henry had become tired of his adventures and spotted a friendly landing pad.

Bob had let the bird loose in his living room while he drove to our house, grabbed the cage, brought it back and lured Henry inside. Then, he took the cage and bird back to our trailer.

So, Henry Budgerigar was back in his cage! For the rest of the afternoon, we couldn't talk about anything but Henry's adventure. We discussed the distance between our two places, more than a mile as the crow (or budgerigar) flies, and marveled at the likelihood of the bird flying to an address where he had never been before or the chances that he would land on Bob's head. And, amazingly, he had trusted Bob enough to let him be walked inside.

For many years afterward, we told Henry's story to anyone who would listen. You could say that Henry's experiment with flying wild and free, and his decision to return home, was just a series of coincidences. But if you ask anyone in our family, they will tell you, as far as we are concerned, this was clearly an Easter miracle.

—Jean Anne Feldeisen—

93

When It's Your Own Child

The child must know that he is a miracle, that since the
beginning of the world there hasn't been, and
until the end of the world there will not be,
another child like him.
~Pablo Casals

White dogwood blossoms welcomed the spring of 1992 in mid North Carolina. I'd recently started my new job as an emergency room physician in a rural hospital, a busy setting where patients with heart attacks were as common as those with sprains. I'd been taught in medical school the importance of keeping an emotional buffer, to recognize that the tragedies I dealt with beset the patients and not me. After shifts, I'd go home and decompress in the comfort of my wife's arms and words. When I arrived at work on April eighteenth, I had no hint that the day's big crisis would be mine.

It was three p.m., the end of my eight-hour shift, a busy one with the typical flow of car accidents, falls, and illnesses. Finishing up the paperwork on my last patient, a nurse notified me that my wife was on the phone. Not unusual, I expected her to ask me to pick up milk on the way home, or some such errand. Instead of her voice, all that came through the receiver was her sobbing.

"What's wrong?" I demanded. "It can't be that bad."

But it was. During my wife's dance lesson, our four-year-old Lauren had wandered away from the childcare area. She had been found in the otherwise unoccupied weight room, asphyxiated by a two-hundred-pound barbell she had dislodged across her chest. Cyanotic, pulseless, fixed and dilated pupils, she was clinically dead.

On my arrival at the trauma center a half hour later, I found my wife huddled with a friend in the waiting room. "The nurse said that she's never seen anyone recover from such trauma before. She said Lauren may never wake up from her coma."

"No!" I shouted. "No one can predict that."

My wife clung tightly to my arm. "But what if she never wakes up? Or, worse, what if she wakes up and she's brain damaged. I can't even stand to look at her. Oh. Oh. I can never forgive myself. How could I be so careless?"

I hugged her tightly. "Don't blame yourself. And don't give up hope. Even in the few years I've been a doctor, I've seen many miracles. Right now, I'm going to go sit by her side."

"And me?"

"You," I told her, "Pray."

I caught the attention of a nurse who led me into the trauma bay. "The rescue squad performed CPR for fifteen minutes on the way here," she told me.

There, on a gurney large enough to hold a seven-foot man, my precious one lay partly covered by a sheet, a quartet of IVs pushed fluids into her nearly lifeless body. The whoosh of a ventilator choreographed with the beep of a monitor showing her erratic slow pulse.

I pulled a stool up by her side, grasping onto her tiny unresponsive hand. Over the next several hours I let my words ramble, telling her stories, calling her name, and singing songs. Lauren's favorite was "You Are My Sunshine." When I came to the last line, "Please don't take my sunshine away," I could only whisper.

Late that night, a room opened in the neuro ICU. Lauren remained unresponsive, not offering any effort to breathe. At least her heart rhythm had stabilized. The doctor told me not to expect any response for at least twenty-four hours. At the time, it was standard of care to put a patient with a brain injury into an induced barbiturate coma with the hopes that this might rest the gray matter as it recovered.

Friends and family rallied to our plight. Visitors brought gifts and comforting words. I believed in the power of prayers, and hundreds were sent by church members, work colleagues, and extended family.

The minutes stretched into hours. Grandparents called every half hour asking for updates. There was nothing new to tell them. My wife and I nursed cups of coffee, neither of us needing the stimulus to our already frayed nerves.

The sun was just lightening the curtain when our miracle bloomed. Lauren's eyes snapped open, confusion and irritation broadcast in her features. Unable to speak due to the tube down her throat, she could only mouth her words. "What happened?"

The rejoicing of redemption echoed off the walls.

By noon, an astonished neurosurgeon performed a complete exam and ordered removal of the breathing tube. Soon Lauren wiggled free of her restraints and pulled out her IVs. By evening she was moved to a regular bed on the pediatric ward. The next morning, not even forty-eight hours after the accident, we piled her new dozen dollies on top of her in her wheelchair and rolled out the hospital door.

Thirty-years later she's a mother of two young ones, precious grandchildren each with their own sense of adventure. I watch my grandchildren scamper in and out of mischief and think back on that day, and what I learned.

For I learned a valuable lesson. When a patient in dire straits comes under my treatment in the emergency room, I never give up. Miracles happen. Prayers help. Hope is essential. For on that day, God did not take my sunshine away.

— Dr. Philip L. Levin —

94

A Date with Destiny

*It was possible that a miracle was not something that
happened to you, but rather something that didn't.*
~Jodi Picoult, The Tenth Circle

I was nineteen and on my own for the first time. I was both
excited and apprehensive.

I was glad that Wayne, the guy in the apartment on my
right, was very friendly and helpful. If only he hadn't kept asking
me out, it would have been divine to have someone nearby who was
always eager to help.

Wayne was the kind of person who grows on you slowly. At first,
I didn't notice how cute he was. One evening, after he helped me carry
in my groceries, I invited him to have a Coke with me on my small
patio. We were chuckling over something he had said, and I looked
up. It seemed like I was really seeing him for the first time. Had I
really never noticed before those cute dimples in his cheeks when he
smiled, those warm, brown eyes that seemed to perpetually sparkle
as if he were constantly on the verge of laughter, or those perfect,
Crest-commercial-worthy teeth?

When Wayne stood to leave, he sighed and said, "I'm a fool for
punishment, but I'm going to try again. The new movie that's showing
on the Boulevard is supposed to be good. I'd like to see it… with you."

For just a second, disappointment washed over his face. I wish
I had a snapshot of his face when he realized that I had said "Yes" at
last. He beamed with pleasure, and I, in turn, beamed at his pleasure.

We shared our first kiss when we said goodbye. When our lips parted, we were still grinning like idiots.

After the movie, we went for cheeseburgers, fries and Cokes, the typical young couple's dinner date. We lingered in our booth, talking and laughing until Wayne glanced up and realized that we were alone in the diner except for the staff. The busboy was scowling at us as he mopped the floor. "Never in my life has time flown by so fast," Wayne said as he grabbed my hand and led me outside. "It's almost 11:00, and I have to be at work early in the morning." He kissed my hand before he let it go. "Not that I mind. I have enjoyed every minute of my evening with you."

As Wayne drove toward our apartment building, I was gripped by a sudden terror and anxiety. In mid-sentence, Wayne turned to look at me and gasped in surprise. "What's wrong? Are you sick? What can I do?"

"I need to go by Mom's house," I stammered. "Right now!" I added urgently.

Wayne looked stunned. "Now? But why?"

I shook my head. "I don't know why," I said, panic making my voice shrill and sharp. "I just know that I have to."

The only sound in the car as we sped forward was me giving Wayne directions to Mom's house in a shaky voice.

It was a dark, starless night, and we didn't notice the smoke until we were almost at Mom's driveway. I jumped out of the car before Wayne came to a full stop. He caught up with me and grabbed my arm. I struggled to break free.

"Mom!" I cried. "My little sisters!"

Wayne clasped my shoulders and shook me gently. "Run next door and call the fire department. I will stand a better chance of getting inside than you will. Tell me where the bedrooms are."

I called over my shoulder as I ran next door. "Hall to your right. The first two bedrooms on the left are my sisters' rooms. Mom's room is the first door on the right." I wanted to call out to Wayne to please be careful, but my throat was too constricted with tears and fear for me to speak further. As I pounded on the neighbor's door, I heard glass breaking at Mom's house.

After calling the fire department, the couple next door walked with me back to Mom's house. The woman held me tight as I sobbed while we stared at the house, anxiously waiting to see Wayne and my family come through the front door.

Wayne wasn't a large man, and I don't know how he summoned the strength, but he staggered from the house with a sister thrown over each shoulder. The man next door ran to help him lower the girls to the ground and move them away from the house to safety. Wayne looked at me with red, swollen, smoke-blackened eyes.

"Too much smoke, but they're breathing," he said.

"Mom!" I choked out. "Where's Mom?"

Wayne looked bewildered. "She was right behind me," he said, twisting around to stare at the open door. He took two steps to go back inside the house when the man from next door leaped in front of him.

"Son," he said gently. "It's too dangerous for you to go back inside now."

Just then, coughing and sputtering, Mom tumbled out of the door. Wayne and I darted forward to move her a safe distance from the house. As we placed her on the ground beside my sisters, she looked up at me in confusion.

"Is this a terrifying dream, or is it really happening? How did you happen to be here just at this moment?"

Mom passed out before I could answer her, which was just as well because I had no answers for her. She and I would talk about this many times over the years, but I could never give her a definitive answer. Divine intervention. Premonition. Merely a panic attack that had a miraculous ending. I can't say what happened that night, but I can say that I don't care. I'm just grateful that a kind, young man listened to the pleadings of a seemingly unhinged young woman who had finally, after much persuasion, agreed to go out with him.

Wayne's work transferred him to another state a few months after the incident. We kept in touch initially, but the phone calls, cards and letters came less and less frequently over time. Then, they stopped altogether. I still think of him often, though. If not for him and his willingness to make that late-night detour so many years ago, my family might have perished. I have no doubt that Wayne still remembers and talks about his first date with the girl in the apartment next door.

—Elizabeth Atwater—

95

Someone in the Fire

When you open your mind to the impossible,
sometimes you find the truth.
~From the television show, Fringe

I never meant to be a camper. As a child, we didn't do outdoor stuff, save the occasional mountain hike on vacation. But then I married a mountain man. I didn't know it; he was from Chicago, but his heart was in the mountains of Colorado.

Fifteen years and three kids later, we bought a used camper and became a family of camping enthusiasts. I don't love it, but I don't hate it. My husband and kids love it, so I do it for them.

We were spending a couple of nights in Grand Teton National Park. The metal-ringed firepit was on a tiny slant a few hundred feet away from our camper. It was a clear, cool night with shining stars, but the tree lined area darkened our campsite. We had gathered around the firepit in anticipation of roasting s'mores. Our seven-year-old was lounging in his camp chair. My husband had run down to the camper to retrieve the roasting sticks. I was in my chair with our three-year-old on my lap. Ten-year-old Ellie was sitting to my right.

Ellie rocked forward in her chair to scoot closer to the warmth. Suddenly, the chair flew backward, propelling her face-first into the fire. Her feet hung up on the ring as her hands went into the pit, with her long hair cascading into the fire. I saw her entire torso in the firepit.

I screamed and put my three-year-old to the side. When I looked up, my daughter was standing on the other side of the fire, facing me with her arms outstretched. She was looking down at her body. I was at her side in two steps and shocked to see no flames or smoldering clothing. In fact, the smoke seemed to be funneling into the air as if being sucked from her body. I was sure she was on fire. I started to pat her down. "I think I'm okay," she told me in a tiny voice.

I sat her in a nearby chair and began to strip off her fleece jacket. I thought she must be in shock as she didn't cry and she repeated, "I'm not hurt, Mama." Her face looked untouched, and her long hair was flying free without a flame, but I was sure it couldn't be. Her palms and knees must be burned. Her hands didn't even have ash on them. Later, Ellie would tell us she felt like there was a "force field" hovering over the fire that kept her from the flames.

By this time, my husband had arrived, and we were inspecting every inch of our daughter. Her jeggings had a pushpin-sized hole in the knee. Not one inch of her body was singed. Her clothes were not scorched. There was no ash on her clothing. Nothing clung to her hair. It was as if she hadn't fallen into the pit, but I had seen her there. I have no idea how she got out of the fire. She doesn't remember either. She tells us she remembers falling and being on her feet again. She doesn't remember being in the fire or feeling any heat.

I have only one explanation: Someone else was in that fire — an angel that carried my daughter to safety.

— Brittany Teigland —

96

Pressed for Time

When positive attitudes meet with faith, courage, consistency
and perseverance, miracles tend to happen.
~Edmond Mbiaka

The phone rang, breaking the silence that my Walter and I had gotten used to since our son Jeff went to college four years earlier. Now he was pursuing a second degree, in equine management, at the University of Louisville. His goal: to attain certification in the program to qualify him to work in some capacity with horses and the racetrack industry. He has loved horses since his first visit to the track when he was five years old.

I answered the phone. It was Jeff! We spoke briefly before Jeff asked, "Mom, could you put Dad on the phone, too? There's something I want to tell you both." Once Walter was on the line, Jeff announced, "I'm coming home tomorrow. It's spring break, and I have a job interview at Monmouth Park!"

Monmouth Park is a racetrack about an hour away from us. Jeff had spent the last three summers there as a security guard. Now, he was going to interview for a job as a manager. I had secretly worried that his career path would take him far away from us, so I was thrilled.

He told us, "I'm driving home tomorrow. My interview is on Wednesday morning."

"That's wonderful news! I'm glad you took your suit with you. That way, you'll have everything ready." I was happy that Jeff had an opportunity to get a job in his chosen field and still be near friends and family.

We said our goodbyes. We began to plan dinner for Jeff when he arrived home. Within the hour, the phone rang. It was Jeff again. But instead of relaxed and happy, he sounded tense and anxious.

"Mom, I'm getting ready to pack. I found my suit jacket, but I can't find the pants. I've looked everywhere."

"I was sure you packed them both. In fact, I remember seeing the jacket. I'm sure the pants were with it."

"I thought so, too. But I don't have much space here, and I've checked everywhere. I don't have enough time to get another suit. Can you please check my closet to see if they're hanging in there?"

"Of course! We'll call you back."

We launched into action. We checked Jeff's closet, but the pants were not to be found. From there, we checked each of our closets just to be sure the pants didn't mistakenly find their way there; no luck there, either.

Now, we were as desperate as Jeff — so desperate that we even checked the coat and storage closets! Still, Jeff's pants remained missing.

Walter looked at me. "I don't know where else to look. We'll have to call Jeff and tell him."

I felt panicked as I thought of another scenario: Even if we found the pants they would probably need to be cleaned and pressed. Time was against us.

I prayed for a happy if somewhat unobvious solution to our problem. My prayer was simple and straight from my heart.

"Please, dear Lord, help us find Jeff's pants so he can go to that interview. This is so very important to him. He needs Your help right now."

Reluctantly, we called Jeff to tell him that we hadn't found his pants. We also told him that we were not stopping our search. We would check our closets again, just in case.

I said more prayers before finally falling to sleep. I believe that problems always seem to loom less large in the morning. I wasn't so sure about what would happen this time.

In the morning, I woke up with a feeling of dread that changed after praying, asking for the Lord to help us find a solution.

"Please, dear God, please help us to help Jeff. Amen."

I felt better for saying it, but I still couldn't figure out what solution could possibly arise out of our current situation. I was downstairs when I heard Walter calling from upstairs. I got to the base of the steps. Walter was standing at the top with an incredulous look on his face.

"What's the matter? You look as though you've seen a ghost!"

"I think I have — almost," Walter replied as he swung his arm from behind his back. On it hung a pair of pants — *the* pants! They were nicely pressed and neatly folded over the hanger.

I was dumbfounded, as well. I didn't even know where to start the long list of questions that kept popping into my mind. So I started with, "Are they Jeff's pants?" (I just wanted to confirm for my own benefit.)

Walter, still apparently speechless, just nodded.

I countered with another question, the most obvious one, "Where did you find them?"

"In my closet."

"In *your* closet?" I repeated in amazement. Without waiting for an answer, I quickly added, "How could that be?"

"They were in my closet," Walter repeated. "But wait until you hear this."

He had a quizzical expression on his face. He looked mystified, but he continued, "Not only were they in my closet, but they were right in the FRONT of the closet. As soon as I opened the door, they were right in front of me. I don't know how I could have missed them! And the clothes on either side of them had been pushed away. If they were like that last night, I never could have missed them. It's very strange."

"It's not strange. It's an answer to a prayer — my prayer."

We phoned Jeff. "Great!" Jeff responded, sounding much relieved. "I don't know what I would've done if you hadn't found them. I wonder how they ended up there."

Walter reiterated what he had told me earlier. "It is weird, isn't it?"

I corrected him again. "It's not strange or weird. It's the answer to a prayer." I proceeded to give Jeff a brief rundown of what happened since we had spoken and my prayers for him.

"Wow, that's really something," Jeff commented. "But, you have to admit, it is a strange story — but strange in a good way."

We all agreed and said our goodbyes. Jeff was getting ready to leave; he had an eleven-hour drive home.

Wednesday was Interview Day. Jeff was early for his appointment. He didn't say much, but I knew he was both anxious and excited. As he left, I said another quick prayer. "Bless him, Lord, and let him do well today. Thank you for helping him."

Jeff did do well that day; they offered him the job, which he promptly accepted. He moved back home until he was able to purchase a condo closer to the track.

It was everything I could have asked for — and got — because of the miracle of an answered prayer.

— Donna Lowich —

97

Johnny's Ring

*We should not assume; however, that just because
something is unexplainable by us, it is unexplainable.*
~Neal A. Maxwell

"Here, try it on, Mom. I know it'll fit." To appease my daughter, I slipped the ring on my finger, and it fit perfectly. I had to admit that it looked lovely.

"Why don't you keep it and wear it for a while? You miss Johnny as much as I do, and he'd want you to wear it."

"Jacqui, I can't take your ring," I argued.

"We'll just share it, Mom. You can wear it for a few months, and then it'll be my turn again."

I remember our conversation as though it were yesterday instead of more than twenty years ago. Although comforting, Johnny's ring also triggered sad memories about the tragic set of circumstances that had taken place a few years prior.

Jacqui and her husband John lost their firstborn baby boy due to complications from what should have been a fairly routine surgery. Losing Johnny was devastating for our entire family.

When several friends and extended family members included money in their sympathy cards, the young, grieving couple wanted to use some of it for a keepsake that would make them feel close to their baby. They decided on a ring for Jacqui with Johnny's birthstone.

They picked out a simple but sweet opal ring that was perfectly fitting for the purpose. Its delicate presence had Johnny written all over it. Jacqui wore it all the time, so I was surprised when she offered to share it with me.

"Thank you, Jacqui, for such a sweet gesture." I smiled, still admiring the ring on my finger.

"Is that a yes?" She smiled in return.

"I guess it is."

I didn't want Jacqui to have to part with something she cherished so dearly, but because it felt incredibly comforting on my finger, I finally agreed to the sharing plan.

Over the years, we continued to pass the ring back and forth every few months, knowing it was treasured regardless of who was wearing it.

I knew that Jacqui would be stopping by for a brief visit late one afternoon, so I ran upstairs to my bedroom to retrieve the ring from the small wooden box I kept on my nightstand. I'd been wearing the ring for several months, so it was time to return it to her.

Panic shot through my heart when I opened the box and noticed the ring was missing! I did a quick scan of the carpet surrounding the nightstand and didn't see it. After absorbing a bit of the shock, I did a more thorough search.

I could vividly remember removing the ring from my finger the night before and placing it carefully in the box. There was absolutely no doubt about it.

Since my husband was out of town, and nobody had been in my bedroom besides me, it appeared that the ring had vanished into thin air. How was I going to explain this to my daughter?

As I should have expected, Jacqui was very sweet, and I could tell she was concerned about my feelings of guilt. "Mom, I'm sure it will turn up somewhere. Please don't stress over this another minute. It wasn't that expensive."

I still felt bad. The ring may not have been valuable in a monetary sense of the word, but its sentimental value was priceless. I knew Jacqui was sadder than she was letting on.

The next couple of years seemed to go by quickly. Jacqui had moved to a new house about twenty miles up the mountain, and I was looking forward to seeing it for the first time, but other commitments had kept me busy.

It was getting close to Christmas and the anniversary of Johnny's surgery. Curled up on the couch in front of the fireplace, I was mentally reviewing my gift list when the phone rang.

Before I got the chance to say hello, Jacqui was squealing with delight. "Mom, I found Johnny's ring!"

Confused, I asked, "When were you here?" Realistically, the only place the ring could have been was somewhere in my house.

"Mom, I found it while vacuuming under the dining room table here in our new house! It was right there in front of me on the carpet."

I asked if she was certain it was Johnny's ring, and she answered, "Yes, without a doubt." We both agreed it was the best gift we could have asked for.

Although we've never been able to logically explain the ring's incredible two-year disappearance before finding its way to the dining room carpet in Jacqui's new house, I have a strong suspicion that our little boy angel miraculously pulled some strings to make this a very special Christmas for his mommy.

— Connie Kaseweter Pullen —

98

Deep Freeze

Your spirit guides and angels will never let you down
as you build a rapport with them.
~Linda Deir

I was cold enough that I believed I might die. We had watched without much concern as a foot of snow came down overnight on our homes in Signal Mountain, Tennessee, but then the power went out.

Tennessee is not New York. The Public Works Department had done very little prep for the storm — no salting or sanding of roads, no testing of the power grid, and no tree limbs cut back in preparation for the ice that would inevitably accompany the snow and freezing temperatures we were promised.

Meteorologists gave lackluster warnings, but I had not worried. I had personally prepared by stocking up on food, water, and blankets, and by filling the two bathtubs and the sinks in my house with water for the dogs to drink and for flushing toilets if things became dire. As I watched the precipitation cover my road and hide my house from my neighbors, I had a twinge of worry, but I was mostly calm, even though the power went out.

But late on Day Two, the temperature fell dangerously inside the house as the last of our electric heat seeped away through the windows and the dog door. The dogs, Oreo and Sleeper, were shivering. I'd never seen a dog shiver except when he or she was sick, and this scared me. The dogs didn't object to my covering them with blankets; we were all three in my bed with only our heads peeking out. Every blanket in the house was on my king-sized bed. But the temperature in my bedroom was too low to register on my thermostat, and I had no way to keep any of us warm.

I huddled with Oreo and Sleeper on the second night, only coming out to grab quick treats for them or to hold the water bowls up to one dog and then the other. At times, I shivered so hard that I thought my teeth would break. This was before cellphones. I had a landline, but it was a cordless phone and required electricity. I got really scared a couple of times and stood just outside my front door and yelled for help, to no avail. I was certain my dogs and I would be dead by morning.

On the third morning, though, I woke up to a noise. Was that knocking? Was someone at the door in this neighborhood that had yet to see a snowplow and where I hadn't seen cars or humans in days?

My neighborhood was the kind where drivers wave at each other and at pedestrians, and where neighbors drop by, and doors never get locked. At that moment, I was happy for this custom. The dogs didn't even bound to the door to greet the knockers. "Come in!" I shouted, sure it must be my neighbor coming across the field to check on me.

It was not my neighbor. "Can we come back?" a voice called.

"Sure," I called back, trying not to think this was a stupid thing to do. I sat up straight and tried to make myself look as though I'd brushed my hair more than once since the storm started.

A pleasant-looking face appeared, a young woman. "Hi, I'm Chris, and this," another fuzzier head appeared, "is my husband, Matthias."

"We brought some supplies," Matthias said.

And they had. The two chatted with me as they brought in a kerosene heater and a five-gallon can of kerosene, a huge thermos of vegetable soup, and an even bigger thermos of hot chocolate. While Chris helped me straighten the many covers on my bed, Matthias started the heater and warmed some water for my pups to drink. The two were incredibly kind, but I'd never seen them before. "Where did you guys come from?" I asked. "And how did you get through the snow with all this stuff?"

"We live down the road, over that way." Chris waved behind her.

"Everyone is pretty iced in, and we just thought we'd help where we could."

I thanked them profusely as they headed out. How could I ever tell them they had maybe saved my life — and certainly my mind? I took the thermoses and shared the vegetable soup with Oreo and Sleeper. We had a much better day.

The fourth morning brought more of the same. Chris and Matthias came again, traded out my kerosene can for a new one, gave me two new thermoses, hugged me, and went on their way. About thirty seconds after the pair left, I ran to the door. "Hey! What road are you on?" But they were already gone. And there weren't any footprints. Not in my yard, not on my porch. Nothing but perfectly crisp, deep snow.

I sat in front of the heater all that night, with the dogs finally passed out beside me without any covers, thanking God for kind people, and just thinking.

Right before the sun showed its face for the first time in days that fifth morning, I heard the snowplow rumble by, followed by a sand truck. There was a loud sound, and the power came back. We were going to survive.

Two weeks later, I walked the neighborhood trying to find Chris and Matthias. I had bought them gift cards to local eateries to thank them for all they had done, and to return their heater and kerosene. There were only two long roads in my whole neighborhood back then, but I knocked at every door over several days. No one knew the couple or had heard of them. One neighbor said, "If someone got through this road in that mess with a kerosene heater — well, I'd say they were sledding that heater, or God was carryin' 'em." I remembered the lack of footprints in the twelve inches of snow in my yard and on my road after the husband and wife left me that final day.

I didn't ever ponder it aloud, although I told everyone about the couple who had saved me — and saved my baby dogs — from freezing. I wondered for weeks until, as things do, the incident faded in the midst of everyday life and became a memory.

Sometimes, when I get a chill, I think of Chris and Matthias. Were they angels? How did they walk in over a foot of snow without leaving footprints? I can't be sure, but I believe the entire incident was either a dream or a miracle.

But, when you waken from a dream, there's not still a heater in the living room.

— Marla H. Thurman —

99

The Angel and the Baby Mobile

I am convinced that these heavenly beings exist and
that they provide unseen aid on our behalf.
~Billy Graham

Daniel, our second child, was born a week after his dad graduated from law school and got hand-me-downs from Jennifer, his four-year-old sister. He slept in her old crib with her old bumper pads and used the same musical crib mobile. It was shaped like an umbrella. Six animals dangled from it: a yellow bunny, red elephant, blue cat, pink-gingham zebra, dog with pink spots, and red-checkered teddy bear.

To start the mobile, someone had to crank the dial under the umbrella. The umbrella would slowly revolve and play "Lullaby and Good Night." After about five minutes, it stopped turning and playing music.

The mobile was an instant hit with Daniel. Being a newborn, he couldn't do much, but he seemed to enjoy the music.

Rick's study became Daniel's nursery. We placed the crib along the wall closest to the door so we could watch the baby from the living room and kitchen. Rick spent hour after hour studying for the bar exam at the roll-top desk under the window. He kept an eye on the baby and wound the mobile for him from time to time.

Two weeks went by, and Daniel was thriving. By his two-week check-up, he had gained a pound.

One day, while I was fixing lunch, I heard the mobile play a few notes of "Lullaby and Good Night."

I assumed that Daniel was awake and ready to be fed. He had probably shaken out a few notes as he moved about.

But the music went on and on. It played an entire verse of "Lullaby and Good Night."

I went into the nursery.

Daniel was sound asleep.

The mobile was rotating like someone had wound it to the max. Who did that?

Jennifer? She liked to wind up the mobile because Daniel loved it. We had put a stepstool by the crib so she could reach it.

I could see Jennifer outside helping Rick in the back yard, so it wasn't either of them. The only entrance was the back door that led to the kitchen. I would have seen Jennifer or Rick come in.

For the next week, the mobile started on its own at random times. The umbrella spun around, and "Lullaby and Good Night" played and played until it wound down and stopped.

My husband didn't believe me. He's a rational thinker and chalked it up to an over-active imagination.

One by one, I eliminated all possible scenarios and suspects.

It wasn't Jennifer. She wasn't sneaking in and winding it up. A couple of times, it went off when we were together coloring, reading a book, or making cookies.

It wasn't Rick. Sometimes, it happened when he was at work.

Maybe the AC vent was putting out enough air to hit the umbrella and shake out some notes. I tested the theory by blowing as hard as I could on the umbrella. Nothing happened. That meant air from the overhead vent wasn't strong enough to shake out some notes.

Then, I began having strange thoughts, what my husband would call airy-fairy-woo-woo. Daniel loved the mobile. What if he had tele-kinetic powers? Had I given birth to a baby who could move objects with his mind? Nope. Ridiculous.

A ghost? No, I didn't believe in ghosts. Still…

We had bought the house from a man who retired and moved out of state. The neighborhood gossip was that he got married, but his new wife disappeared after a couple of weeks, and no one knew what happened to her.

Had he done something to her? Was she buried in the back yard? More strange thoughts came to mind. When the real estate agent showed us the house, there was a chest big enough to be a coffin in Rick's study and Daniel's nursery. But that piece of furniture left when the owner did.

I ruled out ghosts and evil spirits. I never felt goose bumps. Never went through an aura of cold air. Never felt afraid. Never sensed someone else in the room.

Nothing odd happened in the house except for the mobile starting up on its own.

I exhausted all possibilities and was a step beyond annoyed with my husband. He still thought I was imagining it, even though I now had an eyewitness. Jennifer had seen it, too.

And then one night, when Daniel was four weeks old, the mobile started to play.

Rick and I were in bed watching television. He turned off the volume.

The mobile kept playing… and playing… and playing.

"See?" I said. "I told you the mobile was starting on its own."

We could see Jennifer's bedroom door from our bed. It hadn't opened.

Rick checked on her. She was sound asleep.

He went to the nursery and flipped on the light. He stood for a moment in the doorway and watched the mobile rotate. Then, he said, "I don't know who you are or what you're doing, but you're scaring us. You need to stop."

The mobile stopped playing.

Instantly.

Never again did it play on its own.

It still worked, but someone had to wind it up by hand.

Our third child arrived three years later. We had moved to a new house in a new town. We used the same crib as before. Same bumper pads. Same mobile, although we had a discussion about whether or not we should put it up.

We tried it out. It worked fine. It never started up on its own. Not one single time.

When Daniel was a baby, he would often look up at the ceiling, grin, gurgle, and windmill his arms. I'd twist around and follow his gaze… and see nothing.

I am completely convinced that Daniel was seeing an angel — an angel who knew he loved the mobile and was turning it on for his amusement.

—Lila W. Guzman—

100

Down and Other Divine Duvets

*Your Angels stay with you through each precious day,
loving, protecting, and lighting your way.*
~Mary Jac

ctober 17, 2001, Edinburgh, Scotland. The lease on my flat had ended, and I was packing my things and waiting for my parents to arrive in order to accompany me back home to New Jersey. I decided to stay in a short-term hotel-apartment in the village of Canonmills, just outside of Edinburgh City Centre. This modern flat was in stark contrast to the Victorian tenement that had been my home for the past twelve months.

It had been a difficult year. My boyfriend of six years broke up with me over the phone, and, as often happens during stressful times, I was overcome by writer's block and struggled to complete a paper for graduate school. I decided to return to my childhood home in the United States in order to save money and be with my parents, especially my mother, who was about to undergo her second knee replacement.

As was my habit whenever I moved into a hotel room or temporary accommodation, I checked the entire room before unloading luggage. I was tired and wanted nothing more than to just dive into the king-sized bed with its white sheets and duvet. But since habits, especially good ones, are hard to break, I just had to do my "James Bond checklist."

Yes, James Bond. My dad was an avid fan of 007 and enjoyed visiting Edinburgh, knowing that his favorite Bond, Sean Connery, was born in the Tollcross section of the city. Dad encouraged me to watch the Bond films with him as he claimed they taught valuable lessons about being street-smart, cautious, and taking care of oneself, especially when alone. I surveyed the room, checking the lights, opening the closet, running the faucets and shower, and opening all the drawers. I turned down the duvet on the bed and checked under the pillows. I made sure that the mini refrigerator was cold, and that there were enough amenities and soap in the bathroom. Finally, I looked under the bed and was pleased to see it was free of dust and had been vacuumed thoroughly.

I wasn't always sure about what I needed to look for, as I had never experienced a natural disaster, kidnapping, or other life-threatening situation. I followed my parents' suggestion to not stay in a first-floor room, and I was relieved to see that this room had a sturdy double lock on the balcony sliding door. I was relieved to not see any spiders, rodents, serpents, reptiles, or scorpions (not that they would be here in Scotland).

After what I deemed to be a sufficient checklist, I flopped on the bed and turned off my "James Bond radar," the family code word for a posture of caution and awareness. This philosophy had been underscored by the few classes I had taken in martial arts, which meant always being attuned to my surroundings and not allowing distractions to overcome me.

The following days were spent finishing the paper and handing it in, shopping for groceries for my parents, which we would cook in the mini kitchen, walking to the nearby botanical gardens, and trying not to feel overwhelmed by the sadness that came from the sudden breakup.

Ricardo and I had dated for six years. We met through my best friend Michael, who had been sharing a university flat with him and five other graduate students. Ricardo came from Madrid, Spain, to Edinburgh to study English, hoping that a full immersion in the English language would help him to become fluent.

I always thought that Ricardo and I would get married. My conservative Catholic upbringing encouraged this, and I was delighted when Ricardo spent Christmases with us in New Jersey. But Ricardo endured many disappointments, including his difficulty in finding work as a lawyer in Madrid. He went through a severe depression, which was exacerbated by our long-distance relationship. I had known for many months now that we could not endure this any longer, but I was young, and my idealism fed the naivete that kept me in denial.

Finally, when he called that last time and told me it was over, I experienced heartbreak for the first time in my life. This resulted in a low-grade depression that I could not shake, no matter how much I dived into routine and work.

One afternoon, after a long writing session and walk outside, I sat on the floor near my bed. As I took my hair out of the ponytail holder and bobby pins that held it in place, the holder and pins flipped out of my hand. It was hard to find them on the dark carpet, so I searched with my fingers. As I felt around the area beneath the bed, I grabbed hold of two long, gray feathers.

How they got in was a mystery. Had a bird gotten it?

James Bond checklist: Check windows. Closed. Check coat. No feathers stuck there; the waterproof material was too slippery. Check boots. Clean, not even caked mud on it. Check handbag. No feathers there. Check hair. Nothing.

The feathers were about eleven inches long, gray at the tops and middle and white on the end. They could become writing quills. I set them aside on the desk and turned on the TV.

Next day. Raining all day. Typical Scottish weather. I decided to just stay in, throw out rough drafts of my notes, and get the place ready for my parents. They would be arriving at 11:00 the following day.

The TV was loud as the housekeepers came in and made the bed, vacuumed, and cleaned. I kept busy reading the Saturday newspapers.

After they left, I searched for my shoes, which needed shining. I found them under a chair, but then my eyes did a double take.

What was that?

The gray streaks were undeniable: three feathers!

"Excuse me!" I opened the door and called the housekeepers back in.

"Sorry to bother you, but did you see these while you were cleaning?"

I held up the three feathers, identical to the two I had found the day before.

"No, dearie, we didn't see any feathers. And, mind you, we cleaned every nook in your room. We hoovered and dusted."

One of them winked at me and said, "Aye, you've got your angel's share, haven't you?"

The "angel's share" referred to the whisky that evaporated in the air in the distillation process.

Five feathers rested on my dresser. I held them close to my heart.

When I picked up Mom and Dad at Edinburgh Airport, we held each other close in a lingering bear hug.

"Have you been lonely, sweetheart?"

"No," I said. "Angels have been keeping me company."

— Leonora Rita V. Obed —

Angels on the 401

For he will order his angels to protect you wherever
you go. They will hold you up with their hands so you
won't even hurt your foot on a stone.
~Psalm 91:11-12 (NLT)

I always made a point of avoiding the 401 on a Tuesday. Any other day, the 401 was bearable if you didn't get caught in rush hour, but Tuesdays were the busiest day for deliveries across Ontario, so the rush hour was perpetual that day. However, today was different. I was on a mission that required me to cross fifty miles of the most heavily traveled part of that highway.

Earlier, while I was chatting with my boyfriend, he had casually mentioned that he was engaged — to someone else. Somehow, I remained calm and asked him to meet me close to his home. The drive across the city so early in the morning wouldn't be bad, I reasoned. And it was going to be a quick meeting, so I could be back before the 401 became a parking lot. So, I hoped.

At the time, I had a ten-month-old Siberian Husky that was already over sixty pounds and was sassing me in the special way that only Huskies can. He was adorable, my constant companion, and his favorite word was "car." Normally, Eddie rode in the back seat of the car to keep him safe. Usually, my headstrong pet complied, which he did on the way to the east end.

Mission accomplished; I watched my former boyfriend drive away, Eddie crept into the driver's seat. I turned to get back into the car and smiled at how he must have been trying to protect me. But when I told him to get into the back seat, he refused, vocalizing his intention in his unique Husky language. Finally, he moved into the passenger seat.

"That's not the back seat, Eddie," I warned. He just stood rooted to the passenger seat and looked defiant.

I am tiny, barely tall enough to see over the steering wheel. There was no way I could pick up this stubborn dog and move him. I was also angry, distraught and anxious to get home before I burst into tears.

"Okay, suit yourself." I eyed the seatbelt and wondered if I should strap him in but decided against it. So, I climbed into the driver's seat and started the car. Eddie grinned at me in triumph.

As we merged onto the 401, I could see that it was packed and already starting to slow down. A few car lengths ahead of me, I could see a truck carrying a load of boulders. From what I could see, the boulders were very big, probably two hundred pounds each, at least. They were bouncing like granite beach balls in the back of the truck. The tailgate looked flimsy. I looked in my side mirror, hoping to switch lanes, but there was a police car about half a car length behind me in the next lane. I looked at Eddie. He was staring ahead, obviously enjoying the front-row seat to this new adventure. I smiled. His joy was infectious.

As the gap closed between the truck and my car, my smile disappeared, and panic set in. I could see now that the wooden tailgate was far too flimsy to hold these huge rocks. By this time, the police car was passing me, with its siren on and lights flashing, obviously intent on pulling over the truck. I prayed that I would have time to pull in behind the police car before the boulders smashed through the gate. A split second later, my worst fears materialized.

Dreamlike, I watched the first boulder bounce on the pavement directly in front of me, rapidly closing the gap between it and my car. I took my foot off the gas and tapped the brakes, desperately trying to widen the gap between us. I watched as the boulder rose again right in front of my windshield. Too shocked to feel anything, I knew it would be nanoseconds before it smashed through the windshield. I turned to Eddie, who was looking at me, and said, "We're dead."

Suddenly, the car lifted. I looked out my window and saw the numbers on top of the police cruiser and the flashing light. There was a loud bang beneath us, lifting us both out of our seats. My seatbelt held me in, but I still hit the roof of the car. Eddie was thrown onto the floor in front of the seat. He looked like a ball of fur.

Then, my car touched the ground again, ever so gently. By this time, the truck had been pulled over, and the officer was getting out of his car. I was so shocked that I kept driving.

Seconds later, when my mind was working again, my first thought was that Eddie was hurt. I took the next exit ramp and pulled over to the side of the road as soon as it was safe to do so.

I got out, examined Eddie, and then helped him into the back seat. Confident that he wasn't hurt, I glanced at the road behind my car, worried that I might be leaking every fluid in my car since the boulder had hit us so hard. The underside of my car had to be damaged. There was nothing.

Still, I decided to take the car to the company I always went to for oil changes.

There, I pulled into the oil-change area and asked the service rep to check the underside of the car.

He was back in a few minutes.

"Your car is fine, ma'am. Why did you think it was damaged?"

"I was driving on the 401, behind a truck with a load of boulders, and one came out and smashed the underside of my car."

The guy's jaw dropped. "A boulder? You drove over a boulder on the 401?"

"No, I didn't drive over it. It bounced on the pavement in front of me and was going to go through the windshield, but something picked up my car…"

Then, my jaw dropped as the reality of what had just happened washed over me.

"Your car lifted?" He glanced nervously back at the line of customers behind me.

I started to cry. "Yes, I could see the numbers on top of the police car beside me."

The guy continued to stare at me.

"It was an angel who picked me up!" I added.

Eddie was in the seat beside me again. He licked me as if to say, "I believe you."

"You know, there are angels so big that they can plant one foot in one continent and one in the other, so why can't one be big enough to pick up a little car?" I said.

The guy looked longingly at the line of customers behind me. "Okay... You can go now, lady. No charge."

— Esme Fen —

Meet Our Contributors

Monica Agnew-Kinnaman was born in England in 1918 and served in a WWII anti-aircraft artillery regiment. She now resides in Colorado. Since age ninety-six, she has written and published children's books (*Samson's Adventures*), a memoir of dog rescues (*So This Is Heaven*), and eight stories in *Chicken Soup for the Soul* anthologies.

Sharon E. Albritton studied journalism at Fullerton College in California. She and her husband are currently enjoying retired life in the Lakelands of South Carolina. Sharon is an active member of her church where she leads a prayer ministry. This is her third story to be published in the *Chicken Soup for the Soul* series!

Jetta B. Allen received her Bachelor of Arts in English from Mississippi College. She and her husband live in North Carolina and enjoy activities with their two sons' families. After retirement, she began writing children's fiction and adult devotionals. E-mail her at jsballen@yahoo.com.

Valerie Archual is a children's author, a travel writer, and is honored to be a part of the Chicken Soup for the Soul family once more! Aside from clicking away at the keys, she enjoys spending time with her family and three tabbies. And as far as angels and miracles go, she most definitely believes in both!

Elizabeth Atwater lives in a small village in North Carolina where she and her husband, Joe, raise standard bred race horses. She fell in love with the written word at six years old, and her love for reading quickly developed into a love of writing. Her first endeavor at writing was a poem for her mother on Mother's Day.

Katrin Babb lives on a small farm with her family. She has been published in multiple magazines as well as the *Chicken Soup for the Soul* series. She also has a blog titled "Mission Log of the Diabolical Baby Brigade."

Dave Bachmann is a retired teacher who taught language arts to special needs students in Arizona for thirty-nine years. He now resides in California, writing poems and short stories for children and grown-ups.

Paul E. Baribault is the author of four children's books available on Amazon, along with two recent works in adult non-fiction: *Our Brilliant Eternity* and its sequel *Comedy & Grace*. Through the years he has written plays, screenplays, and a collection of sonnets. Learn more at www.Ourbrillianteternity.com.

David-Matthew Barnes is the bestselling author of sixteen novels, three collections of poetry, seven short stories, and more than seventy stage plays that have been performed in three languages in twelve countries. As a producer, he has helped bring forty films to the screen. He lives in Sacramento, CA.

Kerrie Barney lives in the beautiful city of Albuquerque, NM.

Christina Barr writes to inspire others and to share the many times God has touched her life. She is the children's picture book author of *Run with your Heart* and a previous contributor to the *Chicken Soup for the Soul* series. She is married and blessed with two children: Dominic and Rose.

Dianne E. Beard is a freelance writer, intuitive mindfulness teacher and speaker who is passionate about helping others access their wisdom through stillness. She lives in the Outer Banks, NC and spends her spare time exploring its endless gems on foot, bike, kayak or whatever gets her up close and personal with nature.

Following a career in Nuclear Medicine, **Melissa Bender** is joyfully exploring her creative side. She was named Woman of the Week by the local FOX affiliate for her inspirational writing and is a regular guest on San Antonio television. Contact her at www.facebook.com/chicvintique.

Bari Benjamin is a former English teacher turned psychotherapist in private practice in Pittsburgh, PA. She began writing in middle school and discovered the joy of expressing her thoughts and feelings in journals. She plans to complete her memoir book of letters to her adopted daughter.

Francine L. Billingslea has been published in over seventy publications, including several in the *Chicken Soup for the Soul* series, *Whispering Angel* books, *Thin Threads*, *BellaOnline Literary Review*, and *The Rambler*, as well as authoring an inspirational memoir titled *Through It All and Out On The Other Side*.

Tamra Anne Bolles recently retired from teaching for Cobb County schools, and she is ready to embrace new adventures. A member of Alpha Delta Kappa for educators, she received her Bachelor of Arts in Journalism from the University of Georgia, and her Master's in Instructional Technology from Georgia State University.

Carolyn Bolz worked as a bilingual elementary school teacher in Rubidoux, CA for twenty-five years before making a career change. She now enjoys writing articles and poems and speaking at special events.

Theresa Brandt is a writer who shares her life with her three sons, the most wonderful boyfriend, two Border Collies, three cats, and a Holstein Steer. You can find her writing, gardening, walking, crafting, cooking, and hanging out with family and friends. She writes for the local newspaper and is working on a novel.

Loreen Martin Broderick is a Wisconsin native living in Tennessee. She received her M.A. in Counseling and Psychology from TTU. A recipient of the 2003 Beulah Davis Outstanding Writer Award, this is her fourth story published in the *Chicken Soup for the Soul* series. Her great joy is time spent with her three grandchildren.

Tammy Brown received her Bachelor of Arts from Ferrum College and her Master of Arts from Virginia Tech. She is currently the coordinator of adult education at the Probation and Parole center for Tazewell County, VA.

Beth Bullard is the author of *Tragically Beautiful Essays of Love, Loss, and Hope, Sandwiched: Essays on Life from the In-between*, and a contributor to the *Chicken Soup for the Soul* series. Beth lives on a small farm in Colorado with her children and a menagerie of animals. Learn more at bethbullard.com or @bethbullardauthor.

Lindsey Burpee earned her bachelor's in modern languages from the University of North Georgia. In her spare time, she enjoys traveling with her husband, creating arts and crafts, and spending time with her Weimaraner/Italian Greyhound.

Eva Carter is a frequent contributor to the *Chicken Soup for the Soul* series and has a background in dancing, photography, finance, and telecommunications. She was born in Czechoslovakia, grew up in New York and is now living in Dallas, TX with her husband and two cats.

Sara Celi is a romance author and journalist. She lives in Ohio with her husband and daughter.

Tess Clarkson, a former professional Irish dancer (Broadway's *Riverdance* and Michael Flatley's productions) and financial regulation lawyer based in New York, she now is a writer living in Missouri with her husband and dogs. She's certified as a yoga teacher, astrologer, and end-of-life doula, and is working on a memoir.

John Danko lives and works in St. Clair, MI. He's married with one son. John enjoys biking, outdoor activities and writing.

Born in Ottawa, Ontario, living in Quebec, **Julie de Belle** is a retired teacher. She published her first collection of poetry in both French and English in 2013, as well as various publications and translations online and in magazines. In addition, Julie has three other stories published in the *Chicken Soup for the Soul* series.

Mary Grant Dempsey is a retired teacher and former owner of an independent book shop. Her writing has appeared in newspapers, magazines and seven books in the *Chicken Soup for the Soul* series. She worked as a freelance writer for a local newspaper and has published a book of her short stories.

Melissa Edmondson is honored to have another story appear in the *Chicken Soup for the Soul* series. She is a real estate paralegal by day but enjoys writing as a hobby. She has published her own book of essays (*Lessons Abound*) and a book of poetry (*Searching for Home*). She is also the proud new Mimi to granddaughter, Evelyn.

Kimberly Ellenwood is a life-long lover of writing and reading and has a large book collection she's proud of. She has a daughter and a husband who fill her days with joy. Kimberly also enjoys knitting, crocheting and all things crafty. She hopes someday to publish her own novel and is currently working on several.

Joanna Elphick is a law lecturer, Dr. of Metaphysics and Humanistic Sciences, and freelance journalist who loves nothing better than hunting cryptids and walking in the countryside with her family and crazy dogs. She is a regular contributor for Future Publishing and also writes novels and non-fiction books.

After retiring from full-time teaching, **Sara Etgen-Baker** began pursuing her teenage dream of becoming a published writer. Since then, she's written over 100 memoir vignettes and personal narratives and is combining them into a yet to be published book, *Shoebox Stories*. She's also written her first novel, *Secrets at Dillehay Crossing*.

Kerry Farraday is an actress/writer/old Irish soul who lives on Long Island with her husband and their Cocker Spaniel, Remy. She is a voracious reader and has more books than she does shelving for them but continues to grow her collection anyway. Kerry loves sports, strawberries, singing, sunflowers, and alliteration.

Jean Anne Feldeisen received a Bachelor of Arts in Philosophy from Stockton University in New Jersey and a Master of Social Work from Rutgers University. She is a mother and grandmother and works part-time as a psychotherapist. She enjoys playing piano, doing yoga, and writing poetry. She lives on a farm in Maine.

Esme Fen is a Canadian writer. Inspired by her former work as a chaplain, Esme's focus is on writing stories about people haunted by their past and their path to healing. Her intention is that these stories will provide hope to those who have been wounded by life. Her debut novel will be published this year.

Gail Gabrielle's writing achievements continue to grow. Family memories are one of her favorite topics. Her children Danielle, Zachary and Alexandra serve as sources of inspiration. A book entitled *Zack Attack* and her website "Gail Gabrielle's Gospel" are both works in progress.

Nancy L. Glass is a retired pediatric anesthesiologist who practiced pediatric hospice care for the last ten years of her career and is now writing a collection of her hospice stories. She earned an MFA in writing from Vermont College of Fine Arts. Nancy enjoys classical music, knitting, bread-baking, hiking, and gardening.

S.M. Green received a Master's degree in English from University of New Mexico in 2006 and began her career as a corporate writer and editor. She enjoys hiking, yoga, movies, reading, baking, and spending time with family. Her alter ego is a published author of more than a dozen romance novels and stories.

Lila W. Guzman writes from her home in Round Rock, TX. Her YA historical novel, *Lorenzo's Secret Mission* (Arte Publico Press), tells the story of Spain's role in the American Revolution. Visit Lila at lilawguzman.com or e-mail her at lorenzo1776@yahoo.com.

Terry Hans is compiling a collection of true, hilarious stories from working forty-five years as a dental hygienist. She's about to publish her book *Laugh, Rinse, Repeat*. Terry enjoys spending time with her family and friends and writing. She attends her grandsons' sporting events and scrapbooks the game stats and photos.

Kat Heckenbach graduated from the University of Tampa with a bachelor's degree in biology, went on to teach math, and then home-schooled her son and daughter while writing and making sci-fi/fantasy art. Now that both kids have graduated, her writing and art time is constantly interrupted by her ninety-six-pound Boxer mix.

Teresa B. Hovatter is a single mother of three, and "TeTe" to five adorable grandsons. She has had a successful real estate career since 1994. Faith and family are her priorities; travel is her pleasure. She is thrilled to be a part of the Chicken Soup for the Soul family and is currently writing her personal story of faith through her worst nightmare.

Rebecca L. Jones is a freelance writer who writes ad copy, Internet content, and for her local newspaper, *The Seaford Star*. In addition, she is currently working on a play and memoir. She is vice president of Delmarva Christian Writers Association. Four felines, four adult children, and one man are the loves of her life.

Trudy Knowles is a retired college professor. She is the mother of five and the grandmother of four. Trudy is the author of *Radishes and Red Bandanas: A Novel of the 1960s*. When she is not writing she is playing pickleball, line dancing, doing yoga, or hanging with her grandkids. Learn more at www.trudyknowles.com.

Shannon Leach lives in Tennessee and is the owner of A Repurposed Heart. Her inspirational stories and books about leadership, life, and loving people focus on encouraging others and reminding them they are not alone. She holds a bachelor's degree in social work and is the co-founder of the non-profit The Fostered Gift.

Dr. Philip L. Levin spent forty-three years as an emergency medicine physician, using his skills at home and abroad, including fifteen medical missions around the world. He has 250 YouTube videos of his travels and other topics. His thirty-two published books are multi-genre, as well as about 300 published articles, stories, and poems.

Victoria Lorrekovich-Miller's work has appeared in *Pithead Chapel*, *Piker Press*, *Kveller*, *Reader's Digest*, *YourTeen.com*, *The Bark*, *Cricket*, and more. She is currently writing a novel about female winemakers. When not writing, Victoria and her husband are riding their Vespas on California's back roads, exploring vintage shops and local bookstores.

Donna Lowich lives in New Jersey with her husband of fifty years. She works as an information specialist, providing information to people affected by spinal cord injuries and paralysis. Her hobbies include cross stitching, puzzles and her three granddaughters. E-mail her at DonnaLowich@aol.com.

Mark Mason is a book illustrator living in Whittier, CA. He has written extensively about his daughter's alcoholism and is an active supporter of bereaved parents whose children have died from substance abuse. E-mail him at got.mark@verizon.net.

Melanie R. McBride is a freelance writer and editor with an M.A. in English and Publishing from Rosemont College. A book lover and previous contributor to the *Chicken Soup for the Soul* series, she hopes to one day write a book of her own. Melanie currently lives in New Jersey.

Robert McGee is an activist, gardener and caregiver living near the French Broad River in Asheville, NC. His stories have appeared in *The Sun*, *Carve*, *The Christian Science Monitor*, *Blue Ridge Outdoors* magazine, NPR's *National Story Project* anthology, *I Thought My Father Was God*, and elsewhere.

Kim Johnson McGuire received her Bachelor of Arts in Literature from the University of California, Santa Barbara. This is her seventh story to be published in the *Chicken Soup for the Soul* series. She lives in Grover Beach, CA where she continues to smile at butterflies sent by her late husband. E-mail her at kimmycat2@msn.com.

Jennell Melancon is a registered nurse from New Orleans, LA. She has a daughter and a son who are thirteen months apart and who share a close bond. Jennell enjoys reading, shopping, and writing short stories and poems. She enjoys finding the silver lining in each of the patients that she has the pleasure of taking care of.

Rhoda Michaelynn and her husband Dave raised two children in Minnesota. After the death of their son, they turned to woodworking and pottery as a form of grief therapy. They have donated more than $35,000 from the sale of their art to support adolescent mental health. E-mail her at Rhoda.Michaelynn@comcast.net.

Michelle Close Mills lives along the Gulf Coast of Florida with her husband, two children, two cats and a little bird. She loves writing about her life experiences, hoping they might help others. E-mail her at michelleclosemills@gmail.com or read more at authorsden.com/michelleclosemills.

Suzanne Weiss Morgen loves words: their power, passion, purpose, possibilities. She writes poetry, stories, and songs as she channels language to bring feelings and thoughts to life. She has had a long career as a singer, vocal coach for singing and speaking, a writer and composer. She lives in California with her husband.

Charlie Morrow is a certified health and wellness coach with master's degrees in Sociology and Psychology from Virginia Commonwealth University and Boston University. She has previously been published in the *Chicken Soup for the Soul* series. Learn more at www.coachcharliewellness.com.

Leonora Rita V. Obed is a fine artist who has exhibited at Trisha Vergis Gallery, Highland Farm (Doylestown), New Hope Arts and the Ewing library. Her poems and stories have been published in the *Kelsey Review*, *Reminisce* and *The Sculpture Foundation*.

Chelsea Ohlemiller is a published author best known for her brand Happiness, Hope & Harsh Realities, a platform that honors grief. Her first book will be published by Revell and released in August of

2024. She lives with her husband and three children in Indiana. Learn more at www.hopeandharshrealities.com.

Nancy Emmick Panko is a frequent contributor to the *Chicken Soup for the Soul* series and the author of award-winning books: *Guiding Missal*, *Sheltering Angels*, *Blueberry Moose*, *Peachy Possums*, and *The Skunk Who Lost His Cents*. Nancy and her husband love being on, in, or near the water with their family. Learn more at www.nancypanko.com.

Adrienne Parkhurst has a B.A. in Psychology from Illinois Wesleyan University and a master's in project management from DeVry University. She spent twenty-plus years in corporate management, then pivoted to freelance writing. Adrienne loves to hang out with her husband, two sons, a chubby cat, and an aloof bearded dragon.

Darlene G. Peterson, a certified court reporter in Canada's Supreme Court of British Columbia, left after many years to pursue a writing career. Published in various areas, she loves to write fiction and non-fiction about succeeding against all odds. Darlene's other loves are animal welfare, gardening and cycling.

Jill Leyda Peterson is the mother of three adult children and lives in Northeast Ohio with her dog, Charlie. She has an associate degree in restaurant management and decades of work experience in the food industry. Jill enjoys baking, sewing, spending time with friends, as well as writing about her life experiences.

Lee E. Pollock has been a salesman, a hardware store owner, and a pastor. He is now retired and spends his time writing and ministering to others. He has two adult children and six grandchildren. This fall he and his wife will celebrate their fiftieth anniversary.

KC Polon graduated from Cornell University. She currently lives with her husband and five children in the rainforest of Costa Rica.

Don Powers is an attorney. His law practice centered on the needs of individuals, families, and businesses. He is a decorated United States Air Force veteran and served in Vietnam during 1968 and 1969. He has flight time in thirty-one different aircrafts. Don's hobbies are dancing with his wife, gold, amateur radio, and reading.

Heather Powers has been supporting her family since high school, refusing to let her father leaving them stop her from achieving her dreams. Her day is taken up by working full-time and going to school, yet she doesn't let that stop her from writing. She's even published a poem book in hopes of helping others.

Connie Kaseweter Pullen lives in rural Sandy, OR, near her five children and several grandchildren. She earned her Bachelor of Arts at the University of Portland in 2006, with a double major in Psychology and Sociology. Connie enjoys writing, photography and exploring nature. E-mail her at MyGrandmaPullen@aol.com.

Michelle Rahn is a wife, mother, grandmother, educator, entertainer, motivational speaker, Ms. Senior America 2004 and... the woman in the walk-in-tub commercial! She believes that choices are part of the legacy that we seniors demonstrate every single day.

Donna L. Roberts is a native upstate New Yorker who lives and works in Europe. She is a university professor who holds a Ph.D. in Psychology. Donna is an animal and human rights advocate and when she is researching or writing she can be found at her computer buried in rescue pets.

Heather Rodin is the author of four books and has had stories published in the *Chicken Soup for the Soul* series as well as other anthologies. She is the mother of six children and grandma to sixteen! Heather serves as Executive Director for Hope Grows Haiti, a registered charity in both Canada and the U.S. She lives with her husband and Australian Shepherd in Ontario, Canada.

Tyann Sheldon Rouw's work has appeared in *Yahoo! Life*, *Huffington Post*, *Scary Mommy*, *The Mighty*, and several newspapers. In her spare time, she enjoys managing chaos, deep breathing, baking pies, wearing her old blue robe, and advocating for those with autism. Follow her on Twitter @Tyann Rouw.

Elissa Rowley lives with her husband and two sons in Rochester, NY. She studied Interpersonal and Organizational Communications at The College at Brockport and currently works at a non-profit. Her passions are yoga, meditation, gardening, writing poetry, candle and balm making, and watching her children grow.

Linda Sabourin lives in the Arkansas River Valley, where she spends her time attending live auctions and selling vintage wares on eBay and Etsy. She is a lifelong Minnesota Vikings fan, cat lover, and bookworm. She loves to write and especially enjoys seeing her stories in the *Chicken Soup for the Soul* series.

Judy Salcewicz lives, writes, and gardens in New Jersey. She loves writing and being a grandmother. She is a cancer survivor who believes in miracles and angels. She is a member of three writing groups and is proud to be part of the Chicken Soup for the Soul family.

Susanne Saltzman, MD is a General Practitioner specializing in Homeopathic and Functional Medicine. She believes the trauma she experienced as a child has helped make her a stronger person and a more compassionate and caring physician. She is currently writing a book on miracle cures from her practice.

Karen Ross Samford came to storytelling through the newspaper industry. The first *Chicken Soup for the Soul* book she read was a gift from her mother. Karen is a mother and grandmother who believes gardening is the best therapy and that every day is an opportunity to learn something new.

Patricia Senkiw-Rudowsky is a Jersey girl. She loves the beach and wandering the Asbury Park Boardwalk in summer. She is a retired child abuse and substance abuse prevention educator. Her mission is to add beauty into the world by sharing the inspirational stories of her life. E-mail her at Storyteller1012@aol.com.

Paula L. Silici is an editor, award-winning writer, and artist whose work has appeared in numerous popular publications throughout the world. There is nothing she enjoys more than working alongside the Holy Spirit whenever she picks up her pen or brush. E-mail her at psilici@hotmail.com.

Maureen Slater is a wife, mother of three and grandmother of eight adorable grandchildren. She enjoys golfing, hiking, bike riding and time spent with family.

Anna I. Smith began writing later in life, and now she can't stop. She is currently working on a book about the virtues of living with Swedish joy. When not writing, she can be found dishing out personal and parenting advice at askthatswedishmama.com, baking, or faking an interest in gardening.

Diane Stark is a wife, mother of five, and freelance writer. She is a frequent contributor to the *Chicken Soup for the Soul* series. She writes about the important things in her life: her family and her faith.

Susan Taylor, previously known as Susan Lynn Perry, is an accomplished writer and author of numerous books, short stories, and articles in both fiction and non-fiction. She lives in the great state of Texas with her family and a very feisty Bengal cat who excels at micro-managing their time and attention.

Brittany Teigland is a wife, mother, music teacher and camper who loves Jesus and wants to share what he has done for her. She would like to thank her mom for helping her put this miracle into words. Brittney writes about connecting people to the Word of God at TonyaAnn.com.

Marla H. Thurman lives in Signal Mountain, TN, with her sweet babies of the canine variety, Tucker and Charlie. The two precious dogs discussed in this story have since gone to heaven without her, but she longs to see them again soon.

Janet M. Todd is a freelance writer from Fremont, NE where she lives with her husband, Tim. After the death of their youngest son in 2005, her writing gravitated toward helping others through their grief. Her goal is to help them understand and cope, while offering hope, by sharing her personal stories and experiences.

Gina Troisi is the author of the memoir, *The Angle of Flickering Light* (Vine Leaves Press, 2021), which won first place for the 2021 Royal Dragonfly Book Award for Memoir. Her shorter works have appeared in *Fourth Genre*, *The Gettysburg Review*, *Fugue*, *Under the Sun*, *Flyway: Journal of Writing and Environment*, and elsewhere.

Lois Tuffin started writing short stories as a child but found real life eclipsed anything her imagination could conjure up. So, she became an award-winning journalist and Editor in Chief of *Peterborough This Week*. She continues to write non-fiction books, blogs, and articles as a freelancer.

Lisa Voisin is a technical writer, a published author, and a graduate of Simon Fraser University's Writers Studio. In her spare time, Lisa enjoys hiking, reading, meditating, and traveling. She lives in North

Vancouver, Canada with her fiancé, their three cats, and, depending on the day, several foster kittens.

Donna Duly Volkenannt is a wife, mother, grandmother, and breast cancer survivor. In 2012, she was awarded first place in the Erma Bombeck Global Humor Contest. A native Saint Louisan, Donna lives in Saint Peters, MO where she believes in angels, miracles and the power of prayer.

Julia Wachuta graduated in 2020 with a bachelor's degree in writing for new media. She is now pursuing an education in copywriting. In her spare time, she also enjoys reading and art.

Dorann Weber is a freelance photographer who has a love for writing — especially writing for the *Chicken Soup for the Soul* series. She is a contributor for Getty Images and worked as a photojournalist. Her photos and verses have appeared on Hallmark cards. Dorann enjoys reading, hiking, and spending time with her family.

Rick Weber won the Casey Medal for Meritorious Journalism for a package on teenage runaways, has been honored twice for column/feature writing by the Associated Press sports editors and is the author of an inspirational biography, *Pink Lips and Fingertips*. He has been published in four other titles in the *Chicken Soup for the Soul* series.

Jane Williams lives in Wisconsin with her husband and Border Collie, Howie. She grew up on a small dairy farm and remains a farm girl at heart.

Meet Amy Newmark

Amy Newmark is the bestselling author, editor-in-chief, and publisher of the *Chicken Soup for the Soul* book series. Since 2008, she has published 193 new books, most of them national bestsellers in the U.S. and Canada, more than doubling the number of Chicken Soup for the Soul titles in print today. She is also the author of *Simply Happy*, a crash course in Chicken Soup for the Soul advice and wisdom that is filled with easy-to-implement, practical tips for enjoying a better life.

Amy is credited with revitalizing the Chicken Soup for the Soul brand, which has been a publishing industry phenomenon since the first book came out in 1993. By compiling inspirational and aspirational true stories curated from ordinary people who have had extraordinary experiences, Amy has kept the thirty-year-old Chicken Soup for the Soul brand fresh and relevant.

Amy graduated *magna cum laude* from Harvard University where she majored in Portuguese and minored in French. She then embarked on a three-decade career as a Wall Street analyst, a hedge fund manager, and a corporate executive in the technology field. She is a Chartered Financial Analyst.

Her return to literary pursuits was inevitable, as her honors thesis in college involved traveling throughout Brazil's impoverished northeast region, collecting stories from regular people. She is delighted to have come full circle in her writing career — from collecting stories "from the people" in Brazil as a twenty-year-old to, three decades later, collecting stories "from the people" for Chicken Soup for the Soul.

When Amy and her husband Bill, the CEO of Chicken Soup for the Soul, are not working, they are visiting their four grown children and their spouses, and their five grandchildren.

Follow Amy on Twitter @amynewmark. Listen to her free podcast — Chicken Soup for the Soul with Amy Newmark — on Apple, Google, or by using your favorite podcast app on your phone.

Thank You

We owe huge thanks to all our contributors and fans. We received thousands of submissions for this popular topic, and we spent months reading all of them. Laura Dean, Maureen Peltier, Susan Heim, Kristiana Pastir, Jamie Cahill, and D'ette Corona read all of them and narrowed down the selection for Associate Publisher D'ette Corona and Publisher and Editor-in-Chief Amy Newmark. Susan Heim did the first round of editing, and then D'ette chose the perfect quotations to put at the beginning of each story, and Amy edited the stories and shaped the final manuscript.

As we finished our work, D'ette continued to be Amy's right-hand woman in working with all our wonderful writers. Barbara LoMonaco, Kristiana Pastir and Elaine Kimbler jumped in to proof, proof, proof. And yes, there will always be typos anyway, so please feel free to let us know about them at webmaster@chickensoupforthesoul.com, and we will correct them in future printings.

The whole publishing team deserves a hand, including our Vice President of Marketing Maureen Peltier, our Vice President of Production Victor Cataldo, and our graphic designer Daniel Zaccari, who turned our manuscript into this beautiful, inspirational book.

Sharing Happiness, Inspiration, and Hope

Real people sharing real stories, every day, all over the world. In 2007, *USA Today* named *Chicken Soup for the Soul* one of the five most memorable books in the last quarter-century. With over 110 million books sold to date in the U.S. and Canada alone, more than 300 titles in print, and translations into nearly fifty languages, "chicken soup for the soul®" is one of the world's best-known phrases.

Today, thirty years after we first began sharing happiness, inspiration and hope through our books, we continue to delight our readers with new titles, but have also evolved beyond the bookshelves with super premium pet food, television shows, a podcast, licensed products, and free movies and TV shows on our Crackle, Redbox, Popcornflix and Chicken Soup for the Soul streaming apps, and DVD rentals at Redbox kiosks. We are busy "changing your life one story at a time®." Thanks for reading!

Share with Us

We have all had Chicken Soup for the Soul moments in our lives. If you would like to share your story, go to chickensoup.com and click on Books and then Submit Your Story. You will find our writing guidelines there, along with a list of topics we're working on.

You may be able to help another reader and become a published author at the same time! Some of our past contributors have even launched writing and speaking careers from the publication of their stories in our books.

We only accept story submissions via our website. They are no longer accepted via postal mail or fax. And they are not accepted via e-mail.

To contact us regarding other matters, please send an e-mail to the webmaster@chickensoupforthesoul.com, or write us at:

Chicken Soup for the Soul
P.O. Box 700
Cos Cob, CT 06807-0700

One more note from your friends at Chicken Soup for the Soul: Occasionally, we receive an unsolicited book manuscript from one of our readers, and we would like to respectfully inform you that we do not accept unsolicited manuscripts, and we must discard the ones that are sent to us.

Chicken Soup for the Soul.

Touched by an Angel

101 Miraculous Stories of Faith, Divine Intervention, and Answered Prayers

Amy Newmark

Foreword by Gabrielle Bernstein

Paperback: 978-1-61159-243-6
eBook: 978-1-61159-941-1

More angel stories filled with hope

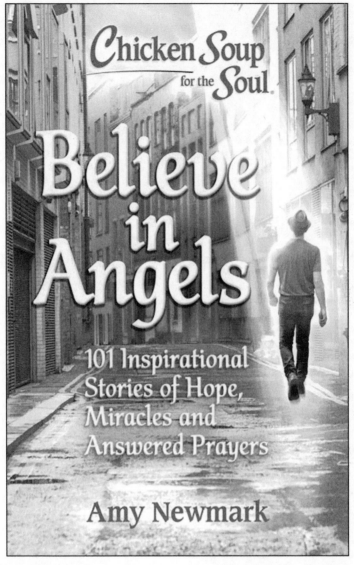

Chicken Soup for the Soul

Believe in Angels

101 Inspirational Stories of Hope, Miracles and Answered Prayers

Amy Newmark

Paperback: 978-1-61159-086-9
eBook: 978-1-61159-324-2

and to deepen your faith

Chicken Soup for the Soul

Miracles and the Unexplainable

101 Stories of Hope, Answered Prayers and Divine Intervention

Amy Newmark

Paperback: 978-1-61159-094-4
eBook: 978-1-61159-332-7

Miracles are all around us